General MacArthur
and
President Truman

General MacArthur
and
President Truman

The Struggle for Control
of American Foreign Policy

Richard H. Rovere
Arthur Schlesinger, Jr.

With a New Introduction by Arthur Schlesinger, Jr.

Transaction Publishers
New Brunswick (U.S.A.) and London (U.K.)

Library of Congress Catalog Number: 91-41848
ISBN: 1-56000-609-9
Printed in the United States of America

Library of Congress Cataloging-in-Publication Data

Rovere, Richard Halworth, 1915–
    [General and the president]
    General MacArthur and President Truman: the struggle for control
of American foreign policy / Richard H. Rovere, Arthur Schlesinger,
Jr.; with a new introduction by Arthur Schlesinger, Jr. — [Transaction
ed.]
    p. cm.
    Originally published: The general and the president. New York:
Farrar, Straus, and Giroux, 1951.
    Includes index.
    ISBN 1-56000-609-9
    1. MacArthur, Douglas, 1880-1965. 2. Korean War, 1950–
1953—United States. 3. Truman, Harry S., 1888-1972. 4. United
States—Foreign relations—1945-1953. I. Schlesinger, Arthur Meier,
1917–. II. Title.
E745.M3R6 1992
973.918—dc20
                                                        91-41848
                                                        CIP

For George Genzmer and Bernard De Voto
Friends and Teachers

Contents

Introduction to the
Transaction Edition

Rereading this book brought back a flood of memories. Richard
Rovere and I wrote *The General and the President* in three or four
months in the spring and summer of 1951. We had met a couple of
years earlier when research on the New Deal brought me to the
Roosevelt Library at Hyde Park. Herman Kahn, the director of the
Library and a man of great charm and wisdom (not to be confused
with the thermonuclear Herman Kahn), had introduced us, and
Rovere and his delightful wife Eleanor soon invited me to stay in
their hospitable house in Quaker Lane during my Hyde Park visits.

My research in the summer of 1950 was abruptly interrupted on
25 June when North Korea invaded South Korea. President Harry
Truman quickly decided that this aggression required a military
response by the United States and other democracies. The United
Nations, free for once to act because of Soviet absence from the
Security Council, called for the withdrawal of the North Korean
forces, and when North Korea refused to comply, set up a U.N.
command under the United States to repel the attack. General
Douglas MacArthur, the American proconsul in Japan, became
commander of the U.N. armies.

A proud and flamboyant personality, MacArthur found himself
in due course waging a two-front war: against the North Koreans
and soon the Chinese in Korea; and against the Secretaries of State
and Defense, the Joint Chiefs of Staff and President Truman in the
United States. The second war became almost as public as the first
and almost as exasperating. On 11 April 1951 the President fired

the General.

As the book recalls, all hell broke loose. MacArthur returned to the United States a conquering hero; Truman became the object of unbridled national denunciation. On 3 May the Senate Armed Services and Foreign Relations Committee opened an extraordinary inquiry into the circumstances of MacArthur's dismissal. MacArthur himself; Secretary of State Dean Acheson; General George C. Marshall, the Secretary of Defense; General Omar Bradley, chairman of the Joint Chiefs of Staff; and other assorted dignitaries underwent a congressional interrogation that in time canvassed the major issues of global strategy.

Dick Rovere and I followed these events with lively interest. The uproar after the General's return prompted us to write a piece that *Harpers* published in July called "The Second Coming of Douglas MacArthur." By this time the subject had us in its grip, and we decided to collaborate on a book. Averell Harriman, whose special assistant I had been in Paris during the first months of the Marshall Plan three summers before, was now back in Washington as in effect the President's national security adviser; and he kept us abreast of thinking in the Truman circle. Dick, who had been writing the "Letter from Washington" in the *New Yorker* since 1948, had excellent sources on the Hill.

We were especially indebted to Senator Brien McMahon of Connecticut for transcripts of each day's hearings. McMahon, who died in 1952, was a witty man with a beautiful wife and a breezy sense of humor. At one point in his senatorial career he had devoted time and energy to sending the diplomat Phelps Phelps to Pago Pago in Samoa; he also expressed the hope that Phelps Phelps would eventually retire to Walla Walla. McMahon was probably the sharpest questioner among the senators.

The collaboration was a really happy one. I wrote the opening section on MacArthur's career up to Korea; Dick wrote the section on the Korean War; and we worked together on the analysis of the congressional hearings. In fact, we really worked together on the whole book, exchanging drafts and (mildly) revising each other's chapters. This accounts for the book's uniform texture. Dick was the better writer, and I learned a lot from him in the collaboration. Writing propaganda for the Office of War Information and then speeches for politicians had nourished a weakness for rhetoric. The graceful and ironic precision of Dick's style stirred me to recapture my respect for the word.

Rereading *The General and the President* also serves as a stimulus to set down second thoughts about the Korean War. Rovere had already done this in his posthumous memoir *Final Reports* (1984). While he was glad that we had defended Truman against MacArthur, Dick wrote, he now wished that we had examined Truman's position as critically as we had MacArthur's. "In retrospect, I think the Truman policy was only slightly less mistaken than the policy MacArthur wanted to pursue. I now think our intervention in Korea was, if not itself a certifiable disaster, a prelude for one." The Korean War, Rovere had come to believe, led directly to the militarization of American foreign policy and indirectly to the disaster of Vietnam. "Where was the American national interest in Korea?" The confusion then and thereafter of national interest with ideological preference—reflexive anti-communism—did incalculable damage, he contended, to the national interest.

My own second thoughts traverse some but not all of this route. The American assumption in 1950 was that North Korea was a puppet of Moscow and that the invasion had been ordered by Stalin as a test of American will. Had we failed to respond in Korea, it was believed, Stalin would be emboldened to launch new probes and sponsor new acts of aggression. People in Europe and around the globe would be confirmed in their fears that Soviet power was invincible, that American big-talk was bluff, that the U.N. was of no use, that communism was the wave of the future. We thought Truman had to act in order to show that the United States was not a fake and that collective security could be made to work.

We know now that the premise of this argument was wrong. The Korean War emerged from the tangled internal history of postwar Korea, not from a Kremlin ukase. Kim Il-sung, as Nikita Khrushchev testified in his memoirs, kept nagging Stalin for permission to invade South Korea, assuring him that North Korean troops crossing the frontier would touch off an explosion in South Korea. Stalin told Kim to go away and think it over.

Kim returned with a concrete plan. "He told Stalin he was absolutely certain of success," Khrushchev recalled. "I remember Stalin had his doubts. He was worried that the Americans would jump in, but we were inclined to think that if the war were fought swiftly—and Kim Il-sung was sure that it could be won swiftly—then intervention by the USA could be avoided." Stalin finally gave Kim the green light; and, when the USA did then jump in, Stalin quickly recalled the Soviet military advisers. Khrushchev asked him why. Stalin snapped back: "We don't want there to be evidence for accusing us of taking part in this business. It's Kim Il-sung's affair."

Still, even if the Truman administration's theory of the war was wrong, this did not necessarily invalidate the American response. What indeed was the alternative? Suppose Truman had stood aside while North Korea defeated and absorbed South Korea. Once Stalin saw that there was no need to worry about Americans jumping in, would he not have been tempted to encourage local communist offensives elsewhere? Would not American acquiescence in North Korean aggression very likely have had many of the grievous consequences the administration feared?

This is one of those unanswerable questions. But I have always been rather impressed by the point Dean Acheson makes in his memoirs: "A school of academic criticism has concluded that we overreacted to Stalin, which in turn caused him to overreact to policies of the United States. This may be true. Fortunately, perhaps, these authors were not called upon to analyze a situation in which the United States had not taken the action which it did take."

I find it hard even today to see what else Truman could have done about Korea. But this is not to gainsay the bad consequences of American intervention: the militarization of the Cold War; the globalization of the Truman Doctrine, heretofore confined by the administration to Greece and Turkey; the acceptance of the apocalyptic view of the Soviet Union set forth in NSC 68, a paper that the Soviet experts George Kennan and Charles Bohlen had opposed and that Truman had declined for many months to endorse; the rise of McCarthyism, a direct by-product of Korea; very likely, the Vietnam disaster too. I do not view these consequences as inevitable, but they were in fact what happened.

The General and the President focuses on a basic constitutional issue: that is, the question of civilian control of the military. For after the initial wrath produced by MacArthur's dismissal had spent its force, Congress and the people concluded that, on balance, the President had done the right thing in firing the General. Truman thereby settled the question of civilian control, one hopes, for all time. If a powerful—indeed,"legendary"—figure like Douglas MacArthur could not get away with defying a very unpopular president, as Truman was in 1951, it will not, I trust, occur to the lusterless generals of a later day even to contemplate such insubordination.

Of course, Truman was considerably helped by the fact that he had on his side not only the Constitution but those other legendary Second World War generals, Marshall and Bradley. As I later suggested in a review of MacArthur's *Reminiscences,* the American military tradition has exhibited two competing strains. The opposing types may be called the roundhead and the cavalier. The roundheads include such men as George Washington, Zachary Taylor, Ulysses S. Grant, William T. Sherman, John J. Pershing, Omar Bradley. The cavaliers include Lighthorse Harry Lee, Winfield Scott, Robert E. Lee, Jeb Stuart, George Patton, Curtis LeMay. In the 20th century the supreme roundhead was George C. Marshall; the supreme cavalier Douglas MacArthur.

The roundhead strain is realistic, austere, laconic, businesslike, modest, grim, and empirical; its tone is understatement; it carries its patriotism in its heart; it regards war as hell. The cavalier strain is romantic, rhetorical, extravagant, self-congratulatory, self-righteous, and mystical; its credo is overstatement; it wears its patriotism on its sleeve. It often agrees that war is hell but implies that it is also the most thrilling and significant of human experiences. The roundhead looks on war as a dirty job; the cavalier looks on it as a divine fulfillment. In 1951 the roundheads backed their President against the cavalier and preserved civilian control of the military as ordained by the Constitution.

If *The General and the President* records the fairly definitive settlement of one constitutional issue, it virtually ignores another— an issue that has assumed vital importance in the years since: the question of the war-making power of the President.

In 1950 Truman committed American forces to combat in Korea without congressional authorization. Senator Robert A. Taft of Ohio, the conservative leader in the Senate, while supporting the decision to respond by force, argued that Truman had "no legal authority" to act on his own. Taft added that he would vote for a joint congressional resolution authorizing American intervention.

Truman did not pretend to legal expertise, but he had as his Secretary of State a most eminent lawyer. Dean Acheson had been a law clerk for Justice Brandeis, whom Truman had known and revered, and was a daily walking companion of Justice Frankfurter. Acheson recommended that Truman *not* ask for a congressional resolution but instead rely on his constitutional powers as President and Commander in Chief and also, though secondarily, on the various U.N. resolutions.

The State Department put together a list of occasions in which Presidents had committed troops to combat without congressional authorization. It was a misleading—indeed, irrelevant—list. These were not actions taken against other states. They were actions, well within the scope of international law, taken to defend the lives and property of American citizens against stateless and lawless bands—angry mobs, savage tribes, revolutionary uprisings, brigands, pirates. Such incidents provide no precedent at all for warfare against a sovereign state. Nor, as the administration also argued, do obligations under the United Nations Charter vacate the constitutional provision giving Congress the exclusive authority to authorize war. The U.N. Charter does not supersede the U.S. Constitution.

That is all clearer now, after Vietnam, than it was in 1951. Insofar as Rovere and I thought about the issue then, we agreed that the President had the constitutional authority to go to war without congressional authorization. Alas, Truman set a precedent that emboldened subsequent Presidents to ignore Congress and regard war as a presidential prerogative. I have no doubt today that on this fateful constitutional question Schlesinger and Rovere were wrong, that Truman and Acheson were wrong and that Taft was right.

On a much smaller point, I cannot forbear repeating a sentence from the preface Rovere and I wrote when *The General and the President* was reissued in 1965 (under the title *The McArthur Controversy and American Foreign Policy*). "On page 235," we said, "we appear, to our present astonishment, to be making a claim to having given the language the word 'unilateralism.' It hardly seems possible that we deserve any such distinction. All we can say is that if we do, we are now properly regretful." My edition of the *Oxford English Dictionary* threw no light on this momentous question, so I applied to that eminent custodian of the language, William Safire. Mr. Safire referred me to the *OED Supplement*, which finds uses of "unilateralism" in 1926 and 1935 (Punch in 1935: "Laugh heartily when politicians talk about 'unilateralism'"). However, the next citation is 1959, eight years after *The General and the President*, so Rovere and I perhaps share a measure of guilt for helping put the word in general circulation.

In the last decade, American and British official archives have been opened for the Korean years. Specialists on Asia have offered new insights. The revisionist fever of the 1960s challenged the orthodox view, and historiography is now entering the period of post-revisionist synthesis. A number of valuable studies have recently widened and deepened our knowledge of the Korean War. In view of the improvement in both data and perspective, why, one might wonder, bother to republish a book written without benefit of classified documents and published two years before the war ended?

I am hardly a dispassionate witness, but I do think there is a case for republication. *The General and the President* is an illuminating document of the day, a secondary source transmuted into a primary source, a faithful rendition of the atmospherics of the time, providing first-hand portrayals both of the hysterical reaction to MacArthur's dismissal and of the calming influence of the Senate hearings. It recalls odd facts: that in 1951 MacArthur's salary as a top general was $18,761 a year and that he had to pay for a suite in the Waldorf what Rovere and I plainly thought in 1951 to be the extravagant price of $130 a day. Witnesses "know better than does posterity," Tocqueville wrote in the notes for his unpublished second volume on the French Revolution, ". . . the movements of opinion, the popular inclinations of their times, the vibrations of which they can still sense in their minds and hearts."

I would, with some immodesty, venture a second reason for republication; and I feel free to do so, since credit for the art of the book belongs more to my collaborator than to me. But I do feel that *The General and the President* represents a style of political writing that we don't see much of any more.

As commentators on politics, Rovere and I were shaped by Lippmann and by Mencken. Our subject was both to inform and to entertain. We sought to bring out the historical context and to submit geopolitical issues to scrupulous and lucid analysis. At the same time, we composed the book with some care; we looked for vivid and revealing quotes; we aimed at aphoristic formulations; we were much taken by the absurdity of politics against the tragedy of war; we saw irony as the essence of human striving. We aspired to write analytical history with urbanity and wit.

I can't be sure how well we succeeded, but I found myself enjoying the book after forty years. I hope new readers may enjoy it too.

Arthur Schlesinger, Jr.

The MacArthur Controversy

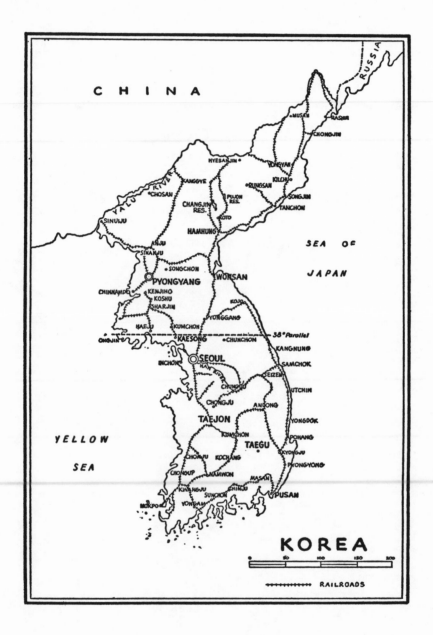

CHINA

RUSSIA

•MUSAN   RASHIN

CHONGJIN

HYESANJIN •   YONGYAN•

KANGGYE   KILCHU
•CHOSAN   CUNGSAN•
YALU RIVER   PUJON   SONGJIN
CHANGJIN   RES.
RES.   TANCHON
KOTO
•SINUIJU   HAMHUNG•

SEA OF

ANJU   JAPAN
SINANJU
•SONGCHON
CHINNAMPO•   ⊚ PYONGYANG   WONSAN
KENJIHO
KOSHU   KOJO
•HARJIN
PYONGGANG
HAEJU•   •KUMCHON
ONGJIN•   KAESONG   •CHUNCHON   38° Parallel
KANGNUNG•
⊚ SEOUL
INCHON•   SAMCHOK
HAN RIVER   SEIZEN
CHUNGJU   UTCHIN
CHONGJU   ANDONG
TAEJON   YONGDOK
KUMCHON   POHANG
YELLOW   TAEGU
CHONJU   KOCHANG   KYONGJU
SEA   PYONGYONG
CHONUP   NAMWON   MASAN
KWANGJU   CHINJU   ⊚PUSAN
SUNCHON
MOKPO•   YONGAM

KOREA

0   50   100   150   200

┿┿┿┿┿┿┿ RAILROADS

I

The Second Coming of Douglas MacArthur

"General MacArthur's place in history," the President of the United States told the country and the world when he announced that the General had been relieved of his several commands in the Far East, "is fully established"

No less controversial statement was made in the course of the great controversy that shook the country in the spring and summer of 1951. And if what the President said (or had said in his behalf, for he slept soundly in Blair House while the stunning news was being given out) was true at one o'clock in the morning of April 11, its truth was to be heightened and broadened in all its meanings during the weeks that followed. Douglas MacArthur's place in history was larger on April 11 than it had been on April 10—larger and of a very different order.

On April 10, MacArthur bore some of the most resounding titles, symbols of towering trusts and responsibilities, that any military man had ever borne. As Supreme Commander of the United Nations Forces in Korea, he was the first United Nations general in history, the first leader of a large-scale military action ever undertaken by a world organization. He was, in addition, Supreme Commander for the Allied Powers in Japan, a man for whom the Emperor was a deputy, and Commander in Chief of

United States Forces in the Far East. He was known to his countrymen as a gaudy, imperious, and contumacious military personality, a daring and valorous field officer, and a writer and
orator who made effective and unashamed use of the rhetoric of
war and conquest, combining with it, very often, an imagery
drawn from both Christian and Oriental mysticism.

He was a singular figure in an army whose generals mostly
looked and talked like board chairmen and county-court judges.
With gladiatorial features and bearing, with a voice that could
trumpet and drum, he looked the part of the "heaven-born general," to use Pitt's phrase for another empire-builder, Robert
Clive, who was also a mystic, an orator of parts, and a military
prodigy. Since the death in 1945 of Lieutenant General George
Patton, Jr., who carried two pearl-handled pistols wherever he
went and sometimes shot chandeliers with them, MacArthur was
our only general whose manner and appearance could support a
reputation for old-fashioned derring-do. He supported a very
handsome one. In the native idiom, he could run faster, jump
farther, dive deeper, and come up drier than anybody. But there
was more to the reputation than that, and more to MacArthur
than reputation. He was a man of high native intelligence and
wide learning. As the first American proconsul, he was a military
statesman of great ability and a gifted administrator. He was an
American prophet honored at home largely because of the lavish
ways in which he was honored, and in some quarters despised,
abroad.

Yet, for all that, MacArthur was not, up to the moment of his
abrupt dismissal, a central figure in the American consciousness.
He was more a character in American history than a participant
in American life. The MacArthur legend was vivid—the most
doltish of schoolboys could have supplied several details of it—but
the General himself was something less than a vivid household
figure. His name stirred the public emotions, but it did not engage
the private ones, except, perhaps, among fellow members of his
officer caste and among the enlisted men who had served with

him in the Southwest Pacific in the Second World War. Like most characters in history, like most heroes of legends, however large, he was to a degree a spectral, disembodied form. This was probably truer in his case than in others, for in his case the reputation, the legend, the history, and in a real sense the man had been made on the far side of the Pacific during a fourteen-year period in which MacArthur, busy first with soldiering, then with affairs of state, then with soldiering again, had not once set foot in the continental United States.

But when MacArthur, a week after being notified of his discharge in Tokyo, flew inward from the perimeter of American power, he made a similar journey toward the center of the American consciousness. Indeed, it can be maintained that for several strange, electric days he *was* the center of American consciousness. It is doubtful if there has ever been in this country so violent and spontaneous a discharge of political passion as that provoked by the President's dismissal of the General and by the General's dramatic return from his voluntary, patriotic exile. Certainly there has been nothing to match it since the Civil War. Now that the passion, true to passion's form, has largely spent itself, there is a tendency on the part of those who never liked it to deny that it ever existed; now that the President has clearly regained much, if by no means all, of his lost prestige, there is a tendency to deny that he ever lost very much of it. Yet it has to be recorded in all candor that, in the two or three weeks that followed the recall, the American citizen, as encountered in the street, in the railway coach, at the supermarket, the saloon, the gas station, and the barbershop, seemed a deeply aggrieved and affronted man. He took MacArthur's recall as if it were an outrage to his own person.

It apparently did not matter to him that, by law and tradition, the President of the United States is entitled to the loyal service of commanders who either share his views or are willing to accommodate themselves to them; it apparently did not matter that one of the few facts disputed by neither side was the fact of MacArthur's public disapproval of the President's policy, expressed in his repeated statements to the effect that the President's policy made it impossible to complete the mission the President had assigned him; it apparently did not matter very much, in those days, that the American citizen, so far as anyone could determine from all our imperfect indices of public opinion, was more in sympathy with the ends of the President's policy than with the ends of the General's. Notwithstanding all that, the citizen was on MacArthur's side. His private emotions had become deeply engaged.

Normally, in this country, we do well to be on guard when we are told about outraged public opinion, about groundswells of emotion and mass indignation. For one thing, we know that most people go through life without experiencing so much as a moment of inner turbulence over political matters. For another, we know how adroit the American press has become in exaggerating, when exaggeration suits its purpose, the volume and extent of such political feeling as exists at any given moment. In this instance, however, the press was far less active than usual in its efforts to work up the public. In the history of the Truman administration, there had been at least a dozen presidential acts that had been far more sternly condemned than the dismissal of General MacArthur. In point of fact, a great many newspapers which customarily oppose the administration as a matter of course supported it in its conflict with the General.* It was not the urg-

* The explanation may be that editorial writers, having been called upon to say a great deal about the Constitution in the past twenty years, have studied the document closely and become familiar with its provisions on the rights and powers of the President. Close study, or even casual study, could lead to no rational conclusion but that the President, whether or not his wisdom on matters of policy was exceeded by the General's, was fulfilling his constitutional obligations in discharging General MacArthur. Among the newspapers which habitually opposed Mr. Truman but took his side in this affair were the New York *Herald Tribune*, the Chicago *Daily News*, the Washington *Post*, the Washington *Star*, the Baltimore *Sun*, the Boston *Herald*, the Denver *Post*, the Portland *Oregonian*, the Birmingham *News*, the *Wall Street Journal*, the St. Louis *Post-Dispatch*, the Minneapolis *Tribune*, the *Christian Science Monitor*, and many others. The Hearst and McCormick papers were full of wrath over the dismissal, but their wrath was not notably more formidable than it had been over a number of other recent episodes.

CIVILIAN AUTHORITY
IN THE UNITED STATES

HERBLOCK
©1951 THE WASHINGTON POST Co

ing of the press that caused a sea of telegrams, mostly angry and abusive, to wash over the White House. Partisans of both sides agreed that the response was the greatest in recent history. In the Roosevelt administration, the only event which had a comparably jolting effect, and which appeared to bring about a comparably spontaneous disapproval, was the announcement of the President's plan to enlarge the Supreme Court. In the first twelve days after that announcement, the White House received 1,966 letters and telegrams. In the first twelve days after the announcement of General MacArthur's dismissal, the White House received 27,363 letters and telegrams.

Congress, of course, also hears from the public. The Washington office of Western Union was handling, at the peak of the protest, a daily volume of telegrams far beyond anything it had ever known before. The almost spastic nature of the reaction can be felt in many of the telegrams inserted in the *Congressional Record* by recipients: "IMPEACH THE LITTLE WARD POLITICIAN STUPIDITY FROM KANSAS CITY." "RUN THE UNITED NATIONS BACK TO SWITZERLAND." "WE WISH TO PROTEST THIS LATEST OUTRAGE ON THE PART OF THE PIG IN THE WHITE HOUSE." "IMPEACH THE IMBECILE." "IMPEACH THE RED HERRING FROM THE PRESIDENTIAL CHAIR." "JUST HEARD PRESIDENT TRUMAN'S SPEECH [on his reasons for recalling MacArthur]. PLEASE IMPEACH HIM." "IMPEACH THE JUDAS IN THE WHITE HOUSE WHO SOLD US DOWN THE RIVER TO LEFT WINGERS AND THE UN." "THIS IS ANOTHER SELLOUT OF OUR COUNTRY TO THOSE DIRTY BRITONS WHO RUN THE FAR EAST WHILE OUR SONS GIVE UP THEIR LIVES FOR BRITISH DOMINATION AND DIRTY DOLLARS. IT'S JUST MORE DIRTY POLITICS." "IMPEACH THE B WHO CALLS HIMSELF PRESIDENT." "WHEN AN EX-NATIONAL GUARD CAPTAIN FIRES A FIVE-STAR GENERAL IMPEACHMENT OF THE NATIONAL GUARD CAPTAIN IS IN ORDER." "SUGGEST YOU LOOK FOR ANOTHER HISS IN BLAIR HOUSE."*

* Some day these telegrams, and all the other data on the public's response to MacArthur's dismissal, will provide grist for the mills of the social psychologists—better grist, perhaps, than their mills are now capable of handling. It is not to our purpose here even to attempt an explanation of the phenomenon, but we call to the attention of the psychologists Eric Hoffer's observa-

It cannot be concluded that impeachment or any other such drastic remedy was favored by the mass of Americans, but there is not much reason to doubt that a majority of the people, in their first reactions, were for MacArthur. When Americans go to baseball games carrying portable radios and tune the radios in on a political speech, we can be sure that political apathy has been at least momentarily conquered. At baseball games throughout the country, during the half-hour in which MacArthur addressed Congress on April 19, the crowds (such as they were, for all crowds were smaller than usual that day) paid as much attention to the General's speech as to the event they had paid cash to see. The speech happened to coincide with the annual Boston Marathon, which normally draws a quarter of a million spectators; there were fewer than half that many on hand in 1951, and enough of those who showed up brought along portable radios to allow the whole crowd to hear the address.

From Honolulu, MacArthur's first stop on his flight home, to San Francisco, where he first touched mainland soil, to New York, where on April 19 he took up temporary residence in the Waldorf-Astoria Towers, frenzied, importunate crowds were on hand to greet him. In New York, which staged its demonstration on April 20, the day after the speech to Congress, the Police Department estimated the crowd at 7,500,000, a preposterously fat figure but one which has to be compared with another preposterous figure, the 4,000,000 counted by the same Police Department when another General of the Army, Dwight D. Eisenhower, returned in

---

tion, in *The True Believer*, that people follow a leader "less because of their faith that he is leading them to a promised land than because of their immediate feeling" that he is leading them away from the present, along with the following communication printed in the *Record:* "AMERICAN EAGLE IS DEAD. LONG LIVE AMERICAN EAGLE. AMERICAN EAGLE WAS A FAITHFUL BIRD. SHE WAS ONE HUNDRED AND SEVENTY-FIVE YEARS OLD WHEN DONE TO DEATH BY PARASITES. SHE ALWAYS FLEW HIGH. SHE NEVER WINKED HER EYE. AMERICAN EAGLE WAS DONE TO DEATH BY PARASITES KNOWN AS 'FIVE-PERCENTERS,' 'MUSCLE-INNERS,' 'TRAITORS,' 'HOMOSEXUALS,' 'PINKOS,' 'SEX PERVERTS,' 'GANGSTER POLITICS,' 'RFC GRAFTERS,' 'DEEP FREEZERS,' 'GIMMICK PATRIOTEERS,' 'MINK COATERS,' AND THOUSANDS MORE PARASITES OF LIKE SPECIES."

triumph from another war. Where other peoples strew the paths of heroes with flowers, Americans, and New Yorkers in particular, affectionately dump litter on heroic heads. The New York Department of Sanitation, which probably approaches statistics a bit more circumspectly than the Police Department, reported that the MacArthur litter weighed in at 16,600,000 pounds; the previous record had been 3,600,000.

On very short notice, New York threw together the biggest, most bedazzling show in its frenetic history. There were streamers on the spires of Trinity Church. Forty thousand union longshoremen struck for the afternoon; the harbor people were left with nothing much to do but keep their whistles tied down, which nearly all of them did. School children and office workers were given the afternoon off; even the pajama-clad intimates of psychiatric wards were brought outdoors to watch the spectacle. Eighteen victims of hysteria—none of them from psychiatric wards—had to be carted away from the demonstration.

The homecoming was in every respect an extraordinary affair. Not only was it staged for a general stripped of authority; it was staged for a general who, only four and a half months earlier, had been forced, through apparent bungling on his part, to order one of the most tragic retreats in the history of American arms. It is easier now than it was in April 1951 to recall that in December 1950 there had been more than a few Americans who felt that MacArthur should come home, not for confetti showers, but for a sober investigation of the defeat of his armies on the Yalu River front in North Korea. Chinese Communist armies, whose intervention, MacArthur had assured the President a few weeks earlier, was most unlikely, had swarmed across the border from Manchuria, had torn through the middle of the thin line MacArthur had strung out across the peninsula to drive the South Koreans back in panic and wild disarray and split apart the major United States forces.

There were plenty of people then—among them, no doubt, some participants in the later orgy—who felt that he should be recalled for mismanagement and miscalculation. On December 6, 1950, the New York *Herald Tribune,* a Republican newspaper, published an editorial brutally entitled "MacArthur's Disaster," inveighing scathingly against what it called the "colossal military blunder" along the Yalu. "It is becoming increasingly difficult," it observed, "to put confidence in the military capacity of a headquarters which has so gravely compounded blunder by confusion." MacArthur, it concluded, "can no longer be accepted as the final authority on military matters."

The administration, as we now know, came within an ace of superseding him then, but, for reasons of its own, failed to do so. Had it done in December what it finally did, for quite different reasons, in April the protests might have been negligible. After the December retreat, *Look* magazine, which was scarcely an administration organ, published a report from Korea saying that MacArthur "grossly miscalculated the intentions, strength, and capabilities of the forces against him. And no nation in the spot we are now in can string along with a leader whose ill-considered decision . . . precipitated and magnified the swift disaster."

The swift disaster was swiftly enough forgotten. MacArthur, recalled not for military blundering but for attempting to usurp the diplomatic function, returned and rode the streets, not in a cart but in a conqueror's Cadillac. After his speech to the Congress, he rode down Pennsylvania Avenue to the Washington Monument grounds under an air cover of jet fighters and bombers in formation. In the circumstances, it would have been sheer insanity for the government to have given him anything less than the full treatment. He had been greeted at the airport by the Secretary of Defense and the Joint Chiefs of Staff (the President sent his military aide, the highly vulnerable General Harry Vaughan, an act which was strictly in accordance with protocol but for which, naturally, he was heavily belabored), and he again encountered the same group, each member of which had concurred in the dismissal, along with many other dignitaries, on the platform on the Mall. He was given a seventeen-gun salute and a silver tea service.

As for the President, he was burned in effigy in an uncounted number of towns. In his first public appearance after the dismissal, at the opening of the Washington baseball season in Griffith Stadium, he was twice booed by crowds; according to the best recollection of the White House correspondents, it was the first time a President had been booed at a ball game—where the crowds are normally in a relaxed and nonpolitical mood—in exactly twenty years. In Milwaukee, a crowd did not boo while Senator Joseph McCarthy of Wisconsin characterized the President as a "son of a bitch" and ascribed MacArthur's recall to the machinations of a White House clique besotted by "bourbon and benedictine." Senator Jenner of Indiana was listened to attentively and respectfully when he explained, "This country today is in the hands of a secret inner coterie which is directed by agents of the Soviet Union." In Ponca City, Oklahoma, a dummy of Secretary of State Dean Acheson was soaked in kerosene and publicly cremated, while in Los Angeles a newspaper, the *Herald-Examiner*, suggested a variant on Senator McCarthy's bourbon-and-benedictine hypothesis. Considering Mr. Acheson's role, and speculating on the circumstance of the President's being asleep when MacArthur's dismissal was announced, it asked, "What put President Truman asleep at the very crisis of his own career? Maybe the State Department gave him some kind of mental or neural anodyne."

Some reactions were violent, some somber. In Los Angeles a man who didn't like his wife's point of view on MacArthur smashed a radio over her head; in Seattle a critic of MacArthur had his head shoved into a bucket of beer, and held there. Flags were lowered to half-staff in Eastham, Massachusetts, in Oakland, California, and in many other communities between Cape Cod and San Francisco Bay. The day the recall was announced, the Los Angeles City Council adjourned "in sorrowful contemplation of the political assassination of General MacArthur." The Michigan Legislature memorialized Congress in a recurrent resolution which began "*Whereas,* at one o'clock A.M. of this day, World Communism achieved its greatest victory of a decade in the dismissal of General MacArthur" and went on through *Whereas* after *Whereas* in disapprobation of those "who plotted the destruction of a great man at a potential sacrifice of our soldiers in Korea." The Florida and California legislatures passed resolutions similar in tone. All in all, it was an eventful period in the history of the Presidency: booed in public and publicly burned in effigy, the incumbent had been described by responsible officials as an assassin, a rumpot, a son of a bitch, a plotter, and a heedless sacrificer of American lives; he had been characterized in the *Congressional Record* as a fish, a pig, a stupidity, a B, and a traitor. All this, no doubt, was nothing compared to what was being said in private.

The fever reached its pitch at 12:20 P.M. on April 19, when General MacArthur addressed the joint meeting of the Senate and the House of Representatives. Standing on the House rostrum, a platform from which, ordinarily, only heads of state may present their cases, he delivered a speech that was in part an *apologia pro vita sua,* in part a vigorous formulation of the foreign policies which he was urging on the Republic as more honorable and more efficacious than those which its elected officials had been following. He drew the largest radio and television audiences anyone had ever drawn. He broke a host of records that had been set only a short time earlier when millions of Americans had ignored their jobs, their families, and their food to hear and to watch a Senate Committee question a celebrated gambler and entrepreneur named Frank Costello, reputedly the king of the whole American underworld. It takes quite a man to compete for the attention of the American people with an underworld king, but MacArthur bested Frank Costello very handily.

"I address you," MacArthur began, "with neither rancor nor bitterness in the fading twilight of life, with but one purpose in mind: to serve my country." He summarized his convictions about

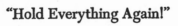

"Hold Everything Again!"

Asia's recent past, its turbulent present, and its promising future; stated his program for ending the Korean war; said that his military views had been "shared by practically every military leader . . . including our own Joint Chiefs of Staff"; argued that "in war there is no substitute for victory"; and drew to a close by recalling a barracks-room ballad popular in his youth "which proclaimed most proudly that 'old soldiers never die; they just fade away.' And like the old soldier of that ballad," he went on, "I now close my military career and just fade away, an old soldier who tried to do his duty as God gave him the light to see that duty. Good-bye."

The atmosphere when he finished was moist and devotional. Two members of Congress said that it was the greatest speech that had ever been delivered. "It's disloyal not to agree with General MacArthur," one United States senator said. Some people were so deeply affected by the speech that they thought it must have been celestial in origin. This was an unexpected development. In the Philippines and in Japan, where the pantheons are capacious and stand always in readiness for new annexes, MacArthur had long been regarded by some people as a figure of supernatural proportions; it was not, however, to be supposed that Americans, most of whom have been taught how Moses, a man on excellent terms with God, had only seen Him revealed obscurely in a burning bush, would associate the General with deity. Americans are much given to hero-worship, but not, as a rule, to idolatry. As David L. Cohn observed, it should have been possible for every American to admire General MacArthur to the fullest measure, yet bear in mind the fact that he happens to be "an Arkansas-born military officer who likes a breakfast of three-minute eggs, toast, tea, and a short nap after lunch." But this was not to be. "We heard God speak here today," Representative Dewey Short, a man educated at Harvard, Oxford, and Heidelberg and a Missourian who has sometimes carried the indigenous skepticism to extremes, cried out in the House of Representatives,

"God in the flesh, the voice of God."* (When Herod allowed his auditors to say that his was "the voice of God" and did not disown the compliment, an angel of the Lord smote him.)

Ex-President Herbert Hoover did not go so far as to deify MacArthur, but he did speak solemnly of him as "a reincarnation of St. Paul into a great General of the Army who came out of the East." In this air of palpable spirituality, there could have been nothing irreverent in the conjecture of a Washington correspondent, made when MacArthur failed to show up just on time for a later appointment, that difficulties must have been encountered in getting him unnailed from the cross.

MacArthur's return—his second advent, so to speak—was in itself an event of large moment. It does not happen very often in this country that the blank indifference which is said to account for slow rhythms of history is even briefly overcome. In our century, only a handful of Americans—the two Roosevelts, Wilson, Bryan, and a few regional and sectarian figures like Huey Long and Charles E. Coughlin—have achieved triumphs similar to MacArthur's. Most of theirs were of greater duration than his, but if the fires he lighted burned only briefly, at least they burned higher and hotter than any of the others.

The future, though, is less likely to remember MacArthur for his conquest of apathy than for the series of challenges he threw down before the government of the United States and, by extension, before the governments and peoples that have associated themselves with us in the present world crisis. These challenges were made in the Senate investigation which got under way in the Senate Office Building on May 3, three weeks and a day after his dismissal and two weeks after his speech to Congress. The tides of emotion were by then visibly receding; the salutary effect of this was to make the issues easier to perceive. The controversy— or the Greater Debate, as someone with a well-developed sense

* Observers in the gallery noted down this remark. In the *Congressional Record,* which allows every Congressman to revise his remarks, he is quoted as saying, "We saw a great hunk of God in the flesh, the voice of God."

of continuity called it—began as an inquiry by the Senate Armed Services and Foreign Relations committees into the circumstances of the General's dismissal. It speedily, and inevitably, broadened into an inquiry that dealt with the most basic problems of global strategy, problems that are the immediate and intimate concern of all the civilizations that today are threatened by Communism. "Never before in the history of Western parliaments," *Time* magazine said, "has there been an examination of fundamentals so painstaking in detail, so sweeping in scale." It can fairly be wondered whether, in view of what was being examined, the examination was painstaking enough, but of the magnitude of the issues there can be no reasonable doubt. They were the issues of survival, which is to say the issues of life and death.

II

A General and His Legend

THE AMERICAN YEARS

The MacArthur controversy was much larger than MacArthur. Indeed, as the Senate hearings ground on into the summer of 1951, there were times when MacArthur seemed to have little part in them. There were long stretches of testimony in which his name was not mentioned; for days at a time, the discussion turned to events and issues which had no bearing on his dismissal. It was the very breadth and comprehensiveness of the controversy, of course, that made it an event of such high importance. It was part of a basic conflict in American life that would have existed even if he never had. This conflict antedated his dismissal, antedated the Korean campaign, antedated even the last great war. It will continue, in one form or another, for years certainly and perhaps decades.

Nevertheless, it is perfectly clear that it was Douglas MacArthur who brought matters to a head at a particular stage of the conflict. It was MacArthur who turned the Great Debate into the Greater Debate. Now, "debate" and "controversy" and "conflict" are polite words for what was and is in reality a grim struggle for political power, a war for the American mind. The MacArthur phase of this war was a battle which took place in a congressional hearing-room partly because certain people believed that certain facts to be brought out would prove advantageous to their side, partly because the congressional investigation has become in our day one of the great theaters of political operations. But those who took part, a group of Senators on one side of a conference table and a procession of military and diplomatic leaders, led off by MacArthur, who appeared as witnesses across the table, were not engaged in a cool, dispassionate search for the truth. They were engaged, to violate the martial metaphor, in disseminating what they regarded as the truth they already possessed. Without exception, they had long since taken their stand on all of the major issues, and it is doubtful if, even on the minor issues, a single one of them was led to alter his stand in any way.* This was in fact and in essence a battle, possibly a crucial one, in a war—a contest for the power the American people are able to bestow. In it, MacArthur's remarkable personality was a large factor.

And it might be a factor in battles as yet unscheduled. MacArthur was a man of advanced years—he turned seventy-one three months before his recall—but he was still vigorous, and there were no known limits to his ambitions. In 1944 and 1948, he was a figure to be reckoned with in Republican presidential politics. In 1951 he did not himself endorse the MacArthur candidacy, but he did not—except very late in the preconvention campaign—discourage the MacArthur booms. As he himself put it, "I can say with due humility that I would be recreant to all my concepts of good citizenship were I to shrink because of the hazards and responsibilities involved from accepting any public duty to which I might be called by the American people." Barkis was willing; whether he was eager is impossible to say. But there were por-

---

* It should be noted that by far the better part of the congressional floor debate on MacArthur took part between April 11 and May 3, in other words *before* the hearings which were to provide the material for the debate. In those three weeks, almost every Senator and almost every articulate Representative declared himself. By the time the hearings got started, most of them had talked themselves out on the subject and the floor discussion turned once more to letter-carriers' wages, Hollywood communism, tariffs, the economics of Florida vegetable growing, the setting aside of May 28 to June 4 as Tom Moore Week, and other matters dear to Congressional hearts.

tents. In the delirium that surrounded his speech to Congress, it passed almost without comment that, later in the same afternoon, he made a brief, patriotic address to the convention of the Daughters of the American Revolution. "The complexities and confusion," he told the transported ladies of illustrious descent, "resulting largely from internal subversion and corruption and detailed regimentation over our daily lives now threaten the country no less than it was threatened in Washington's day. Under these harmful influences, we have drifted far away . . . from the simple but immutable pattern etched by our forefathers." In subsequent speeches to state legislatures, he would enlarge upon this theme.

This country had not seen many personalities like MacArthur's. It is striking that the man who had shown himself to have so overpowering an appeal to millions of Americans, an appeal largely independent of doctrine and capable of inducing a kind of mass amnesia in the susceptible, was not cast in any of the typical American molds. This is not to say that there was anything un-American or sinistral about him but merely that the elements of his style could not easily be associated with those traits which Americans possess, or hope to possess, themselves and which in normal circumstances they respond to with warmth. He was lofty and impersonal. Though he had little self-concern, he had great manifest self-regard. He prided himself on his austerity. Once, reading a manuscript of an article about himself, he penciled in a suggestion that he be characterized as "austere" rather than, as the author had it, "remote." Of course, he was remote, too, as any man must be when he was the object of a passionate and competitive adoration in his entourage, and when he had an overriding sense of mission and destiny. He was commanding, imperious, imperial, ascetic, humorless, flamboyant, not necessarily pompous but full of pomp.

As a military man, MacArthur's punctilio separated him by light years from generals like Omar Bradley and Dwight Eisenhower, who represent a type which up to now has had great appeal to a people retaining ancestral memories of a day when the militia elected its own officers. If he was close to anything, it was to the French military tradition—St. Cyr and the Polytechnique*— and to the Bismarckian tradition in statesmanship. He knew "the trade of being a king," a knowledge which served him and his country well in Japan, without ever being taught it.

As illustration, take a simple contrast between MacArthur and Eisenhower.

Eisenhower had a well-publicized habit, in the last war, of greeting some previously unknown enlisted man by extending a hand and saying, "My name's Eisenhower." In a sense, the act may have been disingenuous. It had been suggested to him by a celebrated war correspondent, who explained that it would make a nice front-page box for newspapers throughout the world, which it certainly did. It was a fake, but the point is that it was a particular kind of fake. Eisenhower's ready acceptance of the idea showed not only that he was, in fine American style, game for a good publicity stunt, but that he was prepared, at a time when the world was ready to compare him to Caesar and Hannibal and Alexander, to have the world think of him as a blood brother to the traveling salesman. MacArthur's approach was different. When he strode ashore at Leyte, his little speech, no doubt as well-rehearsed as Eisenhower's, was "I have returned. Rally to me. Let no heart be faint."

MacArthur's Caesaresque words may very well have been better suited to the occasion than Eisenhower's. After all, it was important to give people a sense of confidence, to ask them to take up the American cause, and it was not at all important, not immediately important anyway, to have people look upon their liberator as an unspoiled son of Abilene. But Eisenhower's words were those of a man who adhered to an American tradition, while MacArthur's were those of a man who seemed to be deliberately rejecting the tradition of Grant and Joe Hooker and the McAuliffe

* Or to the cavalier tradition—see page 265.

who simply said "Nuts" at Bastogne and, in particular, of the Commodore Schley, who, after the Battle of Santiago, said "There is glory enough for all."*

The sources of personal power are too deep for definition— except by great artists and, sometimes, by psychoanalysts. How one man thinks of himself is something no other man can say. MacArthur might or might not think of himself as a messiah, but he did have a messianic style. There was an old episode in New York one day not long after the speech to Congress. At a conference in the Waldorf, his aide, Major General Courtney Whitney, was asked by some reporters if there was any possibility that the General might be dissembling just a trifle when he disclaimed political aspirations. General Whitney, who always saw the press for MacArthur, said that the General had anticipated just such a question and had directed that those who asked it be referred to John 20:20-29. There, as the reporters learned after some rummaging around for a benefaction of the Gideon Society, is to be found the story of Doubting Thomas, the gloomiest apostle and the one who could not believe in the Resurrection "except that I shall see in His hands the print of the nails and thrust my hand into his side." Then Jesus appeared, and Thomas reached forth his hand, and was convinced. Jesus said, "Thomas, because thou has seen me, thou hast believed: blessed are they that have not seen and yet have believed." It was a strange identification.

---

* On leaving Corregidor in 1942, MacArthur had said, "I shall return." The Office of War Information thought that this assurance would make a good impression throughout Asia and asked MacArthur if he would allow it to change the sentence to "*We* shall return." (The first person singular had left rather an ashen taste in the mouths of the men who knew they would be called on to return somewhat in advance of him.) MacArthur refused to permit this distortion. His attitude was out of line not only with Schley's but with that of many American commanders in the past. "We have met the enemy and they are ours," Oliver Hazard Perry said. William Tecumseh Sherman is commonly believed to have said "Hold the fort, for I am coming." What he actually signaled General Corse was "Hold out—relief is coming," to which the signaled reply was, "We hold out." Although he never said it, legend has Pershing saying, "Lafayette, we are here." Stilwell came out of Burma saying, "The Japs ran us out . . . We took a hell of a beating."

Yet there were other sides to MacArthur. The bottled-in-bond messianic type is, as a rule, full of self-concern. Hitlers, Mussolinis, Stalins, and Perons ride in armored cars. They may feel that fate, or history, is on their side, but they don't altogether trust fate. They are wary of airplanes; in fact, they are not much given to travel of any sort; they employ battalions of bodyguards; they build the sturdiest of bomb shelters. It was lack of self-concern that set Churchill and Roosevelt, who both had a strong sense of destiny and mission, apart from the messiahs, and the same thing seems to set MacArthur apart. He was thoroughly reckless about his person. Also, MacArthur had made a deep impression on many men who rear at a messiah as a bull rears at a red flag. Roger Baldwin, the guiding spirit of the American Civil Liberties Union, was such a man. He called on MacArthur in Japan, found him full of charm and sympathy and returned to report that "in all matters involving democratic principles and methods, I found not a single point of disagreement and a surprisingly sound conviction—for a military man—of the loftiest values of civilization."

If MacArthur were wholly consumed by messianic compulsions, he would not have had the insight to say, as he did before Congress, that what Asia seeks is "not imperious direction" but "friendly guidance, understanding, and support," or that "what the people strive for is the opportunity for a little more food in their stomachs, a little better clothing on their backs, a little firmer roof over their heads, and the realization of a normal nationalist urge." To most messiahs, what the people of Asia and everywhere else need most of all is messiah.

MacArthur's philosophy of government was no easy thing to grasp. He gave voice, as he did in Congress, to wildly New Dealish ideas about the Orient, and he borrowed heavily from the New Deal in the Occupation of Japan, but he could cut his corners sharp and quickly revert to "the immutable patterns etched by our forefathers." In 1943, he had a weird correspondence with a Nebraskan Congressman, A. L. Miller of Kimball, a former state governor of Lions Clubs. MacArthur was in Australia at the time, and the Congressman gave him a briefing on developments on the mainland, reporting that "unless this New Deal can be stopped this time, our American way of life is forever doomed." MacArthur promptly replied that "I do unreservedly agree with the complete wisdom and statesmanship of your comments." He added dark allusions to "the sinister drama of our present chaos and confusion."

It was a strange thing to be said by a man who was fighting so hard to keep that drama on the stage. Encouraged, Lion Miller sent out an amplification of his earlier report, and received from MacArthur an expression of thanks for the "scholarly" correspondence and a reaffirmation of sympathy. "Like Abraham Lincoln," MacArthur said, "I am a firm believer in the people." When the letters were released to the press, MacArthur incredibly said that "I entirely repudiate [the] interpretation that they were intended as a criticism of any political philosophy or of personages in high office." A lively MacArthur-for-President boom was on at the time.

Time affords useful perspectives for a clear view of MacArthur. He sprang from an intense and dedicated military tradition. The life of his father encompassed the life of the United States Army from Fort Sumter almost to the First World War. Arthur MacArthur, New England-born, Wisconsin-raised, enlisted in the Union Army at sixteen. He saw action at Perryville, Stones River, Chickamauga, and Atlanta. For valor at Missionary Ridge, he was thirty years later, awarded the Congressional Medal of Honor. He stuck by the Army through its decline in the dreary seventies and eighties, serving it for nearly twenty years on the frontier, where, as "The Boy Colonel of the West," he established the MacArthur habit of harvesting newspaper sobriquets. Douglas MacArthur was born at Little Rock, Arkansas, on January 26, 1880. In the nineties, Arthur MacArthur rose again with the Army and became a national hero as the pacifier of the Philippines. He led most of the big campaigns against Aguinaldo's *Insurrectos* and finally captured Malalos, the rebel capital, and in 1900 became military governor of the Islands. He died picturesquely in 1912 while delivering a speech at his regimental reunion in Milwaukee.

Arthur MacArthur was able, energetic, and obdurate; old General Enoch Crowder, who had been his aide in the Philippines, once said the two MacArthurs were the most headstrong men he had even known. The years in the Philippines were the high point of the elder MacArthur's life; they probably contributed to his son's emotional attachment to the Islands, to his feeling about the Far East's importance for American security, and to his dislike of civilian authority.

In 1900, when General MacArthur was still having trouble with Aguinaldo, William Howard Taft arrived in Manila as a civilian commissioner overflowing with a cheerful determination to win the "little brown brothers"* with kindness and schoolteachers. MacArthur refused to go down to the boat to greet Taft, assigned him to one small room in the governor's palace and treated him with cold indifference. Taft assured him that he would still be in military command and exercise great power, to which MacArthur replied, "That would be all right, if I had not been exercising so much more power before you came." Taft later wrote the Secretary of War a description of the father which had more than a contemporary relevance. Arthur MacArthur struck him, Taft told Elihu Root, as

a very courtly, kindly man; lacking somewhat in a sense of humor; rather fond of profound generalizations on the psychological conditions of the people; politely incredulous, and politely lacking in any great consideration for the views of anyone, as to the real situation, who is a civilian and who has been here only a comparatively short time, and firmly convinced of the necessity for maintaining military etiquette in civil matters and civil government.

Washington backed Taft, and in 1901 MacArthur was relieved of his command. In a few years, when Taft became president, he passed over MacArthur in choosing his Chief of Staff. Years later,

* *Oh, he may be a brother of William Howard Taft,*
  But he ain't no brother of mine.   —Soldier's song.

Taft's son did his level best to make it up to the son of Arthur MacArthur.

MacArthur, not much chastened, returned to the United States and after a short time delivered a speech casting grave doubts on the patriotism of German-Americans. Theodore Roosevelt, who had no patience for soldiers meddling in politics, cracked down without mercy. An officer who thus spoke out of turn, he said, "is unfit to hold a commission in the National Guard."

His son, by this time, was already carving out an army name of his own. Douglas MacArthur was never less than promising. He led the class of 1903 at West Point, making, it is said, the highest scholastic record anyone has ever made there. He was rousingly handsome—the late Hugh Johnson, a classmate, said young MacArthur was the best-looking man he had ever seen— and his career, both social and military, was adroitly managed by his mother, a Virginian who set great store by adroit social management. When she learned that the mother of Ulysses S. Grant III had moved to West Point to attend to her son's interests, she determined that a MacArthur should lack no advantages possessed by a Grant, so she swept up the Hudson in full sail and anchored fast for four years. It is said that she gave a superb performance.

After graduating, MacArthur served briefly in the Philippines, seeing his first action in skirmishes with brigands; was a military aide to Theodore Roosevelt; went out to Japan for a short hitch; helped seize Vera Cruz in 1914; was briefly superintendent of the old State, War, and Navy Building; and became the first press officer in War Department history. The work he turned in was always first-class. General Robert Eichelberger's first memory of MacArthur goes back to 1911 or 1912. A fairly raw second lieutenant, Eichelberger had just arrived at camp. He was told that the two coming men of the Army were there. One was Captain MacArthur; the other was Lieutenant George Catlett Marshall.

In France, MacArthur served with distinction and valor. A major by then, he proposed over the heads of his superior officers the project of a "Rainbow Division"—a kind of All-American division made up of National Guard units from many states. In time it was set up, and in time he became its commander. He took part in the Champagne-Marne and Aisne-Marne defensives and in the St. Mihiel, Essey, Pannes, Meuse-Argonne and Sedan offensives. In the authoritative view of Newton D. Baker, Wilson's Secretary of War, he was the best front-line officer the country had. He was the youngest division commander in France and the youngest officer of general rank in the Army, at that time. Later, he was to be the youngest Chief of Staff and the youngest superintendent of West Point in history. The papers had found him a fetching figure and liked to call him "the D'Artagnan of the A.E.F." After serving for a while with the occupation forces in Germany, he came home with two battle wounds, a trunkful of decorations and clippings, and enough memories of adventure and wartime kudos to nourish a vast discontent through the years of peace.

In the twenties, MacArthur, like Winston Churchill and Charles de Gaulle and other figures of a heroic cast, was miserably out of place. It was no age for heroes; for a professional soldier of MacArthur's stripe, it all but was impossible. Given his limitations along with his abilities, there seemed almost nothing for him to do except do nothing. He could not fly the ocean like Lindbergh, or explore the poles like Byrd; he would not turn to business like Hugh Johnson, or to politics, like Leonard Wood. The Army was his dedication; he could conceive no alternative. Nevertheless, the United States was a wasteland, the Army a withered vine.

Luckily, he managed, after finishing up as Superintendent of West Point, which was largely a matter of distasteful bickering with Congress over money, to escape into the Philippines for a few years. This was shortly after his marriage to Louise Cromwell Brooks, a giddy and very rich divorcee who provided MacArthur's one fleeting contact with the jazz age ("Marriage of Mars to Millions"—newspaper headline). Mrs. Brooks, who was the stepdaughter of Edward T. Stotesbury and who, after divorcing MacArthur married the actor Lionel Atwill, had been General Pershing's official hostess, and it was gossiped around Washington that the Manila job was an exile. Exile or not, it was, for a time, a happy return to the family fief. But even in Manila, he tasted gall. The marriage was a failure and a rather public one at that. The Manila papers were full of stories. She divorced him in Reno in 1929. He was back in Manila at the time. Late in 1935, once again in Manila, he met Jean Faircloth of Murfreesboro, Tennessee; he married her in 1937. It has been, by all accounts, a most successful marriage.* In 1938, the second Mrs. MacArthur gave birth to the General's only child, Arthur. The dynasty can continue.

In spite of the two Philippine assignments, he spent most of the twenties in the United States. Those years were notable chiefly for his service on the court-martial of Brigadier General Billy Mitchell, the prophet of airpower, and for his service as President of the American Committee for the Olympic Games. The Mitchell affair is one from which he has not yet quite extricated himself. He and Mitchell had known each other as boys in Milwaukee, where the Mitchells and the MacArthurs were the most prominent military families. It seems a peculiar piece of jurisprudence to have appointed MacArthur to the court-martial, but peculiar or not, it was done. His role in the trial is still enigmatic. Certain of MacArthur's friends have claimed for years that MacArthur voted

* In *MacArthur the Magnificent*, a richly ripened biography by the sportswriter Robert Considine, it is said of the first marriage that "MacArthur's world and the world of beautiful Louise Cromwell Brooks were . . . as spiritually unconnected as . . . two planets. MacArthur was a soldier full of a soldier's precision and impatience with civilian frivolity. His life had been the cushionless life of an Army outpost, of West Point, and of rough campaigns. The life of fashionable young Mrs. Brooks was wholly different . . ." It may be that this polite tabloid prose hits the nail squarely on the head. A more ambitious tracing of the origins of MacArthur's traits than we have been able to undertake here might very well lead inward, past all the manifestations of Prussianism, to the Puritan marrow of his bones. If MacArthur married Society in Mrs. Brooks, he married Army in Miss Faircloth. A Daughter of the Confederacy and a Daughter of the American Revolution, she was reared from birth to be a soldier's wife.

against conviction. The Luce publications assert this as a fact, and a fact it may be, but MacArthur himself, perhaps respecting the sanctity of court-martial proceedings, has never publicly disclosed his vote. According to one legend, a newspaperman with a dubious sense of propriety went through a wastebasket after the trial and found there a mutilated slip of paper marked "Not Guilty. Douglas MacArthur." Once in a letter to Senator Alexander Wiley of Wisconsin, MacArthur wrote that his part in the trial was "fully known" to Mitchell, who, MacArthur went on, "never ceased to express his gratitude for my attitude." In George Kenney's *The MacArthur I Know*, Kenney, both an airman and a MacArthur enthusiast, does not say that MacArthur voted for acquittal, but he suggests that MacArthur was the man who "prevented the court from sentencing Billy Mitchell to a dishonorable discharge from the Army." He quotes Mitchell as saying, in 1933, "A grand guy, Douglas MacArthur, and a true friend. Some day people will realize how good a friend of mine he was back there in 1925." In Isaac Don Levine's life of Mitchell, it is more or less taken for granted that MacArthur voted to acquit, but the only approach to documentation is a letter Mitchell wrote to H. H. Arnold, who was to command American air forces in the Second World War, shortly after MacArthur became Chief of Staff. "There is a much better set-up in the War Department than there used to be," Mitchell wrote.

Mitchell's own recollection of the trial in a manuscript written in 1935 and left in the hands of friends shortly before his death in 1936 expresses not gratitude but deep resentment. Mitchell wrote:

Douglas MacArthur, I believe, will be the first to admit that I was right, when the next war comes. He regrets the part he played in my court-martial. May he be brave enough to say it openly.

and further on, Mitchell says:

MacArthur, whom I admired for his courage, his audacity and sincerity, surely could not be part of this! But there he was, his features as cold as carved stone. I had fought under his father . . . We had even discussed what might be done some day if Japanese Imperialism should embark on a southward course. And here was his son, a brave soldier, appointed to strip me in mid-career, in an argument over a machine which might some day save the Philippine Islands. He is back there now [1935] directing the organization of the national defense of the Commonwealth Government, which no battleships could protect from air attack. Planes and nothing but planes can hold those possessions. Perhaps by this time MacArthur can see it all with an open mind. . . .

But MacArthur certainly had not grasped the significance of my trial in 1925. I still believe he erred honestly. Men grow in stature by admitting their own mistakes. Douglas has developed that quality. But perhaps I am a better judge of planes than of men.

However MacArthur voted, he must have found the whole affair painful, like most affairs in those days. It would be possible to construct a tenable theory of MacArthur's present character by saying that its most salient and extravagant elements are the product of a kind of delayed rebellion against the twenties and parts of the thirties. They were frustrating, imprisoning years. His most important activities—the Mitchell affair, the Olympic games, and the sad rout of the Bonus Marchers in 1932—were unworthy of him. The best he could do was to charge the activities with the heroic emotions he must have felt stirring inside him. It was sometimes more than the activities could bear. The Mitchell trial was certainly no occasion for wearing "features as cold as carved stone"; the campaign on Anacostia Flats was no occasion for wearing burnished boots and a full complement of decorations. But he had to make the most of intractable materials. There had to be some make-believe. As head of the Olympic Games Committee, he constructed a fantasy world in which his role was that of a man rescuing the American people from grossness and degeneracy through athletics. In a communiqué to President Coolidge, we get some insight into how intractable materials may be forced to yield.

In undertaking this difficult task [he wrote] I recall a passage in Plutarch wherein Themistòcles, being asked whether he would rather be Achilles or Homer, replied: "Which would you rather be, a conqueror in the Olympic Games or the crier who proclaims who are conquerors?" And indeed to portray adequately the vividness and brilliance of that great spectacle would be worthy of the pen of Homer himself. No words of mine can adequately portray such great moments as the resistless onrush of that matchless California eight as it swirled and crashed down the placid water of the Sloten; that indomitable will for victory which marked the deathless rush of Barbuti; that sparkling combination of speed and grace by Elizabeth Robinson which might have rivaled even Artemis herself on the heights of Olympus . . . I can but record the bare blunt facts trusting that imagination will supply the magic touch to that which can never be forgotten by those who were actually present.

MacArthur was Chief of Staff of the Army from October 1930 until October 1935. The most celebrated feature of his long tenure—he was the first Chief of Staff to succeed himself—was his rout of the limp and ragged hordes of Bonus Marchers from the back lots of Washington on July 28, 1932. Two incompatible lines of explanation are currently employed to justify his role in that lamentable campaign. One is that the Bonus Expeditionary Force, as it came to be known during its two-month encampment, was a Communist conspiracy and that MacArthur's destruction of it was an early victory in democracy's struggle with communism. The other is that MacArthur simply gritted his teeth and carried out the harsh orders of his superiors.

As to the first theory, it is true that there were Communists in the B.E.F., and it is doubtless a fact that their numbers and their influence grew during the long and squalid bivouac on Anacostia Flats. But to see the B.E.F. as nothing but a Communist conspiracy is possible only to those who regard the crash of 1929 as nothing but a fiction of Communist propaganda. When fifteen million people are unemployed, Russian agents are not needed to produce a march on Washington.

The theory that MacArthur had no choice in the matter has more to recommend it. He acted under orders—orders from President Hoover, who at four o'clock on the afternoon of July 28 telephoned the Secretary of War, Patrick Hurley, and directed immediate evacuation of the B.E.F. by the military. Hurley passed the orders along to MacArthur, who might, if he had wished, have sped them further along the chain of command; it is not customary for chiefs of staff to go into the field and direct operations there, particularly against an army equipped mostly with barrel staves and stones. There is no doubt that the means chosen were MacArthur's. He had tanks and mounted cavalry from Fort Myer massed for the advance. The tanks and the gleaming sabers of the cavalrymen were chiefly for display purposes, and there may have been some merit in his later explanation that what was clearly a ridiculous show of force for the occasion was actually the way to get the job done with the least bloodshed and skull-cracking. He wished to scare the marchers away, not drive them away, he said; but in the end some blood was shed, some skulls were cracked.

It will always be an open question whether MacArthur chose the least destructive means; what is something less than an open question is the dignity of MacArthur's own conduct. Shedding his white linen suit, he slipped into his most dashing get-up. Directly the skirmish was over, he issued an on-the-spot communiqué, complete to the last subjunctive. "Had the President not acted today," he said, "had he permitted this thing to go on for twenty-four hours more, he would have been faced with a grave situation which would have caused a real battle. Had he let it go another week, I believe the institutions of our government would have been severely threatened." It was still a gray time for a "heaven-born general," a time requiring compensation in fantasy.

Anacostia Flats was the Army's only engagement during MacArthur's period as Chief of Staff. His day-to-day performance satisfied Herbert Hoover, and it impressed Franklin D. Roosevelt sufficiently to lead to reappointment. MacArthur fought a sturdy, unyielding battle of words against the prevalent pacifism* and

* At a University of Pittsburgh commencement, he declared: "Pacifism and its bedfellow, communism, are all about us. In the theaters and picture shows, newspapers and magazines, pulpits and lecture halls, schools and colleges, it hangs like a mist before the face of America, organizing the forces of unrest, undermining the morale of the working man. Day by day this cancer eats deeper into the body politic."

against the preoccupied, neutrality-minded Congress. At first, he fell in with the Hoover retrenchment policy, which affected the War Department most of all. But Roosevelt provided new encouragement and new ideas; with characteristic resourcefulness, for example, the new President contrived to have some of the costs of defense written off as relief expenditures. Between them, the two men managed to save the Army from starvation; it was no fault of theirs that it continued to suffer from galloping malnutrition. "For the first time since 1922," MacArthur was able to write in 1935, "the Army enters a new fiscal year with a reasonable prospect of developing itself into a defense establishment commensurate in size and efficiency to the country's minimum needs."

His military prescience was less estimable than his feats with the outstretched hand. During those years, officers like Charles de Gaulle in France, J. F. C. Fuller in England, Heinz Guderian in Germany, and, in this country, Colonel Adna Chaffee began to see something of the shape of wars to come: *Blitzkrieg* and armored warfare and strategic bombing. MacArthur was by no means blind to the future, but he saw it through a glass not so much darkly as bifocally. "Tanks, planes, submarines will be the decisive weapons in the next war," he said. "Mass movements of airplanes and huge concentrations of tanks will win the battles." But he also said, in his 1932 report, "The evolution of the mounted trooper into the mechanized cavalryman will necessarily take place over a considerable period of time, and will become practically complete only when machines have been developed capable of performing every function heretofore devolving upon the horse."

Six months after MacArthur became Chief of Staff, he disbanded the mechanized force which, since 1927, had been patiently, and, in the view of most students of the problem, brilliantly built up at Fort Eustis by Colonel Chaffee. In this force were mechanized infantry, engineers, and artillery as well as tanks. Chaffee was developing, in a necessarily small laboratory, theories and methods of organization which were observed admiringly and often emulated by the German General Staff. MacArthur had different ideas, which were studied but not widely borrowed. It was his belief that those machines which could perform at least some equine functions should be organized not as a separate unit within the military establishment but should be integrated with other units. Breaking up Chaffee's American *Panzers*, he divided their armored cars and tanks between the infantry and the cavalry.* It was not until after the fall of France that we took up where Chaffee had been forced to leave off.

"The time has come," Billy Mitchell had said in 1924, "when we must modernize our national defense . . . and organize it in a simple, direct, and efficient manner. This can be brought about by creating a Department of National Defense, with service departments for the Air, the Army, and the Navy." Exactly this was done a quarter of a century later, and when MacArthur testified at the Senate hearings in 1951 he said that "I believe it is the gravest possible mistake in the use of the armed forces . . . to draw lines of demarcation between ground troops, air troops, and navy troops." He said that the value of integration had been proved in Korea, where the co-ordination of the "three fighting services has

* Here is his explanation, as given in his 1931 report: "There have been two theories advanced to govern the application of mechanization . . . The first is that a separate mechanized force should be so organized as to contain within itself the power of carrying on a complete action, from first contact to final victory, thus duplicating the missions and to some extent the equipment of all other arms. The other theory is that each of the older arms should utilize any types of these vehicles as will enable it better and more surely to carry out the particular combat tasks it has been traditionally assigned . . . In the initial enthusiasm of postwar thought the first method was considered as the ideal one . . . continued study and experimentation have since resulted in its virtual abandonment . . . Accordingly during the last year, the independent "mechanized force" at Fort Eustis has been broken up. The cavalry has been given the task of developing combat vehicles that will enhance its powers in roles of reconnaissance, counter-reconnaissance, flank action, pursuit, and similar operations. One of its regiments will be equipped exclusively with such vehicles. The Infantry will give attention to machines intended to increase the striking power of the Infantry against strongly held positions ѵ . . . I feel that the continued observation of [this] basic doctrine now promulgated to our Army will have far-reaching and beneficial effects in future training and readiness for emergency."

been as complete as I could possibly imagine. They have worked as a team. The responsiveness of each service to the desire and wishes of the other has been almost perfection." It was probably an amiable overstatement—unless in the Far East there is a sublime harmony that cannot be achieved in Washington—and it was assuredly a repudiation of an old conviction. "The line of demarcation," MacArthur had said in his 1932 report, "between the Army and Navy is clear-cut and permanent in character. . . . Certainly the necessity for tactical co-operation in isolated instances of combined action cannot be considered as a sufficient reason for revolutionary changes in higher organization." He was later to tell George Kenney that he regarded his opposition to a single Department of National Defense with a separate department for Air as "the greatest mistake of my career."

In the thirties, MacArthur was enthusiastic about certain other forms of integration. He wanted tanks integrated with horses, and in 1934 he had a vision of sweating down all types of military aircraft into one: "The three types that, in major quantities would compose the G.H.Q. air forces are attack, pursuit, and bombardment. . . . [These] types are beginning to blend, and I personally believe that within the next ten years, you will probably see such a marked improvement that one type will do the work that is now divided among the three types." He was enthusiastic about reintegrating the Air Corps with the Army, from which it had been largely de-integrated by the Air Corps Act of 1926, establishing a separate Assistant Secretary of War for Air. In 1933, the Air Corps went back to the Army General Staff, a development for which MacArthur was not directly responsible but which he told the House Military Affairs Committee he looked upon as thoroughly sound.

Still, the truth, in all likelihood, is that MacArthur saw things as clearly as most of the men around him at the time. He was no Mitchell, no Guderian, no de Gaulle. But even some of the things they said have an absurd ring today. By the calendar, 1933 was only a few years ago, but in terms of ideas it was centuries. It must be established that MacArthur is not God; it must also be noted that it is not of record that Marshall, Eisenhower, Malin Craig or any of MacArthur's contemporaries were much shrewder; Eisenhower, indeed, who from February 1933 was MacArthur's personal aide and intimate adviser, drafted many of MacArthur's reports. It is of record that Billy Mitchell's shrewdness cost him his career. As for Adna Chaffee, who can identify him today?

For the rest, MacArthur lived on in Washington, a somewhat old-fashioned and incongruous figure in the days when Rexford Tugwell, Benjamin Cohen, Thomas Corcoran, Harold Ickes, Henry Wallace and Jerome Frank were the names with which to conjure. His mother, proud and watchful as ever, was still with him. Nearly every day, when not detained at the War Department, he would drive back to Fort Meyer to lunch with her. Within the Army itself, MacArthur exercised an anxious supervision which was based, some critics felt, on his calculation as to whether officers could be counted on to be MacArthur men. In Eisenhower he reposed great trust; and, for his Deputy Chief of Staff, he selected first Major General George Van Horn Moseley, who later achieved a brief notoriety for his pro-Fascist political activities in the late nineteen thirties, and then Major General Hugh A. Drum. Other officers he consigned to exile. The most famous case was that of Colonel George C. Marshall, who, having just returned to active command after four years at the Fort Benning Infantry School, was suddenly ordered by MacArthur to go to Illinois as Senior Instructor for the National Guard. Marshall, convinced that another long absence from the troops would be fatal to his army future, addressed to the Chief of Staff the first request for special consideration he had ever made in the Army. MacArthur rejected the request out of hand; Marshall left for Chicago within a week. "Those first months in Chicago I shall never forget," Mrs. Marshall has since written. "George had a gray, drawn look which I had never seen before, and have seldom seen since." For Marshall the exile lasted till early 1936 when he was suddenly promoted to brigadier general. "General Malin

Craig was now Chief of Staff," Mrs. Marshall noted. "The waiting was over—General Marshall was back with troops."

For MacArthur, the waiting continued. A man destined for great things, he seemed condemned to growing old in mediocre times. Glory recollected in fantasy remained his most satisfactory solution. In the summer of 1935 the veterans of the Rainbow Division met for a reunion in Washington. MacArthur, turning his eyes from the alphabetical agencies and the pacifists and the imbecile congressmen, tried desperately to restore through words the magic days of courage and heroism.

It was seventeen years ago—those days of old have vanished tone and tint: they have gone glimmering through the dreams of things that were. Their memory is a land where flowers of wondrous beauty and varied colors spring, watered by tears and coaxed and caressed into fuller bloom by the smiles of yesterday. Refrains no longer rise and fall from that land of used-to-be. We listen vainly but with thirsty ear for the witching melodies of days that are gone.

How flat the present! how magnificent the past!

Ghosts in olive drab and sky blue and German gray pass before our eyes; voices that have stolen away in the echoes from the battlefield no more ring out. The faint far whisper of forgotten songs no longer floats through the air. Youth . . . strength . . . aspirations . . . struggles . . . triumphs . . . despairs . . . wide winds sweeping . . . beacons flashing across uncharted depths . . . movements . . . vividness . . . radiance . . . shadows . . . faint bugles sounding reveille . . . far drums beating the long roll . . . the crash of guns . . . the rattle of musketry . . . the still white crosses . . . And now, we are met to remember.

But the stupid importunities of the present kept breaking in: this was the other side of the medal. The congressmen, the columnists, the pacifists, the reformers—they buzzed pestiferously around him. One day he could stand it no longer and filed a libel suit against Drew Pearson and Robert S. Allen, who had treated him with contempt in their Merry-Go-Round books and were after him again in their column. The objectionable articles had given national distribution to a number of unflattering anecdotes about MacArthur that had for some time been going the rounds in Washington and at Army posts. The Chief of Staff's suit charged the reporters with a desire to bring his good name and reputation into "disastrous scandal, ridicule, and professional disrepute before his superiors, associates, friends, neighbors, acquaintances, and the public in general."

But even this rebounded. Reconsidering, he abandoned the suit, perhaps because he thought it beneath his dignity, which it unquestionably was. He had asked $1,750,000 from the columnists; he ended up paying the costs of the suit, which were large. "No apologies or retractions," Pearson and Allen later stated, "were given or asked for." Returning to Washington in 1951, he said the experience brought back "poignant memories of former military service here, when life was gentler and happier." He was either rising to the occasion or thinking back to his young manhood, before the First World War, for the life he had known when he had last seen Washington was, for him, stale, flat, and unprofitable.

He found a familiar way out of it. In 1934, the United States began the liquidation of its most exotic adventure in colonialism. The Tydings-McDuffie Act, passed that year, provided for the full independence of the Philippines by 1946. The Islands would have more than a decade in which to adjust themselves to the harsh necessities of nationhood. Of these necessities, one of the most puzzling, both to Franklin Roosevelt and to Manuel Quezon, the first President of the Commonwealth, was defense. The United States obviously did not intend to free the Islands for the benefit of some other colonial power; the Filipinos did not propose to exchange one master for another. In November 1934, Quezon addressed a formal request to the War Department asking for a United States military mission for the Philippines. Informally, he let it be known that his government would welcome Douglas MacArthur as its chief military adviser.

Quezon's reasons were clear enough. The presence in Manila of the retiring American Chief of Staff would heighten the prestige of the new commonwealth all over the Orient. MacArthur was both a first-class military organizer and a first-class name. The name had special meanings for the Filipinos. It somehow dramatized the progress of the Islands to have the son of their conqueror become the servant of the new state.

MacArthur's reasons were no more obscure than Quezon's. At fifty-five, he was by no means ready to go on the shelf. Even had he been physically less resilient than he was, the thought of retirement would have been abhorrent. Next to professors emeritus and over-age dentists, probably no professional man commanded less respect in the America of 1935 than a retired army officer. He could, of course, have stayed on in the Army. But he was cursed with too much rank. There was nowhere for him to go but down— nothing here for him to do but grow old assailing the unkind seasons. The Philippine offer was a godsend. It not only provided him an escape from the vexations of American politics; it offered a scene in which his character could expand to its true proportions. In those days, the white man in the Far East still had an exalted status by the mere fact of color. When he clapped his hands, the native boys came running. For white generals, they ran especially fast. Nationalism was stirring, to be sure, but it was not the headlong force it was later to become. Only a few Filipino radicals would object when the American general received a salary higher than that of their President, a salary which enabled him to live a princely life in his penthouse on the Manila Hotel. Authority in Manila still commanded its due recognition. The man of authority there was safe from the intrusions of the press and the complaints of the legislators.

MacArthur made a quick exit in the fall of 1935, leaving Washington, as it had been his wish to do, while still Chief of Staff of the United States Army. It was a bitter disappointment that he was divested of the title before his arrival in Manila.* He valued

* He had been most eager to have General George S. Simonds succeed him. Simonds was a staunch and capable figure, but Roosevelt didn't take to him. In fact, he once told James A. Farley that he had extended MacArthur's term

the title but one cannot examine his subsequent career without concluding that he has always been happiest when away from the people who granted it.

MacArthur is our greatest military expatriate; he was as much in rebellion against our civilization as ever Henry James or Henry Miller was, and he probably symbolized the non-homesick American better than they ever did. There is no reason to suppose that he ever longed for Little Rock or Milwaukee or Fort Meyer or pined away for the long, lonesome wail of the locomotive whistle. Between 1935 and 1951, he saw the mainland only once—in 1937, when he came on a business trip with Quezon. When he made this last visit to America, the Neutrality Act was ten days old. On one side of the world, as he left America in 1937, Neville Chamberlain was just taking over as Prime Minister of Great Britain; on the other, toward which he was heading, there was a minor clash between Chinese and Japanese troops on Marco Polo Bridge, near Peiping.

THE ROAD TO BATAAN

MacArthur's routine of life was quickly established, and he threw himself with energy into his new job. He had brought a small planning staff with him, headed by the Major Eisenhower who had served him so usefully in Washington. But for a time the chief manifestations of the new dispensation were more superficial. When Quezon made MacArthur a field marshal in 1936, MacArthur proceeded in his best bravura fashion to live up to a rank too magnificent for the United States Army. *The Army and Navy*

---

simply in order to remove Simonds from consideration, since Simonds would then not have time enough to serve out a full term as Chief of Staff before he reached the age of automatic retirement. Shortly after MacArthur left Washington for Manila, Roosevelt announced the appointment of Malin Craig. MacArthur, hearing the news in Larami, Wyoming, said "No better selection . . . could possibly have been made." But his fellow officers say that he was furious and that he never forgave Roosevelt for the appointment.

Journal told of a Manila parade in this period: "Standing beside the President at the review was General MacArthur, dressed, according to press dispatches, in a white uniform of his own design made of sharkskin material, with four stars on his shoulder, a red ribbon at the base of his lapels, with his General Staff insignia on his left breast." This description unaccountably neglects the fine, gaudy, gold-braided cap, also a MacArthur original.

But it should not be thought that this passion for regalia necessarily reflected MacArthur's direct personal preferences. The obligations of military command often have a convulsive impact on sensitive individuals, splitting them into two distinct personalities: the private personality, reserved for wife, family and the officers' club; and the military personality, employed in the command of troops. The maintenance of morale in the Army depends in great part on a sense of confidence in the commander; the commander, as a consequence, must devise means to project himself as an individual in a way which makes an unforgettable impression on the troops. Insensibly, almost, he heightens existing traits and invents new ones, and in time the military personality diverges further and further from the original.

MacArthur recognized that he faced a difficult morale problem in the Philippines. His defense program would never succeed unless the Filipinos developed an active and unquestioning confidence in his wisdom. He therefore had to impress them with a sense of his authority, if not of his infallibility. The rhetoric, the military swagger, the remorseless gold braid were, in part, the response of a naturally histrionic personality to a situation where histrionics became almost a part of policy.

Yet histrionics always present a danger. In the long run, the public personality may begin to swallow up the private, the actor may begin to believe in his own role. This danger is doubtless the greater when the actor lacks humor and succumbs to the spell of his own rhetoric—greater still when there are no dramatic critics. Manila exposed MacArthur to fatal temptations while relieving him from the restraints once imposed by his contemporaries in the Army. His sense of remoteness from the mainland seemed to increase every year. In 1937 he took a tremendous step of separation and resigned from the United States Army. His worst suspicions about the tendency of things at home were very likely confirmed in 1939 when Roosevelt, in appointing a new Chief of Staff, passed over General Hugh A. Drum, who had been MacArthur's Deputy Chief of Staff, to appoint the former Senior Instructor of the Illinois National Guard. Later the same year, MacArthur and Eisenhower, after many years of close association, came to a parting of the ways. The field marshal in Manila was more isolated than ever.

More isolated, more remote, more lofty—even Paul V. McNutt, the experienced and affable high commissioner of the Philippines, not a man notably phased by pomp or circumstance, confessed, "I wouldn't hesitate to call President Quezon Manuel, but I never called the General 'Doug.'" He was becoming a truly formidable figure, nourished by an atmosphere which rewarded both benevolence and despotism; and he provided his formidability with the necessary external trappings.*

But all was not regalia and ritual for MacArthur. Beneath the trappings, he was engaged in deadly serious work. His mission was to organize Philippine defenses and train Filipino forces so that by 1946 the Philippine Republic would be able to defend itself against invasion. In accepting this mission, MacArthur was flying in the face of informed military opinion. As early as 1909, long before the modern bomber had reduced the protective value of the sea, the Army and Navy Board had abandoned the belief

---

* It may not be frivolous to suggest that one other MacArthur quality which induced inferiority feelings on the part of those near him was his cool and immaculate appearance on the hottest of tropical days. While collars wilted and creases dissolved around him, MacArthur would remain detached and unaffected. This immaculacy, however, was perhaps less a triumph of will than an accident of biology. At a later stage General Robert Eichelberger would write with some bitterness, "The sun poured down mercilessly, and my uniform was soggy and dark with wetness. I remember my astonishment that General MacArthur, despite the sweltering heat and the vigorous exercise, did not perspire at all."

that the Philippines were defensible against any opponent (meaning Japan) which had really set its heart on conquering them. For that reason, Washington discarded the thought of building important bases in the Philippines. Twenty years later Major General Johnson Hagood, after his tour of duty as commanding general in the Philippine Department, stated the general opinion when he told President Hoover, "It is not within the wildest possibility to maintain or to raise in the Philippine Islands a sufficient force to defend it against any probable foe." Nor did prospects seem much better of a successful defense by means of aid from the United States, as envisaged in the War Department's old Orange plan. "To carry out the present Orange plan, with the provisions for the early dispatch of our fleet to Philippine waters," Brigadier General Stanley D. Embick, commander of the Manila defenses, wrote in 1933, "would be literally an act of madness."

This was strong language from Generals Hagood and Embick, particularly when one remembers the studied caution of most military prose. But MacArthur boldly rejected the counsels of pessimism. The Philippines, he said, would be defended; and his plan which he submitted to Quezon in 1936, was guaranteed to transform potentiality into reality. "I am certain," MacArthur said in a speech to the army officers that year, "that no chancellery in the world, if it accepts the opinions of its military and naval staffs, will ever willingly make an effort to willfully attack the Philippines after the present development has been completed."

He was to say much the same thing again and again in the next few years—often in terms so unguarded that it sounded as if he were talking about the Filipino capability of 1938 and 1939 rather than the capability hoped for by 1946. Thus, after war had broken out in Europe in 1939, he would predict that "invasion would cost the enemy, in my opinion, at least a half million of men as casualties and upwards of five billion of dollars in money to pursue such an adventure with any hope of success. Would it be worth such a staggering cost?" Such statements have often been unfairly quoted against MacArthur by men who forget the "if" generally imbedded somewhere in the text—"if the present national defense plan is earnestly and thoroughly carried out."

In part, no doubt, MacArthur's air of certainty was "campaign oratory"; it was as much a part of his campaign to give the Filipinos hope and confidence as his new uniform and his scrambled-egg cap. But if it were that alone, if he had no real belief that the Philippines would be defensible by 1946, he was engaged in an unforgivable deception of Quezon and of the new nation. The best evidence is that MacArthur was engaged in no such deception. Against the whole weight of military thinking, he had convinced himself of the defensibility of the Islands. His military optimism was not put on for purposes of morale. It reflected his essential estimate of the situation.

He planned to raise a regular army and, through universal military training, a reserve; and he counted upon American support for bombers, artillery and other heavy weapons. But the heart of the program (and MacArthur's contribution to the strategic philosophy of Philippine defense) was his system of naval patrol. "The purpose of the Philippine Plan," as he defined it himself, "is to assure an active and carefully planned defense of every foot of shore line in the inhabited islands of the Archipelago." His solution was to employ a flotilla of fast torpedo boats: "a relatively small fleet of such vessels, manned by crews thoroughly familiar with every foot of the coast line and surrounding waters, and carrying, in the torpedo, a definite threat against large ships, will have distinct effect on compelling any hostile force to approach cautiously and by small detachments."

Generalizing cheerily from Gallipoli ("that abortive undertaking") in terms which would hardly have appealed to Winston Churchill, MacArthur argued that in the future "armies and navies will undertake with extreme reluctance any similar operation"—that is, attacking a defended coast. With his fleet of 65-foot Q-boats buzzing around the islands, everything, he felt, would be under control except against the mightiest of armadas. "In all history there is no example of this kind of attack being attempted on a comparable scale, since the invasions of Greece by the Persians in the fifth century B.C. were mainly accomplished by land marches. Even so, those invasions resulted in complete failure."

In last resort, the MacArthur plan stood or fell on its success in denying the use of territorial waters to hostile ships through speedboats and bomber patrols. From the viewpoint of most competent observers, it fell, and badly. The total coast line of the Philippines, it was pointed out, was longer than that of the United States; yet even the much larger American fleet did not pretend to have "an active and carefully planned defense of every foot of shore line." MacArthur's mosquito fleet was limited in range; its operations were dependent on favorable weather; and, in no case, could these toy boats hope to deal with the destroyers which Japan had in such abundance.

Indeed, as the years went on, it seemed increasingly clear that, even if his plan were "earnestly and thoroughly carried out" it would not provide an adequate defense for the Philippines. In time Quezon, MacArthur's first and strongest backer, began to succumb to MacArthur's critics and to find the Field Marshal's confidence increasingly hollow. By late 1940 the President was ready substantially to repudiate the whole MacArthur theory. The Philippines could not be defended, Quezon said at last in a public speech, even if every last Filipino was armed with modern weapons.

Only the General himself remained unperturbed. In the end, of course, his thesis would never be put to test; war would strike long before 1946, the year of the plan's scheduled fulfillment. The experience of that war hardly supports the theory of Philippine defensibility, urged so gallantly in the face of so much skepticism. MacArthur's own signal contribution to that war would be a series of amphibious operations on a scale which made Gallipoli seem like small gear. When the war was over and MacArthur addressed the Philippine Congress in 1945, he quietly, if obliquely, abandoned his old theory. "No nation, however powerful," he said, "may with safety rely exclusively upon its own defense potentiality. . . . Defense is no longer national; it has become international." So far as the Philippines were concerned, Douglas MacArthur seemed to have been wrong, and Johnson Hagood right.

In any case, by the end of the thirties it was clear that 1946 would be too late. In 1940 Japan assumed an increasingly dark and menacing posture in the Pacific. It was these developments which filled Quezon with his increasing pessimism. But MacArthur, in the face of all the portents, retained his optimism. He affected not to understand the fear of Japan. "It has been assumed," he observed in 1939, "in my opinion, erroneously, that Japan covets these Islands. Just why has never been satisfactorily explained. Proponents of such a theory fail fully to credit the logic of the Japanese mind."

The phrase "logic of the Japanese mind" struck a note which MacArthur would sound with increasing frequency in the next decade. He began to fancy himself a master of Oriental psychology, and those around him systematically confirmed his impression that he was the only American who understood Asia. So far as Japan was concerned, he argued that "strategically, possession of these Islands would introduce an element of extraordinary weakness in the Japanese empire. . . . Economically, Japan would gain nothing by conquest." Moreover, any such adventure would expose Japan to the risk of foreign intervention. "If committed to such an attack the Japanese position would become desperate if such intervention should materialize on the part of a nation equipped with a powerful fleet." In brief, the oracle said, Japan would court suicide if its aggression provoked the United States.

The bitter events of 1940 and early 1941 did not significantly alter MacArthur's estimate. In May 1941, in his precise and confident way, pacing the floor in his office, MacArthur explained to a *Time* reporter why the United States need not fear Japan. Germany, he said, has told Japan not to stir up trouble in the Pacific, because Japan is helping Germany more by not fighting than she would by actually going to war. As a threat, Japan can do several things. She ties down the American fleet in Pearl Harbor; she ties down British and Imperial troops in Malaya. And if Japan did enter the war, he said with unusual emphasis, the Americans, the British and the Dutch could handle her with about half the forces they now have deployed in the Far East. The Japanese Navy, MacArthur said, would either be bottled up tight or destroyed.

His certitude was irresistible. It is a rule of modern warfare, he continued, that complex industrial nations cannot fight much more than four years of war. In two months, Japan's war in China would be four years old; decay was already rotting the foundations of Japan's economic and military structure. "Resources have been burnt out, Japan has overspent itself. . . . The morale of the people is worsening." The Chinese war was hopeless: "China is like an accordion; the more the Japanese push in, the more force it gains." (MacArthur, who is never one to waste a good phrase, would in another decade compare the war in Korea to an accordion, while urging an enlargement of the war to China.)

In Washington, Roosevelt and Marshall, Henry L. Stimson and Cordell Hull looked on the Japanese situation with considerably less than MacArthur's complacency. Through the long summer of 1941 they worried over the tension in the Pacific, while the Japanese moved into Indo-China and seemed ready to drive on wherever they could in southeast Asia. In July MacArthur was recalled to active duty in the United States Army and made commander of U.S. Army Forces in the Far East (USAFFE). The warnings from Washington began to have some effect on MacArthur; at the same time, MacArthur's optimism began to have its effect in Washington; and the success over Germany of the Flying Fortresses based on Britain suddenly gave Marshall and Stimson a flicker of hope that these mighty new bombers, based on the Philippines, would be capable of blockading the China Sea and smashing a Japanese invasion.

As a consequence, our Pacific strategy was altered in August and the Philippines were suddenly given the highest priority on military equipment. A force of B-17's was flown in; other material followed. On October 6, 1941, Stimson told Hull that "we needed three months to secure our position" in the Islands. So far as MacArthur was concerned, they would have the three months—and more. While he was now at last willing to admit the possibility of Japanese aggression, he declared repeatedly, with his customary confidence, that there was no reason to fear it before April 1942.

General Lewis H. Brereton, arriving from the United States in November 1941 to take over command of the air force, was assured that nothing would happen before next April. "The mobilization and training schedule of the Philippine Department and of the Philippine Army," he noted in his diary, "was based on that assumption." This was MacArthur's prediction and party line, in spite of all the gloomy messages from Washington. "Looking back on that prediction, and remembering hindsightedly that the Japs were even at that hour massing to hit us," General Jonathan M. Wainwright, the hero of Bataan, later testified, "I'd like to stress this thought: MacArthur believed that nothing was going to happen before April 1942."

Washington kept up its warnings. On November 28, General Brereton wrote in his diary: "Two messages from the War Department alerted us to the possibility of an attack by Japan at any hour." Other cables in the next taut days spelled out the message. The breakdown of negotiations was anticipated momentarily, the War Department told MacArthur; all military, naval and air installations were to prepare themselves against surprise.

On December 2 the air corps radar set showed tracks of Japanese aircraft off the Luzon coast. Colonel Harold H. George, the brilliant young air force officer, commented, "It's my guess they simply were getting their range data established—possibly a rendezvous point from Formosa." The next day Clark Field reported a strange plane high over the field just before dawn. George said grimly, "They've got all they need now. The next time they won't play. They'll come in without knocking." On December 4 Brereton scribbled in his diary that unidentified aircraft, estimated at from 9 to 27 bombers, had been approaching within 20 miles of the shores of Lingayan Gulf. "Presumably, they were making trial navigation flights to familiarize themselves with the air route."

Warned from above, warned from below, the MacArthur headquarters maintained equanimity. General Arnold had cabled from Washington for a report on the state of vigilance. On December 6, MacArthur finally replied for Brereton: "All air corps stations here on alert status. Airplanes dispersed and each under guard." On December 7, Brereton notified all fields and commanders that they were to go on 'combat alert' as of dawn on Monday, the 8th. But Douglas MacArthur's high command, secure in its hope of Philippine defensibility, secure in its gospel of no danger till April 1942, secure in its mastery of the "logic of the Japanese mind," refused to be panicked by warnings of attack.

With the shock of Pearl Harbor, reality pierced the MacArthur fantasy. In the air corps detachment, at least, the reaction was swift. The B-17 crews were alerted; Colonel George ordered that the bombing-objective folders, outlining the targets on Formosa, be brought to the staff conference. "We were ready," Colonel Allison Ind recalls. "We had been ready ever since that grim warning of November 27."

At five in the morning of the 8th, General Brereton requested permission from General Richard Sutherland, MacArthur's chief of staff, to mount all the available B-17's for previously assigned missions against the enemy. Sutherland agreed in principle (according to Brereton's diary) but said that he first must obtain General MacArthur's authority for daylight attacks. "When I left General MacArthur's headquarters," Brereton wrote, "I was under orders to prepare our heavy bombers for action but not to undertake any offensive action until ordered." At 9 o'clock Sutherland advised Brereton that planes were not authorized to carry bombs at this time.

On his return to Clark Field, Brereton was told that hostile aircraft were operating over Luzon. He phoned Sutherland again and warned him that, if Clark Field were attacked successfully, he would be unable to operate offensively with the bombers. "I again requested authority to carry out offensive action." Sutherland reaffirmed his decision that "the present attitude is strictly defensive." But, at ten minutes after ten, Sutherland called to say that General MacArthur had now decided that a photo-reconnaissance mission could be sent to Formosa. The men at Clark Field were incredulous: the camera did not seem to be the indicated weapon against the Japanese a few hours after Pearl Harbor. At about eleven o'clock, Brereton received another call from Sutherland, this time informing him that bombing missions could be executed. Six precious hours had been lost waiting for orders from MacArthur.* Brereton instantly directed the commanding officer at Clark Field to load all available B-17s with bombs and brief the crews to attack known airfields in southwest Formosa.

At noon the loading and the briefing were still under way. The planes (in spite of the Brereton-MacArthur cable to Arnold) were not fully dispersed; some of the B-17s stood in line, wingtip to wingtip. It was nine hours after the assault on Pearl Harbor—nine hours wasted because of the strange lassitude and indecision in headquarters. At about thirteen minutes after noon, a wave of Japanese bombers suddenly dove down out of the sky. There had been no warning; communications with the single radar set in northern Luzon had broken down.

The raid was short but devastating: two waves of bombers, with dive bombers and strafers, shot up the field. Most American planes were caught on the ground or on the runway; a few barely

---

* The Japanese themselves were baffled by the delay. Their own bombing of the Philippines had been held up by fog; hence they were certain that they had lost all chance of destroying U.S. airpower by surprise, and they feared that American bombers would now be able to smash the invasion forces in Formosa. Captain Shibita, the senior Japanese staff officer on Formosa, told interrogators of the U.S. Strategic Bombing Survey in 1945: "We were very worried because we were sure after learning of Pearl Harbor you would disperse your planes or make an attack on our base at Formosa. We put on our gas masks and prepared for an attack by American aircraft." Captain Shibita's anxiety was unnecessary.

managed to take off. When General Wainwright arrived at Clark Field a few moments later, planes and buildings were in flames, with great pillars of black smoke whirling into the sky. Of the shiny new B-17s, the pivot of the defense of the Philippines, more than half were wrecked and smashed; over 20 first-line fighter planes were gone; 200 American airmen and ground personnel were killed or wounded; the destruction of ground equipment alone was staggering. The Japanese lost only two planes in the Clark Field raid.

With one blow the Japanese had smashed any hope of defending the Philippines. Who was responsible? In 1951 the question was still clouded and obscure. Admiral Kimmel and General Short were relieved of their commands and pilloried across the country for failing to anticipate the Japanese surprise attack at Pearl Harbor; but MacArthur remained almost unscathed in spite of the fact that, with nine hours' clear warning—Kimmel and Short had none—he did not anticipate the attack at Clark Field. A congressional committee spent months in a detailed investigation of the Pearl Harbor affairs, but no committee has ever looked into the far less forgivable fiasco in the Philippines. "The lightness with which this cardinal military sin was excused by the American high command when committed by Regular Army officers," Major General Claire L. Chennault later declared of the Clark Field affair, "has always seemed to me one of the more shocking aspects of the war . . . It is high time the American people made it their business to find out more about why the men they paid for twenty years to provide for the national defense were so pitifully unprepared for the catastrophe that nearly engulfed us all."

The MacArthur party line was quickly established. When George Kenney went out to the Pacific to take command of the U.S. Air Force, Sutherland told him that the loss of our planes on the ground was all Brereton's fault. MacArthur himself later put it forcibly to Clark Lee of the International News Service: "I got rid of those incompetent, bungling nincompoop airmen who were with me in the early days of the war." The General even denied on September 27, 1946, that he had ever received from Brereton any recommendation to bomb Formosa, or that he knew anything of such a recommendation having been made.

Probably the local unpreparedness—the inadequate dispersion, and so on—must be charged to Brereton. One air force officer later described a photograph made by an American pilot in flight over the stricken field, showing, through a frame of sweeping smoke, a row of four B-17s neatly lined up. Other photographs, taken on the ground, all told a "nauseating" story of half-measures. "This entire set of photographs was removed from my desk a few nights later," the officer added. "No one seemed to know what happened to them. Whether they were removed by order, I do not know—nor do I have any ideas as to whose order it might have been."

But it is hard to lay the ultimate blame on Brereton. When General Arnold sent him a scorching cable after the disaster, Brereton replied for the Air Force, "We had done everything in our power to get authority to attack Formosa on 8 December but had been relegated to a 'strictly defensive attitude' by higher authority." For all the Sutherland disclaimers and the MacArthur denials, this statement seems essentially true. Existing air force records—particularly the headquarters log—bear out Brereton's claim that he requested authority to bomb Formosa. "Neither General MacArthur nor General Sutherland," Brereton later declared, "ever told me why authority was withheld to attack Formosa after the Japs had attacked Pearl Harbor."

MacArthur's denial that Brereton ever made any request may mean that Sutherland never bothered to pass Brereton's request on to him. On other occasions, certainly Sutherland did not hesitate to take responsibility on his own shoulders. Yet it seems unlikely that Sutherland would have dared make so considerable a decision as this one without checking with his commanding officer. On the whole, one must assume that, here as elsewhere, MacArthur's capacity for imaginative reconstruction of the past went into play when he made his statement in 1946. With an imagination as lively as MacArthur's, who could blame him for confusing imagination in the end with reality?

The reasons for his paralysis that fatal morning thus remain unknown. In his 1946 statement, he claimed that "the over-all strategic mission of the Philippine command was to defend the Philippines, not to initiate an outside attack." Conceivably, in the astonishment and confusion, he may have supposed that the Pearl Harbor attack was a local incident, perhaps precipitated by the Japanese fleet in defiance of the government, and that he must therefore refrain from retaliation until an overt act was committed against the Philippines. Yet General Marshall had ordered MacArthur to execute "all the necessary movement required in event of an outbreak of hostilities with Japan"; and in this he specifically included air raids against Japanese forces and installations. Perhaps MacArthur's confidence in his understanding of the "logic of the Japanese mind" dictated some more inscrutable explanation. In any case, his interlude of daze and uncertainty was decisive. The price of MacArthur's vacillation was the flame and wreckage of Clark Field.

With the elimination of the Air Corps as a serious weapon, the Philippine campaign went into a new phase. At this point, it should have been clear—if anything was clear—that the U.S. and Filipino forces could no longer hope to prevent an invasion of the islands. But MacArthur's vacillation did not end with the Clark Field raid. He reacted slowly and uncertainly to the new situation. His mind seemed still to be fixed on his grandiose plan for the defense of the entire Philippines. He refused to acknowledge the necessity of preparing for an eventual retreat to the peninsula of Bataan and the island fortress of Corregidor.

Yet his own plan for commonwealth defense, if it ever was tenable, was clearly useless after December 7, 1941. At best, it was not to go into effect until 1946; the flotilla of fast torpedo boats had never floated; half of MacArthur's air strength had been destroyed or damaged. The Philippine soldiers, moreover, though brave, were untrained; in all MacArthur's time as field marshal, he had not been able to give his army effective field exercises or even target practice.* The obvious move in such circumstances was to resort to the classical solution for the defense of the Philippines. Familiar in broad outlines in all the textbooks, known in its 1941 version was War Plan Orange No. 3 (WPO-3), this plan called on the defending forces to fight delaying actions against the invaders and gradually to withdraw into the peninsula of Bataan. MacArthur regarded it as a "defeatist plan," however, and for sixteen days refused to put it into effect.

This refusal had little effect on the actual fighting; WPO-3 envisaged a gradual and hard-fought withdrawal. Where it was crucial was on the question of supply. By failing to invoke WPO-3 until December 23, MacArthur wasted sixteen days which the Quartermaster Corps might otherwise have devoted to stockpiling food, medical supplies and material on Bataan. Part of the Supply Section of WPO-3, for example, was the building up of a rice depot at Cabantuan; here 50,000,000 bushels of unthreshed rice were stored. In the days after Pearl Harbor, there was ample opportunity to move some of this rice to Bataan; the railroad was open to points south of Lubao, and box cars were available; moreover, the roads were relatively free, and there were plenty of trucks on hand. But nothing was done; not a grain of rice was moved from Cabantuan. Similarly, plans for the evacuation of food and supplies from the port area and the wholesale warehouses of Manila were never carried out. On December 29, when Colonel E. B. Miller and the 194th Tank Battalion took up positions around the strategic Calumpit Bridge, they saw a trail of *empty* trucks winding their way to Bataan.

This battalion, on its own initiative, was able in the next few days to salvage and move to Bataan about 12,000 gallons of aviation gasoline and 6 truckloads of canned food. Other units did

* General George Grunert, Commander of the Philippine Department, had reported to Washington in 1940 and 1941 in unflattering terms regarding the state of training of the Philippine Army. Grunert's estimate of the defensibility of the Islands was realistic and in sharp disagreement with MacArthur's. In October 1941, MacArthur had Grunert sent home.

likewise; but the High Command had failed miserably. It had clung to its illusion that it might drive the Japanese off Luzon long after it should have concentrated its main energy on preparing for the retirement into Bataan. General Wainwright, infected with MacArthur's reckless optimism, wrote later that, on the night of December 23, when "I was working on my counterattacking plans —forlorn as they were now becoming," he suddenly was told that WPO-3 had been at last put into effect. "It was," said Wainwright, "a bitter pill to swallow." This attitude may have been magnificent, but it was not war. MacArthur's refusal to face up to the necessity of retreat meant that the troops in Bataan had to go on half-rations immediately after the withdrawal into the peninsula. In a longer run, it condemned them to weeks and months of hunger and suffering.

Thus the troops retired to Bataan, and MacArthur himself to the island fortress of Corregidor. The Japanese pressed their attack relentlessly; and the Americans and Filipinos, ill-equipped and ill-fed, fought with great courage under the command of General Wainwright. MacArthur himself remained aloof on Corregidor. Most people when they think of Bataan, think of Mac-Arthur. Yet he visited Bataan only once during the months of grim resistance. General Wainwright's description of this meeting is worth reproducing.

"Jonathan," he said, greeting me most cordially as he stepped out of the car, "I'm glad to see you back from the north. The execution of your withdrawal and of your mission in covering the withdrawal of the South Luzon force were as fine as anything in history."

Douglas was a little expansive on some occasions, and I don't mean that unkindly. I just wondered if I deserved such praise.

"And for that," he continued, "I'm going to see that you are made a permanent major general of the Regular Army." That was nice, for I was only a temporary one at the time.

He spoke to the other generals for a few minutes, then came back to me.

"Where are your 155-millimeter guns," he asked.

I told him where the six of them were, and since two of them were fairly close I suggested that he walk over with me and take a look at them.

"Jonathan," he said, "I don't want to *see* them, I want to *hear* them!" It was our only meeting on Bataan.

This single visit moved Wainwright's men even less than it moved Wainwright. Hopelessness had begun to settle over the troops; they felt that everyone had forgotten them; they were the expendables. A sardonic verse expressed their feelings.

> *We're the battling bastards of Bataan:*
>   *No momma, no poppa, no Uncle Sam,*
> *No aunts, no uncles, no nephews, no nieces,*
>   *No rifles, no guns or artillery pieces,*
>   *And nobody gives a damn.*

From their viewpoint, Corregidor, for all its squalor and over-crowding, meant infinite security and incalculable luxury. They disliked MacArthur for staying on "The Rock"; they disliked his communiqués* The Marines disliked him particularly because his communiqués refused to acknowledge the fact that the 4th Marine Regiment was fighting in Bataan. (When the Corregidor radio mentioned their presence after many days, the Navy Department in Washington had to explain that it did not mean that reinforcements had arrived.) The men on Bataan freely predicted to each other that MacArthur would run to safety and leave them to their wretched fate.

An anonymous ballad-maker wrote the "USAFFE Cry of Free-

---

* It is sometimes said that the men who have served with MacArthur regard him ever after as the greatest man alive. This maxim distinctly does not apply to the Philippine campaign. Even the general officers seem to have come away with an abiding distrust. Thus Brigadier General William E. Brougher, who served in Bataan, wrote *apropos* of the MacArthur controversy of 1951: "Russia's whole object in the Korean incident has been to induce the United States to abandon the Marshall concept and go over to the MacArthur plan. In this they have partially succeeded. If the American people are blind enough to permit them to gain the rest of their objective, God help our country. When the security of our country is at stake, I follow George Marshall, one of the greatest Americans of many generations."

dom" to the tune of "The Battle Hymn of the Republic." It passed
from hand to hand during the black weeks of February 1942.

Dugout Doug MacArthur lies ashaking on the Rock,
Safe from all bombers and from any sudden shock
Dugout Doug is eating of the best food on Bataan
And his troops go starving on. . . .

We've fought the war the hard way since they said the fight was on
All the way from Lingayen to the hills of Old Bataan
And we'll continue fighting after Dugout Doug is gone
And still go starving on.

Chorus:

Dugout Doug, come out from hiding
Dugout Doug, come out from hiding
Send to Franklin the glad tidings
That his troops go starving on!

The song was grievously unfair. However mistaken MacArthur
was in not sharing more often the discomfort and danger of
Bataan, it is abundantly clear that his motive was not physical
fear. He never lacked courage. As commanding general, he had
many calls on his attention.

Something lashed him into desperation in his relations with
Washington. He pleaded for reinforcements, as any commander
in the situation must; but, when they did not arrive, he seemed
to regard it as a personal betrayal. Overoptimistic messages from
Roosevelt may for a moment have revived his own excessive
optimism. "Although I cannot at this time state the day that help
will arrive in the Philippines," Roosevelt had cabled to Quezon,
"I can assure you that every vessel avaailable is bearing to the
Southwest Pacific the strength that will eventually crush the
enemy and liberate your native land." MacArthur promptly sent
a message to his troops: "Help is on the way from the United
States. Thousands of troops and hundreds of planes are being
dispatched. The exact time of arrival of reinforcements is un-

known. . . . It is imperative that our troops hold until these reinforcements arrive"

Quezon soon gave up on the hope of reinforcement. MacArthur at first challenged Quezon's defeatism. "I will bring you in triumph on the points of my bayonets in Manila," he assured the Philippine President. But, as time passed with no sign of aid, he too began to feel that they had been sold out by the United States. Washington had promised large-scale reinforcements; now it was failing to deliver. Had it, he must have wondered, ever had any intention of delivering? Had not Washington committed itself to the British view that the war against Hitler must take priority? The men at Corregidor began to talk to the newspapermen about their "enemies" in Washington: Eisenhower, who had come to a chilly parting with MacArthur in 1939 and was now in charge of Philippine war plans in the War Department; Marshall, MacArthur's old military rival; Roosevelt himself, who must regard MacArthur as a political rival.

Quezon, ailing and embittered, began to reconsider the whole question of the Philippines' role in the war. In late January he worked out a startling plan for the neutralization of the Philippines. Both American and Japanese forces, he concluded, should be withdrawn, and the Philippine Army disbanded. Sergio Osmeña, the vice-president of the Philippine Commonwealth, was opposed; but General MacArthur listened to Quezon with sympathy. As Osmeña's intimate personal adviser, Dr. James K. Eyre, Jr., later described MacArthur's state of mind at this juncture: "His own demands for assistance having produced few tangible results, he decided to use to the fullest the one weapon which seemed to be left to him—Manuel Quezon. . . . Having resolved upon this course, he not only encouraged but actually assisted the Filipino leader to prepare his ultimatum to the occupant of the White House."

The MacArthur-Quezon message of February 8, 1942, was an extraordinary document. Besides the surrender proposals, it contained a bitter attack on what it called the bad faith of the United

States Government—"strictures against the American failure to reinforce the Philippines," Henry L. Stimson later wrote, unaware of MacArthur's part in the preparation of the message, "in terms as unfair as they were wholly understandable." With the Quezon cable came a message from High Commissioner Francis B. Sayre giving his conditional support to the neutralization policy. And, along with these two messages, came one from General Mac-Arthur, phrased with care, yet unmistakably throwing its weight on the scales in favor of the Quezon program.

Since I have no air or sea protection, you must be prepared at any time to figure on the complete destruction of this command. You must determine whether the mission of delay would be better furthered by the temporizing plan of Quezon or by my continued battle effort. The temper of the Filipinos is one of almost violent resentment against the United States. Every one of them expected help and when it has not been forthcoming they believe they have been betrayed in favor of others.

The General's military observations were particularly interesting. MacArthur, who insisted in 1951 that the loss of Formosa would drive the United States back to Oregon and Washington, contended in 1942 that we would "lose no military advantage" through the loss of the Philippines. "So far as the military angle is concerned," he added, "the problem presents itself as to whether the plan of President Quezon might offer the best possible solution of what is about to be a disastrous debacle."

Washington was stunned. For Eisenhower it was a "bombshell." Stimson declared it "a serious shock" to himself and to Marshall. Quezon, Stimson said, seemed to act as if the Filipinos had no stake in the war; "worse than that, Commissioner Sayre and General MacArthur appeared to have made no effort to dissuade Quezon from his position and had even given it some support in their messages." The Secretary of War and the Chief of Staff felt that the whole proposal was hideously unrealistic and would be of benefit only to Japan. Neither MacArthur nor Quezon, Stimson wrote, "appeared to appreciate the moral abdication involved in the proposal of a neutralized Philippines."

Stimson and Marshall went immediately to the White House. The President asked Stimson what he thought. To avoid interruption, Stimson rose from his seat and gave his views standing, as if before a court. Roosevelt listened attentively; then he and Sumner Welles, who was also at the conference, both said that they agreed entirely. The four men set to and drafted replies to Quezon and to MacArthur.

The Roosevelt cable to MacArthur of February 9, 1942, is one of the great documents of the war. In essence, it was a lecture on the nature of appeasement, but read with such dignity and respect as to lack any elements of reproach. After all, MacArthur and Quezon were the men on the spot, in the agonizing situation of impending military defeat; and Roosevelt and Stimson understood their extremity. But in this case other considerations had to be overriding. A coalition of free nations had arisen in response to the totalitarian challenge; "we cannot afford to have this line broken in any particular theater. As the most powerful member of this coalition we cannot display weakness in fact or in spirit anywhere. It is mandatory that there be established once and for all in the minds of all peoples complete evidence that the American determination and indomitable will to win carries on down to the last unit." Why should any one think for a moment that appeasement would work, that Japan would respect the terms of neutralization? "Is it longer possible," Roosevelt asked MacArthur, "for any reasonable person to rely upon Japanese offer or promise?"

The lecture struck home. MacArthur promptly replied that he would resist to the end. Quezon, however, flew into a rage and dictated a statement resigning as President of the Commonwealth. "Because of Roosevelt's insulting message," he told the members of his cabinet, "it is no longer possbile for me to serve as President of the Commonwealth. I have been deceived and I intend to return to Manila." For two days, the crisis continued. Eventually Osmeña and MacArthur were able to prevail upon Quezon to withdraw his resignation and stay on in Corregidor.

Had MacArthur's recommendation of February 8, 1942, been followed, he might have gone down into history with men like General William Hull, who surrendered Detroit during the War of 1812. But Roosevelt's staunchness saved MacArthur's reputation, as Roosevelt's orders a few weeks later would save MacArthur himself for greater usefulness in the South Pacific. In the meantime, MacArthur himself was in one of those swings from extreme pessimism to extreme optimism which have characterized his entire military career. On February 8 he had been grimly anticipating "a disastrous debacle . . . the complete destruction of this command." Two weeks later his mood had entirely changed. "With his present forces," he cheerily cabled Washington, "the enemy appears to be unable to make the attack required to destroy me."

But Roosevelt had already decided that MacArthur must leave Corregidor and command the allied forces in Australia. MacArthur balked at first; but he finally obeyed what Roosevelt made into an order. On March 11, MacArthur, accompanied by his wife, young Arthur and the boy's Chinese nurse, boarded a PT boat to begin the long and hazardous trip to Australia. Two days before he left, however, he recommended all the units on Bataan and Corregidor for unit citations—except the Marine and naval detachments. "Sutherland let it be known," Hanson Baldwin has reported, "that this was no oversight; the Marines had gotten their share of glory in World War I, and they weren't going to get any in this one!" On this amiable note, MacArthur left Corregidor.

General Wainwright assumed command of the United States forces. The situation grew more desperate; the food and medical supplies shrank; the Japanese pressed ever closer. By early April resistance was near the point of collapse. Wainwright still got typical messages from MacArthur. "When the supply situation becomes impossible," MacArthur cabled on April 7, "there must be no thought of surrender. You must attack." Two days later Bataan was surrendered. On May 5 Wainwright himself finally capitulated at Corregidor. His simple statement summed up the sacrifices of Bataan.

I have been with my men from the start and, if captured, I will share their lot. Americans shaken by the loss of Bataan should not feel the fall of the Manila Bay forts to be a double tragedy, but rather the exemplification of the grimness of our spirit when we stay to the end with a job to be done.

MacArthur issued a statement at the same time.

Corregidor needs no comment from me. It has sounded its own story at the mouth of its guns. It has scrolled its own epitaph on enemy tablets, but through the bloody haze of its last reverberating shots, I shall always seem to see the vision of its grim, gaunt and ghostly men.

THE ROAD TO TOKYO

In Australia, MacArthur's war entered a new phase. He was at first still oppressed by a sense of failure in the Philippines. Bataan was on his conscience, and for a while he talked about it all the time, in public and in private. John Hersey reported that Major General Pat Hurley, in Australia on a presidential mission, had said that MacArthur seemed to want to relieve Bataan more than anything; some people even feared that this might warp his views of general strategy. MacArthur himself declared his fervent purpose in an historic pledge. The President, he announced, had ordered him to Australia to organize the American offensive against Japan. "A primary purpose of this is the relief of the Philippines. I came through and I shall return."

But he was bitterly—and understandably—disappointed in the resources available to him. American power was limited; the European theater had first call. Like any good theater commander, MacArthur fought hard for supplies and for men, exchanging angry telegrams with General Marshall and the Joint Chiefs of Staff. The ghastly Philippine defeat behind him, he was determined to resume the offensive as soon as possible. But he could not defeat the Japanese with his bare hands. "Must I always," he said savagely to General Robert Eichelberger, "lead a forlorn hope?" Once, in a moment of despair, he cabled Quezon in Washington, asking whether he could have his old job back in the Philippines after the war.

In June 1942, the great Midway victory checked the Japanese drive. It was necessary to follow this up lest the Japanese have time to bind their wounds and return to the attack. The Navy and the Marines stabbed into Guadalcanal and Tulagi in August, beginning a long saga of American heroism. MacArthur in the meantime set up advance lines in New Guinea in preparation for a counteroffensive. In the fall of 1942 American and Australian troops plunged into the New Guinea jungle, fighting under indescribable conditions across the Owen Stanley Mountains toward Japanese bases at Buna and Gona.

There had been criticism of the defective training which MacArthur's troops received both at home and in Australia. "I recall one soldier," Eichelberger has since stated, "who told me that in twenty months of service he had had only one night problem. He asked me how he could be expected to be proficient in night patrolling against the Japanese under those conditions." When Eichelberger questioned the training system at the MacArthur headquarters, however, he was rebuffed: "my opinion was not popular."* But there is little criticism of the spirit with which MacArthur undertook the counteroffensive. The Australian government wanted him to concentrate on defensive operations; but he was determined to recapture the initiative. He drove his troops and commanders almost beyond human endurance; but they survived the terrible rigors of jungle fighting to achieve victory after victory. He replaced generals who could not do the job, and gave

---

* In particular, training in the avoidance of jungle diseases was neglected. As a consequence, malaria was for a time more dangerous to American troops than the Japanese were. In the Buna campaign, over half of the men of the 32nd Division succumbed to disease.

ruthless orders to their replacements. "Bob," he said to Eichelberger when he sent him into the Buna campaign, "I want you to take Buna, or not come back alive . . . Do you understand?" To other men, he made other appeals. When he asked Halsey to become chief of his naval operations, he said, "If you come with me, I'll make you a greater man than Nelson ever dreamed of being!"

Early in March 1943, General George Kenney's bombers, operating under MacArthur's command, smashed a Japanese troop convoy headed for New Guinea in the Battle of the Bismarck Sea. This battle wrecked the enemy strategy in the South Pacific; the Japanese never again tried to move large bodies of troops within range of allied airpower. This development had a decisive effect on American strategy. It meant that it would be possible to bypass Japanese bases, leaving them, so to speak, to wither on the vine, knowing that, after the Bismarck Sea disaster, the Japanese would be reluctant to risk large-scale reinforcement. The "leapfrogging" strategy began to emerge as the basic pattern of the American counteroffensive.

But MacArthur could not begin to move up the Pacific until New Guinea was cleared of Japanese. In 1943 and 1944, with the amphibious attack on Hollandia in April 1944 as the eventual climax, this was his major task. Yet, if he went on the offensive sooner than the Australian government wanted, it is an odd and little-known fact that he was much more slow and cautious than his superiors in Washington wished him to be. As the military history of the Pacific War makes clear, MacArthur, far from urging new offensive activity on an indifferent Washington, actually resisted one attempt after another on the part of the Joint Chiefs of Staff to hasten his advance.

In January 1943, for example, the Joint Chiefs asked MacArthur to submit plans for the capture of Rabaul on New Britain. MacArthur replied that the losses of the Buna campaign and the lack of reinforcements from America would make it impossible for him to undertake new operations without a period of preparation. The Joint Chiefs deferred the Rabaul plan and reduced the immediate scope of MacArthur's objectives. In May the Joint Chiefs began to develop their central thesis for the Pacific War—the idea of moving toward Japan along two axes of advance, one from the South and Southwest Pacific under MacArthur, the other from the Central Pacific through the Gilberts, Marshalls and Carolines under Admiral Chester Nimitz. MacArthur immediately protested against what seemed to him a gravely mistaken division of inadequate American resources. There was no useful strategic objective, he said, in the Central Pacific; everything should be concentrated on his own drive through New Guinea to Mindanao, the southernmost island of the Philippines.

The Joint Chiefs ignored the protest, contenting themselves with reminding MacArthur in July that the war was being run from Washington. At the same time, they urged him to hurry along, suggesting that he now consider isolating Rabaul, instead of attacking it, and then move straight up the New Guinea coast to Hollandia. MacArthur quickly denounced this as a reckless plan. The investment of Rabaul, he said, was essential to the Hollandia operation, since Rabaul was the only possible naval base from which to cover the advance up the New Guinea coast. The Joint Chiefs again ignored his objections and at the Quebec conference in August issued a firm directive, ordering him to bypass Rabaul. At the same time, they provided a new timetable for Nimitz, who was making steady progress in the Central Pacific.

Whatever MacArthur's initial resistance to the directives from Washington, he executed them with incomparable skill. Combining air, naval and ground operations with superb success, ably solving the logistics of the amphibious offensive, he succeeded brilliantly in knocking out the crucial links in the Japanese island chain of defense. The enemy was badly outmaneuvered; allied losses were one-tenth those of the Japanese. In these spectacular campaigns, MacArthur more than made up for Bataan.

After the New Guinea campaign and the capture of Morotai, the Japanese island base to the north, MacArthur was within 300 miles of the Philippines. Admiral Nimitz had made similarly impressive gains in the independent Navy campaign in the Central Pacific. The Joint Chiefs of Staff in Washington were now faced with the problem of where MacArthur and Nimitz should go next. MacArthur and Nimitz offered radically different answers.

MacArthur was still possessed by his determination to liberate the Philippines and by his conviction that American strength was not great enough to sustain two great advances toward Japan. But the Navy wanted to by-pass the Philippines and move directly on Formosa. The capture of Formosa, the admirals argued, would place the allied air forces in a position to strike at the heart of Japan. General Arnold and other men in the Air Force also believed in a direct assault on Formosa. Some air force officers even argued that B-29s, operating from Guam, Saipan and Tinian against Japan proper, could knock Japan out of the war before MacArthur could capture Luzon—an idea MacArthur thought ridiculous.

On March 12, 1944, the Joint Chiefs issued a compromise directive, calling for co-ordinated operations against Mindanao in the southern Philippines, with the choice between Luzon and Formosa deferred to a later date. Three months later MacArthur was summoned to Pearl Harbor for a conference with Roosevelt, Admiral King, and Admiral Nimitz to make a final decision on the Philippines. Nimitz argued vigorously for a plan of leapfrogging the Philippines and instead securing bases on Formosa and the Chinese mainland. Roosevelt asked MacArthur for comment. MacArthur set forth eloquently the military case for taking the Philippines. Later, in a private interview with the President, he presented the moral argument. Was Mr. Roosevelt willing, he asked, "to accept responsibility for breaking a solemn promise to eighteen million Christian Filipinos that the Americans would return?" As he moved to leave, MacArthur felt that his cause was lost. But the President suddenly looked up. "Wait a minute, Douglas," he said. "Come back here." As MacArthur later told the story to John Gunther, Roosevelt's last words were: "Well, Douglas, you win! But I am going to have a hell of a time over this with that old bear, Ernie King!"*

MacArthur's insistence on the Philippine invasion was strongly questioned at the time and in the years since. Critics said that he was sacrificing military strategy—and American lives—to dynastic sentiment. Yet there were potent military arguments for moving into the Philippines. The leapfrogging strategy works well only when the islands skipped are too weak to sustain offensives of their own which might break the allied lines of communication. The Japanese had a big force in the Philippines; moreover, with their bases in Japan and China, they could have made a direct attack on Formosa terribly costly. In any case, MacArthur would have needed the deep-water harbors and the naval bases of the Philippines as staging areas for the massive amphibious invasion then anticipated against Japan proper. "From a purely strategical point of view," Admiral Leahy subsequently wrote, "I was personally in favor of the Philippines operation."†

In October 1944 MacArthur stepped on the invasion beach at Leyte. He delivered a prepared address into a convenient microphone.

People of the Philippines: I have returned. . . . Rally to me. Let the indomitable spirit of Bataan and Corregidor lead on as the lines of battle roll forward to bring you within the zone of operations, rise and strike. . . . For your homes, and hearts, strike! For future generations of your sons and daughters! Strike! In the name of your sacred dead, strike! Let no heart be faint. Let every arm be steeled. The guidance

* The conference had a wonderful effect on MacArthur's attitude toward Roosevelt. In place of his former bitterness, MacArthur now began to speak of him with affection. "You know that the President is a man of great vision," he remarked to Clark Lee, "—once things are explained to him."
† Years later, when Formosa had acquired a new importance, MacArthur half abandoned his strategic case for the Philippine invasion. "I don't know of anything that would be more universal than the concept of the strategic value of Formosa," he observed in the congressional hearings. "As a matter of fact the Navy wanted to go into Formosa rather than the Philippines, and it was largely a moral question that decided the issue." One feels that here MacArthur does himself an injustice.

of Divine God points the way. Follow in His name to the Holy Grail of righteous victory.

It took months of bitter fighting to secure the Philippines. The next step was Japan itself. MacArthur was one of those, like Marshall, who insisted that a large-scale invasion of Japan would be necessary. With Tarawa, Iwo Jima, Okinawa and other amphibious battles vivid in everyone's recollection, this invasion loomed ahead as a horror of bitter-end killing; if American casualties were not to be fantastic, the military leaders believed it essential that the Red Army be induced to enter the war and pin down the great bulk of Japanese land forces on the Asian mainland. Some of the Pacific commanders disagreed with the invasion theory. Lieutenant General Holland M. Smith of the Marine Corps was convinced early in 1945 that the Japanese were about to throw in the sponge; so was George Kenney; but, though both men were excellent in their specialties, few people had much confidence in their judgment on world strategy. MacArthur's views contributed vitally to the Joint Chiefs' conclusion that Soviet participation in the Far Eastern War was indispensable. Their position, of course, led Roosevelt and Churchill to make the Far Eastern concessions at Yalta—concessions designed at military behest to make sure that the U.S.S.R. would enter the war. On March 2, 1945, MacArthur set foot again in Corregidor. Five months later, after Hiroshima and Nagasaki, he accepted the Japanese surrender at Yokohama.

In three and a half exhausting years of war, MacArthur thus fought himself from the defeat and disgrace of Bataan to the triumph of Tokyo. The searing experience of these years was the final phase in the transformation of the Chief of Staff of 1935 to the Supreme Commander and proconsul of a decade later. MacArthur had always been somewhat larger than life; but in a style which had been confined and thwarted by American folkways. Since 1919, his wings had been clipped in America—first by the frivolity of the Jazz Age, then by the reforming zeal of the New

Deal, always by the skepticism and humor of the American temperament. But the Philippines had given him room to expand; and the Second World War placed him in a setting of great events. In a sense, actuality began to catch up with his rhetoric. What was grotesque when applied to the Olympic Games became appropriate when applied to Hollandia or Leyte. The Pacific War rescued him from bathos. MacArthur, so long out of joint with the times, had finally made full contact, and, out of the contact, emerged a new creation: MacArthur the great general, resplendent, disinterested and wise.

Was MacArthur a great general? It must first be asked if great generals are possible in modern war. The tests have changed since the old, chessboard wars of Prince Eugene, Marshal Saxe and the Duke of Marlborough, who were great generals because they were great captains. A general today must be a diplomat, a politician, an industrial statesman, a transportation czar, a publicity expert—all these things as well as a strategist and a tactician. And, in the assembly line of modern war, it is as difficult to distinguish the individual contributions as it is to single out names from the credit list of a Hollywood film. Certainly if the man on top risks the blame of defeat, then he earns the credit of victory. In this sense—and in others—MacArthur was surely a great commander in chief. But this still does not answer the question whether he was a great captain, in the sense that Frederick and Napoleon and Alexander were great captains.

Most of his generals had deep respect for his strategical sense. It is true that Holland Smith, the Marine commander in the Pacific, has been acid in his comments. "MacArthur," he has later said, "was in supreme command in his own theater and could pick his own targets. He picked the easiest. Mine were picked for me by the Joint Chiefs of Staff in Washington, who indicated the objectives and left me the task of capturing them." But this statement is neither fair nor accurate and its author was hardly without prejudice. Yet it is also to the point that after Bataan, MacArthur never really had a field command—that is, he never had a small body of troops dependent on him for detailed tactical leadership (and the full extent of the Bataan failure was concealed till the men of Bataan began to emerge from the Japanese prison camps years later). Thus it was Eichelberger, not MacArthur, who took Buna and Hollandia. It was Halsey, not MacArthur, who had the brilliant idea of going into Leyte instead of Mindanao; it was Sutherland who took the Leyte decision in MacArthur's absence and without clearance with him; it was Halsey who won (after nearly losing) the Battle of Leyte Gulf, and it was Krueger who commanded the amphibious landings— even if it was MacArthur who spoke into the microphone on the beach.

In Europe, Eisenhower, who had MacArthur's equivalent position, has been virtually euchred out of any position in the generalship competition. He will go down as the chairman of the board; when you think of generals in the European theater, you think of Bradley, of Patton, of Montgomery. MacArthur's special triumph was to make people forget who his field commanders were; his greatest triumph of all was to convey the impression that he was the field commander himself, in tactical command in every jungle and on every beachhead.

This was achieved with surprising ease. The MacArthur headquarters from the start established and maintained a tight control over all news coming out of the theater. MacArthur's chief public relations officer, the egregious Brigadier General LeGrande A. Diller, guarded his chief's publicity potential as if it were a gold mine. MacArthur had always shown a canny understanding of the uses of publicity. When Dwight Eisenhower returned from the Philippines, someone asked him why he had broken with MacArthur. His reply was stark and illuminating: "He thought I was stealing his publicity."* But MacArthur's was always publicity

* Relations between MacArthur and Eisenhower got worse during the war. MacArthur used to talk about Eisenhower's "stubborn egotism" and criticize his conduct of the European war. "I could have landed with twenty divisions on the north coast of Germany," MacArthur said on December 21, 1944, "and had Berlin in two weeks." Eisenhower, for his part, was convinced that

by remote control: he held only four press conferences in the first three years of the Pacific war, all off-the-record. Diller, through what one infuriated correspondent called "the most rigid and dangerous censorship in American history," was able to control absolutely the picture of the war as it appeared in the American press. This control was systematically used to exalt the role of MacArthur and to reduce the role of the generals around him.

If newspapermen had been forbidden to mention Omar Bradley's or George Patton's name, and if all the achievements of the Twelfth Army Group or the Third Army had been credited to "Eisenhower's Headquarters," Dwight D. Eisenhower would have a far greater military reputation today. MacArthur applied this simple rule with wonderful success and suspended it only at moments of acute crisis. "If you capture Buna," he said to Eichelberger, "I'll give you a Distinguished Service Cross and recommend you for a high British decoration. Also," he continued, as if bestowing the final accolade, "I'll release your name for newspaper publication." During the grim months of jungle fighting around Buna, the communiqué bore the bland designation "MacArthur's headquarters." Some months later, when *Life* magazine ran a full page photograph of Eichelberger on February 15, 1943, MacArthur was outraged.

MacArthur—or General Diller—took eternal care to propagate the theory of MacArthur as the omnipresent field commander. Thus newspapermen were allowed to report it every time that

---

MacArthur blamed him personally for the failure to relieve the Philippines in 1942. In September 1943, when Clark Lee relayed to Eisenhower a radio description of MacArthur watching from a B-17 what was described as the biggest parachute landing in history, Eisenhower hit the desk a crashing blow with his first and glared at Lee. "Do you believe that?" he asked, "I don't."

The bad relations between Eisenhower and MacArthur seem to have been a factor in the decision to keep Marshall in Washington and make Eisenhower supreme commander of the European invasion. "If Eisenhower were to become Acting Chief of Staff," Sherwood writes in *Roosevelt and Hopkins*, "the regrettable but real lack of cordiality which characterized the relationship between him and MacArthur could become a source of major embarrassments."

MacArthur left Brisbane for the New Guinea front; but they were not allowed to report his return to Brisbane. As a consequence, the impression developed in America that MacArthur spent most of his time at the front, whereas he really spent most of his time—as a theater commander should—in supreme headquarters. Photographs released by MacArthur's headquarters contributed to the false impression. On his sixty-fourth birthday MacArthur paid a visit to Rockhampton, one of the Australian training areas, and had his picture taken in a jeep with Eichelberger. Subsequently the picture was released with the caption: "General MacArthur and General Eichelberger at the New Guinea Front." But the dead giveaway was the nose of a Packard automobile in one corner of the picture. "There weren't any Packards in the New Guinea jungle in 1944," Eichelberger has since pointed out.*

MacArthur's stubbornness was not petty vanity. His egotism included vanity, but rose far above it; it was a great natural fact, like Mount McKinley or Fujiyama. For him, "I" meant the whole of the allied forces—even though he should have known that many of his men resisted this neat identification. Just as he identified his troops with himself, so he identified himself with his theater and his theater with the war. He seems never to have reconciled himself to the grand strategy of fighting Germany first. Washing-

---

* MacArthur missed no opportunity to emphasize himself at the expense of his army commanders: examples could be multiplied indefinitely. Toward the end of the war, General Krueger's psychological warfare division wanted to drop surrender appeals to Japanese units. One day the phone rang in a subordinate office, and a MacArthur aide angrily said: "The General doesn't want anything dropped on the Japanese signed 'Krueger.' He wants it to be signed 'MacArthur.'" Krueger was furious at not being master in his own zone of operations; but he had no choice save to accede. At Leyte, radio broadcasters wanted to use a canned interview with Admiral Kinkaid, the tough naval commander who covered the landings. But Diller killed the idea. "On this great day," he said, "nothing shall be said or done that will detract in any way from the personal publicity or glorification of the commander in chief." The fight with OWI over "I shall return" was in the same category, though it was complicated by MacArthur's conviction that he alone understood the psychological value of "I" in the Orient. American soldiers and sailors might have considered "We shall return" more appropriate; but "I shall return" it remained.

ton's every application of that strategy was taken as a vindictive personal thrust at the General. "There are unmistakable evidences of an acute persecution complex at work," Robert E. Sherwood reported after a visit to the MacArthur headquarters. "To hear some of the staff officers talk, one would think that the War Department, the State Department, the Joint Chiefs of Staff—and possibly, even the White House itself—are under the domination of 'Communists and British Imperialists.'" According to Arthur Bliss Lane, MacArthur even opposed British participation in the Pacific War. The Navy was another cross to bear. "Yes, we've come a long way since Melbourne," MacArthur told Clark Lee in December 1944, "despite the Navy cabal that hates me, and the New Deal cabal." He voiced his persecution complex with vigor— at times less through official channels to his superiors in Washington (Roosevelt once remarked, after a talk with an official just back from a visit with MacArthur, "I wish that he would sometimes tell some of those things to *me*"), than through his own private network of newspaper reporters assigned to his headquarters, visiting congressmen, and other itinerant dignitaries.

His own world excluded all others, and he was at its center. The visible expression of this world was the MacArthur communiqué. His communiqués constituted a problem all by themselves in the Pacific. Their lush and elaborate prose, in a devoted but vulgar imitation of the General's own rhetoric, gave them a special air of South Sea fantasy. And always they came back in the end to the General himself. The Navy, in self-defense, finally produced a derisive ballad toward the end of the war:

For two long years, since blood and tears have been so very rife,
Confusion in our war news burdens more a soldier's life
But from this chaos, daily, like a hospice on the way,
Like a shining light to guide us, rises Doug's communiqué. . . .

'My battleships bombarded the Nips from Maine to Singapore
My subs have sunk a million tons; they'll sink a billion more.
My aircraft bombed Berlin last night.' In Italy they say,
'Our turn's tonight, because it's right in Doug's communiqué.' . . .

His area is quite cosmic and capricious as a breeze,
Ninety times as big as Texas, bigger than Los Angeles,
It springs from lost Atlantis up to where the angels play
And no sparrow falls unheeded—it's in Doug's communiqué.

But it was not just the egotism of the communiqués which made them intolerable; it was their inveterate, chronic, ineradicable inaccuracy. MacArthur was not only the sole commander in the field; but he also was forever destroying a forever outwitted enemy. The communiqués radiated self-congratulation for the surprise achieved, for the enemy units pulverized, for the American lives spared by the brilliance of the generalship. So far as MacArthur's public-relations officers were concerned, even the admiring George Kenney has admitted, "unless a news release painted the General with a halo and seated him on the highest pedestal in the universe, it should be killed. No news except favorable news, reflecting complete credit on an infallible Mac, had much chance of getting by the censors."

The truth was magnificent enough; it needed no adornment; there was glory enough for all. But MacArthur could not resist creating a fantasy picture of the war. The men fighting in the swamps around Buna in 1942 have never forgotten the MacArthur Christmas communiqué. "On Christmas Day," MacArthur's Headquarters piously announced, "our activities were limited to routine safety precautions. Divine services were held." But, as General Eichelberger subsequently observed, "on Christmas Day at Buna —the only place in the theater where there *could* be American Ground Force activities—the fighting was desperate and the outcome of the whole miserable, tortured campaign was in doubt."

The Buna campaign, indeed, set the pattern for the MacArthur communiqué version of the Pacific warfare. Not only did he eliminate the name of the general in the field, thereby creating the impression that MacArthur was personally in command; not only did he invent a soft and comfortable Christmas to soothe the folks back home; but he began with the Buna campaign his practice of announcing victory while the outcome was still uncertain.

As a result, some of the most terrible battles of the war are still almost unknown in the United States. With his total press control, MacArthur could, when it suited him or his public relations officer, reduce battles to skirmishes and expand skirmishes into battles. The fall of Buna, the communiqués suggested, ended the Papuan campaign. But the Americans and Australians in the field knew that Sanananda still lay ahead. The high officers in both armies, according to Eichelberger, "foresaw, as a result of optimistic reports released to the press, the ruin of their own careers—and mine. Sanananda would not be easy."

When some veterans of the New Guinea campaign were reminiscing with Eisenhower after the war, it developed that he had never heard of the battle of Sanananda. Why should he have? It was only a "mopping-up operation." Yet as many Americans and Australians were killed at Sanananda as at Tarawa later in the war. The cost of the Buna campaign as a whole was as great as the cost of Guadalcanal. Still such statistics did not fit into the theory of MacArthur as the man who licked the Japanese practically without losses. According to the computations of Dale Kramer, between the fall of 1942 and the beginning of the Philippine campaign in October 1944, the MacArthur communiqués reported Japanese losses of from 150,000 to 200,000, while the allied casualties listed in the communiqués amounted to 122 killed, 2 missing and 529 wounded.

MacArthur's public relations officers learned nothing from the New Guinea campaign. The Eighth Army, for example, took over in Leyte in the Philippines on Christmas Day, 1944. Eichelberger was told that there were only 6,000 Japanese left on the island. Actually the Japanese Army was still intact. It took several months of the roughest kind of combat to defeat this army; from Christmas Day to the real end of the Leyte campaign, the Eighth Army killed more than 27,000 Japanese. But, so far as MacArthur's headquarters was concerned, the Leyte campaign had officially closed in December and all future operations were "mopping-up." "If there is another war," Eichelberger recently observed, "I recommend that the military, and the correspondents, and everyone else concerned, drop the phrase 'mopping up' from their vocabularies. It is not a good enough phrase to die for."

The same thing happened a few weeks later in Manila. On February 7, 1945, MacArthur announced that Manila was secured. But weeks of fighting were to take place, building-to-building, room-to-room, hand-to-hand, before Manila really fell; only none of this could be reported since, according to General MacArthur, Manila had already fallen. With the fall of Davao City on Mindanao, MacArthur announced victory again. "However, there were many weeks ahead," Eichelberger later commented, "for the GIs who had no newspapers to tell them that everything was well in hand." MacArthur had told Eichelberger that he did not believe there were 4,000 Japanese left alive on Mindanao; when the war ended, 23,000 enemy soldiers came in to surrender.

The Philippine communiqués did more than just give another picture of MacArthur's unbeatable speed and skill. They also continued his policy of special preference for the Army. "You can search MacArthur's communiqués describing the Philippines fighting," Holland Smith has written, "and you will be unable to find a single reference to the Marines." Smith met a young marine who was being flown back from Leyte. The boy was in great pain, but it was not the physical suffering that seemed to worry him. "I don't mind losing a leg, sir," he said, "but at least Doug might have mentioned that Marines were there!" The famous Marine poem hardly did justice to the bitterness of their feelings. The last verse, of course, is classic:

> *And while possibly a rumor now,*
>   *Some day it will be fact*
> *That the Lord will hear a deep voice say,*
>   *Move over God, it's Mac.*

The corrections are now being entered on the historical record. But the communiqués, and not the facts, have shaped the popular picture of the Pacific fighting. Out of this picture MacArthur, a fine hero by any standards, emerged as a demigod. In today's perspective, indeed, the distressing thing about these communiqués is not just their literary debauchery, nor even their fast and loose way with facts; the smoke of battle often does obscure the truth. The distressing thing is that the man from whose headquarters they came has stubbornly refused to correct them, even when the truth later came out.

Thus Communiqué No. 3 reported the sinking of a 29,000-ton battleship by an air force plane north of Luzon. Subsequently MacArthur's headquarters identified the pilot as Captain Colin P. Kelly, Jr., and provided a graphic account of the destruction of the *Haruna*. The whole origin of this communiqué is obscure. Captain Kelly, who was killed on his return home, had radioed in of bombing the ship but not of sinking it. General Brereton, who made an inquiry, states, "How this report got out I have never been able to ascertain. Colonel Eubank, commander of the 19th Bomb Group, did not claim the *Haruna* as having been sunk and was never able to learn how the story originated." Evidently the whole idea was one more flight of fancy from "MacArthur's Headquarters." But more was to come. Captain Kelly and his crew were brave men and authentic heroes; still, subsequent investigation showed not only that they never sank the *Haruna* but that the Japanese used no battleships at all in the Luzon landings. The *Haruna* at that time was on the other side of the South China Sea. Despite various further claims of its destruction, it was still afloat when MacArthur accepted the Japanese surrender aboard the *Missouri*.

There was an even more striking instance when, after the Battle of the Bismarck Sea in early 1943, the air force communiqué claimed that Kenney and his bombers had destroyed 22 ships, 55 planes and about 12,000 men. Tall stories are common in the excitement of battle; and no one should have been astonished when it was later determined beyond any legitimate doubt that the true figures were 12 ships, 20 to 30 planes and about 3,000 men. This was still an honorable bag. But when the Air Force Historical

Section, after a study of captured materials, reported this to Mac-Arthur later in the year, he replied with a cable demanding the court-martial of the officer who wrote the report. On September 3, 1945, MacArthur, reviewing the events of the war in Japan, declared that the Battle of the Bismarck Sea, "in which the Japanese lost a 22-ship convoy," was a decisive engagement. "Some people," he added, a trifle petulantly, "have doubted the figures in that battle but we have the names of every ship sunk."

The Far East Air Force immediately launched another investigation to discover what had actually happened. Japanese naval veterans of the battle were interrogated; documents in the Japanese Naval Office were exhumed and examined. It bcame clear that the MacArthur figures were way off. On September 24, the report was submitted substantiating the earlier report in Washington. The Far East Air Force officer who received it sighed and said, "It is a fine job and I have no doubt the report will be immediately burned." This officer knew his MacArthur. On November 19, 1945, MacArthur's headquarters ordered that the report be destroyed.* Till the day of MacArthur's recall General Charles A. Willoughby, MacArthur's intelligence chief, and the court historians in Tokyo insisted on the original Bismarck Sea story, though, when challenged by other historians, they were never able to document their contentions.

MacArthur alone, of the U.S. theater commanders, ignored a War Department order after the war to turn his headquarters records over to the Army Historical Division. But the patient work of the Historical Divisions of the Army and the Air Force may be counted on, even without the MacArthur records, to expose the true worth of his communiqués. Still the communiqués brilliantly performed their function—which was to provide a MacArthur's-eye view of the war.

* Volume IV of *The Army Air Forces in World War II*, the official Air Force history, states sadly: "No copy of this report was available for transmission to the AAF Historical Office and subsequent attempts to locate the document have been unsuccessful."

The ultimate myth—the climax of the whole series of minor distortions, fabrications and excisions—is that MacArthur won the war against Japan. But a brief glance at the factors which brought about Japanese defeat shows clearly that MacArthur was only one element in a far more complicated picture. This was scarcely MacArthur's fault; he did everything that was expected of him—and more. But the Pacific War was much larger than the MacArthur theater; and the strategy which won the war was not only planned in Washington but was, in crucial cases, imposed on MacArthur over his passionate opposition. The Joint Chiefs, indeed, by sticking to their two-pronged theory of the war, reached the Philippines three and a half months earlier than he had thought possible and six weeks earlier than he had assured them that he could get there himself if everything was concentrated under his own command.

MacArthur's almost peripheral role, moreover, was inherent in the nature of the war. For Japan, an island power, was above all vulnerable to naval attack. And it was the Navy—and particularly the American submarines—which ate away at the life lines feeding Japan its essential quota of oil, war materials, and rice. It was the Navy too which first rolled back the Japanese tide at Coral Sea and Midway; it was the Marines who led the attack at Guadalcanal. Midway and Guadalcanal were probably the decisive battles of the whole Pacific War; Douglas MacArthur had nothing to do with either of them. Nor did he have anything to do with the Marine conquest of Saipan, Tinian, Guam, Iwo Jima; or with the B-29 raids which subsequently took place from these islands and which were probably the most potent factor of all in bringing Japan to its knees. MacArthur did a fine job in the Philippines; but he could hardly have done it without Admiral Halsey and Admiral Kinkaid, nor would the Philippines have made much difference without Admiral Nimitz's drive up the Central Pacific. Truman happened to choose MacArthur to receive the Japanese surrender; but he might with equal justice have chosen Nimitz (as he almost did). The Navy and the Marine Corps won almost all the decisive major actions against the Japanese in the Pacific War.

But the MacArthur myth will die hard—if only because so much genuine achievement underlies it.

THE PROCONSUL

On the eve of victory MacArthur was asked by one of his admirers, Brigadier General Julius Klein, what his post-war plans were. "I'm going to get myself a great big rocker," the General is quoted as replying, "put it on my porch before a small beautiful garden where I can finally spend life as the average American husband with his family in peace and contentment—that is, if the Nips don't get me first." But the very ring of the phrases was all wrong. One can imagine Bradley saying this, or Eisenhower; even Marshall had his passion for retirement at Leesburg; but MacArthur as an "average American husband," rocking on his porch, watching his garden grow, made an improbable picture.

If the work of war was done, the work of peace had yet to begin; and, for MacArthur—this was part of his greatness—peace was bound to be almost as challenging. A non-homesick American, for whom the East provided its special gratifications, he was in no hurry to get home. From the spring of 1945 to the summer of 1950, the man of war was primarily concerned with the works of peace. In the long run, indeed, history may remember him most of all for what he rehabilitated rather than for what he destroyed. Yet it is too often forgotten today that MacArthur left his stamp as proconsul on, not just one, but two countries; and that his first occupation, judged by the fruits, was far less successful than his second.

There is no reason to believe that the General himself would accept this comparison. "A Christian nation, the Philippines stand as a mighty bulwark of Christianity in the Far East," he said before the Congress on April 19, 1951, "and its capacity for high

moral leadership in Asia is unlimited." After a passing reference
to "existing unrest," the General declared firmly that "a strong
and healthy nation" would grow "in the longer aftermath of war's
terrible destructiveness."

He had ruled the Philippines with a strong hand through the
first crucial months after liberation. True, he had formally turned
the liberated areas over to the Philippine government, headed,
since the death of Quezon, by Sergio Osmeña. But it was sym-
bolic that, when the ceremony was over and the General and his
aides tumbled into waiting cars, Osmeña was left without even a
jeep and driver to help him find living quarters. MacArthur and
his headquarters were to make the vital decisions in the weeks
ahead.*

Before liberation, Roosevelt declared that those Filipinos who
collaborated with the Japanese "must be removed from authority
and influence over the political and economic life of the country."
MacArthur translated this policy into his own idiom. "It shall be
my firm purpose," he said in November 1944, "to run to earth
every disloyal Filipino who has debased his country's cause." But
the gap between principle and performance turned out to be wide
and confusing. The gap was made manifest early in April 1945 by
MacArthur's reaction to the capture of Manuel Roxas, one of the
most eminent of the Philippine collaborators.

The problem of collaboration is not simple. It is too easy for
men who spent the war in New York City to become indignant
over the failure of men in more exposed lands to join under-
ground movements and conduct clandestine operations against
an occupying army; and then to become doubly indignant when
such "collaborators" are not harried and persecuted after the war.
But most men are weak; most men are noncombatant by nature.
In one sense, to "collaborate" was to accept what for *l'homme*

---

* MacArthur was equally contemptuous of the attempts of Harold Ickes, as
Secretary of the Interior, to restore civilian authority in the Philippines. This
was particularly infuriating to Ickes, who, with a nice sense of historical
irony, had planned to recapitulate the drama of 44 years before and send
Charles P. Taft to take over from Douglas MacArthur.

moyen sensuel seemed to be the inevitable. And "collaboration" had its own series of gradations and nuances, from those who affected to collaborate the better to resist, to those who joyously welcomed the invading army and betrayed their countrymen to the enemy secret police.

Still, some people collaborated, others resisted. Manuel Roxas had been a political leader in the pre-war Philippines. After Pearl Harbor he had served as liaison officer between the Commonwealth government and MacArthur's headquarters. He refused to flee with Quezon, preferring to try and keep up guerrilla warfare in Mindanao. In April 1942 the Japanese captured him and put him in a concentration camp. At some point in 1942, he underwent a change of heart. He sent an open letter to the guerrillas, calling on them to come in; "your presence in the hills," he said, ". . . is greatly delaying the return of the people to their normal occupations." By June 1943 he was ready to accept membership in the preparatory commission to draw up a constitution for the puppet state. Subsequently he became vice-chairman of the National Planning Board and food czar; here he blamed the rice shortage on the guerrillas. Toward the end he actually became a member of the puppet cabinet. Yet, when the American forces caught up with Manuel Roxas at Baguio in April 1945, MacArthur's headquarters announced the "rescue" of Roxas and the "capture" of four other members of the collaborationist cabinet. When Osmeña asked MacArthur how he had arrived at this interesting distinction, the General replied, "I have known General Roxas for twenty years, and I know personally that he is no threat to our military security. Therefore we are not detaining him."

In a way, MacArthur's decision settled the political future of the Philippines. He later sought to justify his action by claiming that Roxas was "one of the prime factors in the guerrilla movement." Roxas himself co-operated with enthusiasm in developing this theory. "Modesty aside," he cried at one point, "Manuel Roxas was the leader, the leader of the resistance movement in the Philippines!" The evidence for the theory remains obscure. No one has specified the exact nature of his contribution to the resistance. Roxas, like any sensible man following a policy of reinsurance, probably placed a number of bets on each side. The record makes it difficult to quarrel with the conclusion of David Bernstein, the chronicler of the modern Philippines: "If Japan had won the war . . . the top man in the Philippines today would probably have been Manuel Roxas."

In bailing out Roxas, MacArthur was hardly launching a premeditated and sinister policy. His main job at this time was to reconquer the Philippines and to prepare to conquer Japan. He supported Roxas because he knew him and liked him; at the same time, he decided not to disarm the Hukbalahaps, the powerful but Communist-dominated guerrilla groups—another decision which would shape the future of the islands and in a direction diametrically opposite from that of the Roxas decision. Yet, in rescuing Roxas, MacArthur did set in motion a process which would end by rescuing many leading collaborationists. Roxas himself took speedy advantage of his luck to argue that the puppet government had acted "under duress" and that Osmeña should immediately restore all pre-war officials to their jobs, whether or not they had served under the Japanese. And MacArthur himself, over Osmeña's opposition, insisted on reconvening the pre-war Philippine Congress in spite of the fact that it was filled with collaborationists.

MacArthur's tapping of Roxas in 1945 made possible his election as president of the Commonwealth in 1946; and the election of Roxas meant the recapture of power by the rich, conservative groups who would have ruled the Islands under the Greater East Asia Co-Prosperity Sphere. Roxas himself died in 1948. By 1950, conditions were so critical that the United States government sent an economic mission in a last-ditch attempt to avert collapse. The mission was headed by Daniel W. Bell, a Washington banker, and included a utility official and the superintendent of Virginia Military Institute (who had been MacArthur's own Deputy Chief

of Staff). Its report gave a sobering picture of the stewardship of
Roxas and his successors.

Inequalities in income, the Bell Report observed, had become
greater than ever in the Philippines since the war. "While the
standard of living of the mass of people has not reached the pre-
war level, the profits of businessmen and the income of large
landowners have risen very considerably." Rejecting in chilly language the theory that the war was the main cause of the economic
mess, it pointed out that the Commonwealth government had
wasted its sufficient resources through bad planning, inefficiency
and graft. And the Bell Report, for all its severity of tone, gave
only a stolid and colorless picture of the actuality. By 1950 the
Huks, now entirely under Communist domination and thriving in
the economic breakdown, were carrying their defiance to the very
suburbs of Manila; at times, armed escorts were needed to take
supplies from Manila to Clark Field.

Few men today—in the sixties—regard the Philippines as a
"mighty bulwark." But MacArthur had always been sentimental
about the Islands. In 1946 he flew over a place he knew well. "I
kept looking at Corregidor," he said later, "trying to see the scars
of war. But there weren't any. In such a short time, God has seen
fit to cover the scars with fresh green grass and foliage." If this
was true for the vegetation, however, it was hardly true for the
politics.

His endorsement of his second occupation—the occupation of
Japan—has been even more confident. "The Japanese people since
the war," he told Congress, "have undergone the greatest ref-
ormation recorded in modern history." Politically, economically
and socially, "Japan is now abreast of many free nations of the
earth and will not again fail the universal trust . . . I know of
no nation more serene, orderly and industrious, nor in which
higher hopes can be entertained for future constructive service in
the advance of the human race." This statement, with the normal
markdown for MacArthur's superlatives, is more likely to command general acceptance. The American occupation of Japan

has been a staggering achievement; in its strong as well as its weak points, it has reflected the extraordinary personality of the man who ran it.

MacArthur had long brooded about Japan and its role in Asia. His mastery of the "logic of the Japanese mind" had been a good deal less than complete on questions of war; but he may have been closer to the mark on questions of peace. The total destruction of Japanese military power, he told Robert E. Sherwood early in 1945, is likely to involve the destruction of the concept of the Emperor's divinity. This will result, he continued, in a spiritual vacuum and an opportunity for the introduction of new concepts. The Japanese people, moreover, will have inevitable respect for as well as fear of the instruments of their own defeat; believing that might makes right, they will conclude that the United States must be right. "It seemed to be General MacArthur's view," Sherwood reported to Roosevelt, "that the Japanese civil population if treated with stern justice and strength would be more capable of eventual redemption than are the Germans." MacArthur warned against exerting American influence "in an imperialistic manner, or for the sole purpose of commercial advantage"; our influence and our strength, he insisted, must be expressed "in terms of essential liberalism" if we are to retain the friendship of the Asian peoples.

The thinking in Washington was running along similar lines, though at first there was considerable debate over who should run the occupation. The Navy had already set up an elaborate apparatus of Japanese language schools, military government handbooks and draft directives. But MacArthur beat out the Navy once again, and Truman gave him the occupation job. In late August 1945, the State Department, in consultation with War and Navy, sent him a basic directive setting forth the initial post-surrender policy for Japan. This document, breathing a liberal and humane spirit, gave MacArthur fundamental guidance in his control of the military occupation.

MacArthur thus did not invent the occupation policy, though

his own meditations on the subject made him entirely receptive to the original State Department directive. Yet he brought to the task of executing the Washington directive qualities which transformed the whole character of the occupation from a bread-line, soup-kitchen, WPA operation into an extraordinary enterprise of national dedication. Unlike the merely brisk and efficient commanders of the Lucius Clay type, MacArthur felt that he was performing not one more Army assignment but an exalted historical mission. He communicated his sense of high historical significance to the Japanese, swept them up in the great drama and mystery of reconstruction, and gave them a feeling of spiritual purpose in a moment of unsurpassed national disaster. He invested his role, as the Washington *Post* once put it, with a grandeur which his subjects, with their national memories of the Shogunate, found easy to understand.

He, too, must have been swept up in the drama and the mystery, for he revealed in Japan a deeply personal magnanimity that had not previously been notable in his makeup. The Pacific War had been fought with bitterness and hate. Vindictiveness on the part of the victorious general would have been altogether understandable. Yet MacArthur, who could propose the court-martial of an officer for contradicting his communiqués, shucked his native vindictiveness when he steamed into Tokyo Bay and told the vanquished that the problem of making a decent peace was basically "theological and involves a spiritual recrudescence and improvement of human character . . . It must be of the spirit if we are to save the flesh." On the second anniversary of the occupation he would observe that it had brought "to a race long stunted by ancient concepts of mythological teaching the refreshing uplift of enlightenment and truth and reality with practical demonstrations of Christian ideals."

The process was not entirely one of turning the other cheek. MacArthur had his war crimes prosecutions and, especially in the Yamashita case, showed an ardent desire for a speedy conviction at the expense of the customary safeguards of Anglo-Saxon justice. It was an odd juxtaposition—Yamashita, the most western-ized of Japanese soldiers; MacArthur, the most orientalized of American. Yet, though Yamashita himself was not shown to have been personally responsible for the crimes for which MacArthur hanged him, still the emphasis on speed in war guilt cases is not a bad thing. The Tokyo prosecutions were washed up by De-cember 1948, while the German war crimes cases were an open sore nearly three years later. It may be better to keep the pun-ishment for war crimes sharp and limited than to let them become uncertain and protracted.

But this was a minor part of a larger program of demilitariza-tion. At the same time, broad measures for disarmament were carried out swiftly and effectively; and a political purge of a sort accompanied them, though this was not often pressed to the point where it hurt. MacArthur counted much more on his affirmative reforms, devised by his own headquarters and imposed on Japa-nese society, to invoke and sustain the process of "spiritual ref-ormation." He had few doubts about the reality of the refor-mation. "This revolution of the spirit among the Japanese people," he said on the first anniversary of surrender, "represents no thin veneer to serve the purposes of the present. It represents an unparalleled convulsion in the social history of the world."

Whether or not the spiritual regeneration would last, the vari-ety and weight of the occupation reforms were staggering. They affected every aspect of the national life and ended by almost re-making the face of Japan. The Supreme Commander for the Al-lied Powers (SCAP) gave Japan a new constitution, reformed the distribution of land holdings, reorganized the educational system, established a strong labor movement, decreed equality of the sexes, introduced conceptions of civil freedom, abolished the state religion, rewrote the basic legal codes and remodeled the ma-chinery of government. For a time in 1946 and 1947, it was as if Franklin D. Roosevelt and the early New Dealers had been turned loose to make Japan over. John Gunther said he was reminded of nothing so much as of republican Spain in the early thirties.

The most important reforms were those which reordered the balance of power among the groups of Japanese society. MacArthur's land reform program may perhaps be accounted his greatest success.* It was carried out (after a slow start) with dispatch; the tenant farmers were able to buy land without difficulty—indeed, since the resale prices did not allow for inflation, the owners in many cases had their lands virtually confiscated; and, where purchase was impossible, the conditions of tenancy were radically revised in favor of the tenant. "Our objectives," remarked Dr. Edwin O. Reischauer, the foremost scholar of modern Japan, "have gone far beyond those of the Chinese Communists." And the happy consequence of this MacArthur policy was to deprive the Japanese Communist Party of its most potent issue.

SCAP at the same time encouraged the industrial workers to organize for the first time in Japanese history. It provided unbelievable new opportunities for women—a tremendous change in a country where wife had habitually followed husband at a respectful distance when they walked down the street. And it sought to guarantee the permanence of these reforms by embodying them in a new constitution. The constitution itself, drawn up in SCAP under the direction of General Courtney Whitney, imported the brash American principles of 1789 into a nation which had known only Oriental authoritarianism. Sovereignty left the Emperor for the people; the Diet was given new power, as were elected assemblies on the local level; and, in a unique, astonishing and un-American article, the Japanese people "forever" renounced

---

* He has himself observed of the program that it was "extraordinarily successful. I don't think that since the Gracchi effort at land reform in the days of the Roman Empire there has been anything quite as successful of that nature." Little is heard of it among MacArthur admirers in this country, however, since most of them are committed to the thesis that interest in the redistribution of land holdings is a sure sign of crypto-communism; when they hear the words "land reform," they tend to loose the safety-catch on their revolvers.

"war as a sovereign right of the nation and the threat or use of force as a means of settling international disputes." In order to carry out that hope, the constitution continued, "land, sea, and air forces, as well as other war potential, will never be maintained."

The one gross failure of the reform policy lay, unhappily, in perhaps the most crucial field—that is, of heavy industry and banking. This was not for lack of trying; it was rather for a lack of consistent policies. MacArthur at the start became committed to a trust-busting policy which would have carried the fragmentation of industry to an impractical extreme. This tough approach to Japanese economic problems evidently got its start in the thinking of Edwin Pauley's Reparations Mission of 1946-47, in which Owen Lattimore was a dominant figure. It was supported by Chinese sympathizers, who feared the resurgence of a strong Japan, by old-fashioned American trust-busters and free enterprisers, and by the fellow-travelers, of whom there were a good smattering in SCAP. But as the need for the revival of Japanese industry became more apparent, MacArthur began to backtrack; in the end, the same conservative business groups who had controlled the Japanese economy and collaborated with the militarists before Pearl Harbor were back in control again.

In March 1947, MacArthur announced that the spiritual revolution was "probably the greatest the world has ever known," and that the political phase of the occupation was "approaching such completion as is possible." Little was left to be done; it was time for a peace treaty. By 1948, the reforming zeal had passed almost entirely out of SCAP. This was primarily because the overshadowing menace of the Soviet Union had made the economic recovery of Japan take necessary precedence over its social reform. But it was in part too because SCAP itself began to recoil from the consequences of its own zeal. It was fine to have trade unions, but awkward when they called strikes; it was fine to have free speech and a free press, but distressing when they resulted in criticisms of the occupation. SCAP watched apprehensively while a Social Democratic prime minister tried to keep political power; it sighed with relief when he fell in February 1948 and the safely conservative right took over. By assisting in the enfeeblement of the Social Democratic party and by publicly rejoicing over the trend to the right, MacArthur drove many workers and intellectuals leftward toward Communism.* The result was in 1949 and 1950 a dangerous polarization in Japanese politics, and what many observers considered to be a dangerous restoration of the "old crowd" to power. W. MacMahon Ball, the British Commonwealth representative on the Allied Council for Japan, reluctantly concluded, "There has been no fundamental change in Japan's social structure or in the political outlook of her leaders." Yet MacArthur had already reached a conclusion too, and a good deal less reluctantly. "Our primary economic purpose," he wrote in 1949, "has been to lay strong foundations for the development in Japan of a capitalistic system based upon free competitive enterprise."

No one can yet tell whether the "spiritual recrudescence" of which MacArthur spoke has really taken place; nor can backsliding by the Japanese from the high principles of SCAP be charged to MacArthur's account in the bookkeeping of history. No person can create a nation from outside; the best outsiders can do is to create the conditions for the nation's own development. With all its half-measures and compromises, MacArthur's Japan is certainly a place where democratic forces have a fighting chance. This may not be much. But before 1945 they never had even a chance.

As for MacArthur himself, the personal transformation, which had been going on ever since he came to Manila, reached its climax in Tokyo. His remoteness from common humanity became more pronounced and methodical than ever. Except on state business, he almost never mixed with the Japanese. John Gunther doubts whether, in five years in Tokyo, MacArthur talked at length to more than a dozen Japanese officials. He left Tokyo

* MacArthur told G. Ward Price, the British journalist, in March 1949 that he did not think the Japanese Communists had any direct link with Moscow.

only twice from September 1945 to June 1950; he never visited Hiroshima or Nagasaki, never inspected outlying American units, airfields or naval bases. Even in Tokyo he rarely deviated from his fixed path between the American Embassy and the Dai-Ichi Building, where SCAP had its headquarters. He would not even permit a telephone to be installed in his office. This inaccessibility may have been partly design; MacArthur seems to have believed from his theories of Oriental psychology that this was the best way to impress himself upon the Japanese people. But its effect was to achieve for him a deep and eventually almost impassable isolation. As the years went by, he almost seemed to take on the divinity renounced on January 1, 1946 by Hirohito. "We look to MacArthur," said one Japanese to John Lacerda, "as the second Jesus Christ."

Before 1945, MacArthur had many admirers and a large following; but the following in no sense constituted a cult. The MacArthur cult had its origins after the war in Tokyo's Dai-Ichi Building, where high priests conducted daily devotions and sought to make converts of visitors. By 1950, all the independent spirits on his staff had been screened out and only true believers remained. The message they passed along to visiting journalists was that MacArthur was "the greatest man alive" (Major General Edward M. Almond), the greatest man since Christ, the greatest general in world history, even "the greatest man who ever lived" (Lieutenant General George E. Stratemeyer). "He's too enormous," one officer told John Gunther, "too unpredictable, I don't really understand him. . . . No one could." Another said: "I have lived under his domination for so many years that I do not know what to say." One of those who believed MacArthur to be the world's greatest man gave an insight into the thinking of the cult by describing Francisco Franco as the second greatest man. Another insight comes from Philip LaFollette: "There was something about him that kept reminding me of characteristics of my father." No doubt many men were reminded of many fathers.

Contemplating his handiwork, MacArthur found the miracle of the occupation a source of constant wonder. "It is fascinating to go back and read Plato's vision of Utopia," he observed to the head of the Associated Press bureau in Tokyo, "and to see how far we have progressed . . . What a remarkable vision—what intellectual flashes—those old fellows had, living under their backward conditions."* He fully reciprocated the admiration of his staff ("no group has ever done more to merit the confidence, the admiration, and the gratitude of the American people"); but he now drew on new sources of wisdom. "My major advisors now," he said in 1948, "have boiled down almost to two men— George Washington and Abraham Lincoln. One founded the United States, the other saved it. If you go back into their lives, you can find almost all the answers." MacArthur in these years was often in a philosophical mood, pulling on his corncob pipe, letting his mind roam freely among the spacious reaches of history.

The wonder of the occupation, the mounting sense of historic mission, the protective adoration of the staff—all these made the Supreme Commander's headquarters morbidly sensitive to any criticism. MacArthur, as a result, was in fairly continuous conflict with American newspapermen. He practically never saw them (he held almost no press conferences in his five years of proconsulship) except when they were about to depart, at which point they would be called to the General's office for resonant valedictory lectures. MacArthur snubbed newspapermen, rebuked them, threw them out of the country, denied them accreditation, even complained to their publishers when they stubbornly refused to see things his way. In Tokyo there grew upon him the habit of addressing petulant letters and cables to newspapers and

---

* It was doubtless such a remark as this which led *Life* magazine to comment of MacArthur in the spring of 1951 in prose which would have delighted the General himself: "Greece, Rome, the Middle Ages, the Renaissance, the age of Britain's greatness—all the splendid and tragic meanings of the drama of these centuries are the constant prompters of his mind and spirit."

magazines and politicians—the habit which was to develop almost into a mania after the outbreak of the Korean war.

Being a divinity is no mean enterprise: on the whole, only a god can survive it. It was not altogether MacArthur's fault that he was immersed in an atmosphere of adulation and abasement for the five and a half years after V-J Day. Yet part of his personality, at least, sought this atmosphere, and all his personality suffered from it. As time passed and satisfaction settled over the personality, stagnation settled over his command. MacArthur may have felt it a mistake to withdraw American troops from Korea, but he recorded no protest against the decision. He had so little expectation, indeed, of Communist military adventuring in the Far East that he let the training of American divisions in Japan slacken off distressingly. He did not believe a shooting war was imminent as late as May 1950, a few days before the North Koreans started to shoot. This particular lack of prescience was shared, God knows, by many others, and it would hardly matter today if so many things in our present situation did not hinge on estimates of the probability of aggression. MacArthur's forecasts have been almost uniformly wrong: the invasion of South Korea startled him as much as the Japanese attack on the Philippines in 1941.*

MacArthur played an indispensable role for a season in Japan, but it was not a role of permanent indispensability. His eventual departure did not create the vacuum that his admirers anticipated. The fact that it did not, of course, was a tribute to his success in the occupation. The first reaction was one of stunned incredulity; then of fear that this might signal an American abandonment of Japan. But the quick arrival in Tokyo of John Foster Dulles and Matthew B. Ridgway, the one traveling from

* MacArthur himself, interestingly enough, had no mercy for bad prophets. "Can we therefore accept," he observed of the Truman administration on June 13, 1951, "their present and future judgments in the light of past failures without the most serious misgivings as to our future fate as a free and sovereign nation?"

Washington, the other from Korea, went far to reassure the Japanese about American intentions.

As for Ridgway, so far as the Japanese were concerned, the king had died: long live the king! One of his first acts was to install a telephone in the Supreme Commander's office. This may stand as a symbol of his desire to open up communication with the world outside—both with his own troops and with the Japanese. In his first month as Supreme Commander he was out of Tokyo more than MacArthur had been in five years. He mixed freely with the Japanese, saw them socially, and even rescinded the MacArthur rule forbidding them admission to the American officers' clubs. In place of a godlike aloofness there came a courteous, brisk and businesslike efficiency; and the Japanese welcomed the change. "Though the Japanese look upon him with respect and gratitude," Takeo Naoi wrote of MacArthur from Tokyo, "and feel very sorry for fate, they have little real love for him. . . . MacArthur was a towering mountain of unapproachability." The *Oriental Economist* of Tokyo added that, if the General had based his remoteness on the theory that this would impress the Japanese, he had made a bad mistake. "Had General MacArthur gone out of his way to meet more Japanese of various circles, his popularity and the esteem in which he was held would certainly have been still greater." On May 30 the Japanese government withdrew its impulsive proposal to the Diet that MacArthur be made a "state guest" for life with specially created privileges and honors.

Bert Andrews, the head of the Washington bureau of the New York *Herald Tribune,* made a tour of inspection to Tokyo a fortnight after MacArthur's removal. He discovered to his amazement that Tokyo was losing interest in the MacArthur debate, then raging with mounting fury in Washington, and that many Japanese (and Americans, too), when pressed on the point, admitted to the belief that the removal was a good thing. It raised in Andrews's mind the question what the effect on American public opinion would have been "if all the reporters had been allowed to give an objective view of the occupation in the past."

Yet an objective view in the past, while it might have diminished MacArthur, would probably not have significantly diminished the occupation. In a sense, the reaction to his dismissal in 1951 hardly does justice to his achievement of 1945 and 1946. If Ridgway can fill his shoes today, it is still no proof that MacArthur did not do a unique job in the early years of the occupation. For then the overpowering need was for faith, for a *mystique*, for a moral revival in the midst of moral collapse. The powerful and dedicated figure of MacArthur filled that need, as probably no other American general could have filled it. He was the universal father-image in a season of terrible spiritual crisis. But the spiritual crisis came to an end, and so did the desperate need. The time came for the Japanese to cast off their crutches and try to walk by themselves. Life with father was fine, but it could not go on forever. The best opinion is that it went on too long. If this were not true for the children, it was certainly true for the father.

III

Korea: The Political War

MARS' LAST GIFT

"While I was not consulted," MacArthur said in his speech before Congress on April 19th, "prior to the President's decision to intervene in support of the Republic of Korea, that decision, from a military standpoint, proved a sound one."

There is an intimation of grievance in the statement of historical fact, a note of ambivalence and reservation in the judgment. Actually, the statement does nothing like full justice to MacArthur's role in his government's arrival at a decision that was epoch-making in a quite literal sense. It is perfectly true that his opinion was not sought by the President and his advisers between 8:00 P.M. of June 24, 1950, when the word first reached the State Department (via a news agency) that Communist forces from North Korea had invaded the Republic of Korea, to the late evening of June 26, when the President directed preparation of a statement he was to release at noon the next day: "The attack upon Korea has made it plain beyond all doubt that Communism has passed the use of subversion to conquer independent nations and will now use armed invasion and war. . . . In these circumstances, I have ordered the United States air and sea forces to give the Korean government troops cover and support." That decision was made in Washington, more specifically in that part of

97

Washington occupied by Mr. Truman's head.* It is arguable, though, whether the Korean die was cast in the decision of June 26 or in the decision, reached and announced four days later, to "use certain supporting ground units" in Korea.

The second decision was made, if not on MacArthur's responsibility, on his eminent authority. It was MacArthur who, early in the morning of June 30 (Washington time), talked with the Pentagon and advised the immediate use of American ground units. Up to that moment the government had been reluctant to make the commitment and had, in fact, postponed any decision at all until MacArthur's position was known. As soon as he made it known, the Secretary of the Army communicated it to the President, and the President, immediately upon hearing the view of the Commander in Chief, Far East, instructed the Secretary to authorize the use of ground units. If MacArthur had not urged the decision, it might never have been made. His part was attested to by General Bradley in the course of the Senate hearings:

SENATOR MORSE: Is it not true that it was that request of General MacArthur . . . to use troops that constituted the first act or step that was taken by our government in the use of ground troops in Korea?
BRADLEY: Other than to protect the port to cover the withdrawal of nationals, yes.
MORSE: But the Joint Chiefs of Staff, not being on the scene and not having the benefit of a reconnaissance at the front, did not make the recommendation to General MacArthur that he use troops, did they?

* A decision that can be roughly described as enabling had been made the day before by the United Nations Security Council, meeting at Lake Success on Long Island. On Sunday afternoon, June 25, the Council, which was then, providentially, being boycotted by the Russians because of their disapproval of the continued membership of Nationalist China, passed a resolution describing the invasion as a "breach of the peace and an act of aggression," calling for an immediate cease-fire, and asking United Nations members to "render every assistance" in bringing about the cease-fire. By putting the broadest possible construction on this, the President was able to say that his decision was in furtherance of United Nations policy. This claim gave rise to a wrangle that still goes on in law schools. Three hours after the release of the decision, however, it was ratified by the Council in a resolution recommending that "members of the United Nations furnish such assistance to the Republic of Korea as may be necessary to restore peace and security in the area."

BRADLEY: Not that I remember of, no, sir.
MORSE: Did the President of the United States?
BRADLEY: Not that I remember. . . .

General Bradley's memory appears to have served him well: it was confirmed by most of the other witnesses.

The case for the crucial importance of the second, or Mac-Arthur, decision is impressive. It has been the testimony of several men who took part in the conferences at Blair House during the week of June 25—the first one took place as soon as the President returned by plane from what was to have been a bucolic holiday on his brother's farm at Grand View, Missouri—that, while it was from the start the sense of the entire group that Moscow's challenge had to be picked up, it was at the same time the conviction of most that the United States should not take the kind of action that would commit it to Korea, which could have proved either a baited trap or a lost cause, in any and all circumstances.

It was felt, for example, that if the North Koreans accomplished their *Anschluss* swiftly, that would have to be that; there would be no sense in trying to liberate the conquered peninsula or in endlessly harassing its conquerors with our planes and ships. According to Albert Warner, who interviewed most of the conferees for *Harper's* magazine, the Secretary of Defense, Louis Johnson, made it plain that "if Russia or China came in, we would have to pull out. Korea is no place to fight a major war." This view was shared by the Joint Chiefs of Staff and by the civilian service secretaries. (Of course, Mr. Johnson, if his candor had matched his celebrated bluntness of expression, might have gone on to say that no place on earth was a place to fight a major war in June of 1950, since he, Mr. Johnson, had for many months been presiding, reluctantly or otherwise, over a systematic liquidation of American power.) At all odds, it was hoped by most of the conferees, and believed by some of them, that, in lending aircraft and naval vessels to the Republic, we were making not an ultimate commitment, not even a penultimate one, but one that could be withdrawn if circumstances conspired to make that advisable. The planes could, if necessary, fly back to the bases; the ships could steam back to their ports.

In other words, the decision was essentially a political one. If, as MacArthur believes, it proved sound from a military standpoint, that is a welcome but unexpected dividend. Certainly, if the Blair House conferees had been trying to settle the issue on military grounds, they would have decided against intervention. This seems to be something MacArthur, perhaps because, as he said, he had all he could do to keep up with developments in his own theater, has never seemed to appreciate, or even to grasp. Our intervention was undertaken for reasons of American security, but not for the reason that our security would be imperiled if the Republic of Korea, as a geographical entity, fell into unfriendly hands.

Korea was well outside our defensive system in the Pacific. Its role in global strategy had been studied by our military people (few of whom failed to describe it as "a dagger pointed at the heart of Japan"), and they had felt that, in spite of the advantage of controlling it to anyone bent on the defense or conquest of Japan, we would make no strong attempt to hold it in the event of global war. In large part, they excluded Korea because they agreed so heartily with MacArthur that "anyone who commits the American army on the mainland of Asia ought to have his head examined." This country's "defensive perimeter," Dean Acheson said in his speech to the National Press Club on January 12, 1950, "runs along the Aleutians to Japan and then goes to the Ryukus. . . . [It] runs from the Ryukus to the Philippine Islands. . . . So far as the military security of other areas in the Pacific is concerned, it must be clear that no person can guarantee those areas against military attack."

Acheson expressed the view of the Defense Department as well as that of the State Department. He even expressed MacArthur's view. In March 1949, the General had told the British journalist, G. Ward Price, "Our line of defense runs through the chain of

"Hurrah for the One On This Side!"

islands fringing the coast of Asia. It starts from the Philippines
and continues through the Ryukus Archipelago, which includes
its main bastion, Okinawa. Then it bends back through Japan and
the Aleutian Island chain to Alaska. Though the advance of the
Red Armies in China places them on the flank of that position,
this does not alter the fact that our only possible adversary on
the Asiatic continent* does not possess an industrial base near
enough to supply an amphibious attacking force." Later that year,
he told William R. Mathews, of the Arizona *Daily Star*, substantially the same thing. "From the line we hold," he said, "beginning in Alaska and running from the Aleutians through Okinawa
and the Philippines, we can with our air and sea power break up
any amphibious operation of a predatory power embarking from
the Asiatic mainland." In those days, not only Korea but Formosa
was outside the system. The policy may have been wrong, and it
was almost certainly foolish to broadcast it as we did (Acheson
is generally made the goat for this, though MacArthur said the
same things; if Acheson invited aggression by his talk of no guar-
antees, what is to be said of MacArthur's statement that only a
lunatic would fight on the mainland?), but that does not alter the
fact that the policy was policy and was based on the considered
judgment of our military leaders.

The Communist aggression of June 24 changed nothing militarily. Nevertheless, Korea became immediately vital to our *military* security on that day, not as a geographical entity but as a
relatively free society. It became vital because, as MacArthur had
explained to the Philippine Congress five years earlier, "Defense
is no longer national; it has become international." What threatened American security on June 25 was not the possible conquest
of South Korea but the possible conquest of millions of minds
throughout the world. In relative terms, the Soviet Union was
then at the peak of its power. The very impress of its power on
the human mind put all our national interests in jeopardy. A year

* Presumably the Soviet Union. It turned out that Asia could supply quite
a few adversaries.

earlier, we had concluded a strategic alliance with the major non-Communist powers in Western Europe. Millions of Europeans, however, had been opposed to that alliance because they feared that just by joining it they would bring the Russian war machine crashing into their countries. Others were not so much intimidated by Russian power as they were fearful that we would be intimidated by it; that when we saw the magnitude of the job of defending Europe, we would renege on our pledges.

For six months, the United Nations, thanks to Russian bullying and intransigeance, had been in what Trygve Lie, the Secretary-General, had glumly described as a "total stalemate." The Russians seemed to have brought it to a state of decrepitude at the age of five; the most ardent of internationalists were pretty certain that it could be of no use in blocking Russian power. Thus, if the insolent aggression of the North Koreans had gone unchallenged, millions of people throughout the free world, including this important part of it, would have found rich confirmation of their fear that Russian power was in fact invincible, that American big-talk was a shameless bluff, and that the United Nations was a snare and a delusion. Not the development of these attitudes—for they already existed in many places throughout the world—but the extension and strengthening of them offered an incalculable threat to American security. This was why President Truman determined to make at least a limited challenge to Soviet power. He did it not because he thought that the fall of Los Angeles would follow inexorably on the fall of Seoul, but because he wished to show both the Communist world and the non-Communist world that the United States was not a fourflusher and that the United Nations—or collective security—could be made to work.

Once, during a very black moment in the Korean campaign, the President himself stated to General MacArthur some of the political reasons for our original commitment. The message was sent on January 13, 1951, and, if the original was as well worded as the text read at the hearings in paraphrase (to protect the code) by General Marshall, the President's language on that occasion was uncommonly eloquent. We were fighting in Korea, he said, to the following ends:

To demonstrate that aggression will not be accepted by us or by the United Nations and to provide a rallying point around which the spirits and the energies of the free world can be mobilized to meet the world-wide threat which the Soviet Union now poses.

To carry out our commitments of honor to the South Koreans and to demonstrate to the world that the friendship of the United States is of inestimable value in time of adversity.

To lend resolution to many countries not only in Asia but also in Europe and the Middle East who are now living within the shadow of Communist power and to let them know that they need not now rush to come to terms with communism on whatever terms they can get, meaning complete submission.

To inspire those who may be called upon to fight against great odds if subjected to a sudden onslaught by the Soviet Union.

To lend point and urgency to the rapid buildup of the defense of the Western World.

To bring the United Nations through its first great effort in collective security and to produce a free world coalition of incalculable value to the national security interests of the United States.

To alert the peoples behind the Iron Curtain that their masters are bent upon wars of aggression and that this crime be resisted by the free world.

To labor the essential point no further, the decision to lend ships and planes to the Republic of Korea was a political one. But the negative feature of it, the withholding of ground troops at the first, *was* a military decision, and, in reversing it, MacArthur played the largest part.

Korea, unfortunately, in some ways, had not been part of Mac-Arthur's command before June 26.* It came under his command ("Mars' last gift to an old warrior," he called it) at 10:17 that

* The occupying forces there in late 1948 and early 1949, the 24th Corps, were technically under him. But, as he said at the hearings, "My responsibilities were merely to feed them and clothe them in a domiciliary way. I had nothing whatever to do with the policies, the administration, or the command responsibilities in Korea until the war broke out."

evening, when he received teleconned orders to put air and naval forces into operations below the Thirty-eighth Parallel. "I was knocked on my heels," he is reported to have said. If he was, he quickly righted himself. Acting promptly upon receipt of instructions, he sent jet F-80 Shooting Stars (the tough, efficient planes that became known as the workhorses of the war) and F-82 Twin Mustangs into action (before the orders came, he had sent over ten F-51 Mustangs as part of our regular military-aid program) and ordered B-29 Superforts to commence bombing North Koreans in South Korea. The light cruiser *Juneau* and four destroyers set off to deal with Communist amphibious forces which had come ashore on the east coast.

But the deterrent effect of the American effort was nil. On June 27, Seoul fell without a fight. The Republic's government, shouting over its shoulder the brave word that "the Republican Army is fervently counterattacking. . . . We will persevere," fled to Taejon, ninety miles south. Two of the Republic's seven divisions had been hopelessly shredded. Many troops were drowned or penned up on the wrong side of the river: to outsmart the pursuing enemy, some military geniuses blew up the main bridge across the Han, thereby pitching into the water hundreds of their own soldiers on the bridge at the time and cutting off the retreat of thousands more.

On Thursday, June 29, MacArthur left Tokyo to inspect the disaster. It was one of his characteristically gallant undertakings. The weather was vile; his personal pilot would make the trip only when the General put his request in the form of an order; his C-54, the *Bataan*, was unarmed, and there was no assurance of a fighter escort for it; on its way to its uncertain destination (Kimpo airport, near Seoul, was in Communist hands; most other fields were under attack) it was set upon by a Russian Yak, which it eluded. Landing on the Suwon airstrip, which was under intermittent enemy fire, MacArthur set off with Syngman Rhee, the Republic's president, for an eight-hour tour of the front.

Long before it was over, he was persuaded that the air and

naval support ordered by the President could never do the job. There was no ground-to-air communication between Korean troops and American planes; the American pilots had not had enough tactical practice for their rigorous assignments; furthermore, even if pilots and liaison had been all anyone could ask, Lieutenant General George Stratemeyer's Far East Air Forces had only a total of some four-hundred fighters, sixty-odd bombers, and one troop-carrier group. This force was scattered over the entire command; the whole of it might not have made much of an impact on the massive North Korean offensive during the early days, and the whole of it could by no means be immediately spared for South Korea. Naval equivalents of these unprosperous conditions applied to the Seventh Fleet, which was charged not only with helping in Korea but also, by the terms of the June 26 order, with the neutralization of Formosa.

MacArthur reported to the Pentagon in the early hours of Friday, June 30. Long before then, Washington had been getting piecemeal reports through Tokyo, and the near-impossibility of the North Korean situation was almost as clear to President Truman and to members of the National Security Council, which had met at five o'clock on Thursday afternoon, as it had been to MacArthur on the embattled peninsula. If the Republic could be saved at all, it could be saved only by American ground troops. This much was understood by President Truman and all his advisers; but most of them were still reluctant on Thursday to make the commitment American policy had so long shunned—ground troops on the mainland of Asia.

It was agreed to postpone further action of any sort until MacArthur's opinion was on the record. He gave his opinion to Secretary Pace and General Bradley. He not only said that the use of ground troops was the only action that offered any hope of saving the Republic, but he advised that it be taken right away. He requested, according to General Bradley, immediate "authority to send over one regimental combat team and build it up [to] two divisions." He may previously have thought that such a commitment was lunacy; but either the General, like the President, like the Secretary of State, like just about everyone else, was seeing certain matters in a new light, or else they all regarded a peninsula as being in some odd sense not part of the mainland. Mr. Pace got the President out of bed at four in the morning and gave him the essence of MacArthur's report. The President did not ask for time to think or to consult his advisers. Having heard MacArthur's opinion, he immediately instructed Mr. Pace to send in the troops.

If Warren Austin, our ambassador at the United Nations, was right in saying that the decision marked "the dawn of a new day in international collaboration," MacArthur deserves a generous measure of the credit for bringing it about.

American policy in Korea, up to the dawn of Ambassador Austin's new day, does not make a very inspiring story. It does not make a particularly discreditable story, either. At Cairo and at Potsdam, we had agreed with our allies to establish Korean independence. At Potsdam, in July 1945, it was determined that the deliverance of Korea from the Japanese would be carried out by American and Russian troops, and a few weeks later it was settled that American troops would receive the Japanese surrender in the territory south of the Thirty-eighth Parallel, Russians in the territory north.

This improvisation—"a fortuitous line resulting from the exigencies of war," the State Department called it—has been the source of a good deal of hilarity, what with stories about farmhouse beds bisected by the Parallel and about junior officers in the Pentagon laboring over maps to divide Korea by four o'clock one hot August afternoon. Yet, if one accepts the government's case for admitting Russia to the war against Japan in the first place, the solution appears to have been perfectly reasonable. It seemed to be in the public interest to have the Russians stop somewhere. In August, General Christyakov's troops came down 100,000 strong from their bases near Vladivostok. Since the 72,000

American troops assigned to Korea under Lieutenant General John R. Hodge could not keep their engagement there until September 8, the Russians might have overrun the whole country if a line had not been decided on in advance.

The Parallel, which once, at the turn of the century, Czarist Russia had proposed as a dividing line between Russian and Japanese spheres of interest in Korea, was just about at Korea's fifty-yard line; above it, in the Russian zone were more square miles but fewer people than below it, in the American zone; there was nothing much wrong with the Thirty-eighth Parallel except that, as James F. Byrnes, who was Secretary of State when the Potsdam and Moscow conferences were held, has said in his memoirs, "What was intended as a military convenience [became] a closed boundary between the Soviet and American zones of occupation." And, when there were no more Soviet and American zones of occupation, it still divided Korea, a luckless country which had undergone its first known partition in 108 B.C.

Not much of the blame for the continued partition of Korea can be attributed to American policy. Some experts on the region have held that, if our authorities had been wiser in the ways of Korean politics, they might, in 1946 and 1947, have encouraged a group of moderates who enjoyed widespread support in South Korea and whose prestige in North Korea was large enough to make the Russians do business with them. But they frankly admit that asking wisdom in the ways of Korean politics* is asking quite

* Even today, no one seems to know the number of political parties in Korea, much less the shadings of doctrine which distinguish one from another. In *Korea Today*, a book published in 1950 by a man who was perhaps the leading American student of the country, the late George McCune, passed the buck to our military and State Department representatives in Korea. McCune cited one United States government source which put the number at 20; he cited another which said there were 32, of which 15 were rightist, 10 leftist, and 7 neutral, whatever that may mean. *Time* magazine has reported the existence of 39. John Gunther, as always the connoisseur of the stupendous and superlative, says, in *The Riddle of MacArthur*, "There arose before Hodge's bewildered eyes no fewer than *seventy* different political parties," and then goes on to top his own figure by reporting that of "authorities" who put the number at "more than two hundred."

a lot of American authorities and that, to wring concession from the Russians, the moderates would have had to let the Russians do some wringing, too.

As things stood in 1945, there was probably no more hope for Korean unity than for German unity. The American members of the Joint Commission—which consisted of American and Russian military men representing the four trustee powers: the United States, the United Kingdom, the U.S.S.R., and China—advanced many proposals during the three years of occupation, none of which met with Russian favor. Finally, the United Nations, acting on an American suggestion, set up a commission to organize elections in Korea; the Russians boycotted the commission, and when the elections were held on May 10, 1948, they were held in South Korea only. A National Assembly, with seats left vacant for representatives from the Soviet Zone, began functioning, and in August 1948 the Republic of Korea became a sovereign nation. The Democratic People's Republic of North Korea became theoretically sovereign on September 9, 1948.

The faults of American policy during the military occupation and in the period after the formal occupation but before the withdrawal of American troops were the familiar faults of impatience and unwarranted optimism. If it was asking too much of Americans that they take in all the intricacies of Korean politics, it would nevertheless seem that our people might have accepted with slightly more forbearance the fact that the situation *was* an intricate one. Much of the trouble lay with General Hodge, an earnest and industrious but rather fidgety man. His problems were of a sort that MacArthur might have handled with great adroitness; but the Koreans, with their exuberance and their endless spats over their complicated and preposterous politics, bothered Hodge no end. Although there is no reason to think that he ever bore them anything but good will, he said and did all kinds of tactless things.

A short time after his arrival, the Seoul press was quoting him as having said that "Koreans are the same breed of cats as Japanese." He denied having said it, but it has the sound of authentic Hodgean anthropology. It didn't take him long to find out that it was always simpler to get things done by putting Americans— or in many cases the old Japanese authorities—in charge than by turning them over to the disputatious Koreans. In their zone, the Russians, who weren't too concerned when paper work was not done to an office manager's taste, made a great show of turning everything over to the Koreans as rapidly as possible—except, of course, a few key jobs in the police and educational systems. Hodge saw only that the situation among Koreans was, as he reported, "chaotic, with no central theme except a desire for immediate independence." He exacerbated this desire by repeating that "military government is the only government in Korea" and by letting Japanese-trained police handle the local Communists with their quaint Japanese techniques.

Hodge's subordinates, finding in Syngman Rhee, a Princeton man and a Methodist, someone they could easily understand, let the impression get about that Rhee, whom they encouraged to go to Washington to lobby for immediate independence and the withdrawal of American troops, was the American favorite. Rhee had never been the people's favorite. (Though he managed to hold on to his presidency as a kind of compromise candidate, his Nationalist Party retained only 22 of its 71 seats in the 410-member National Assembly in the elections that were held a month before the invasion.) Hodge had to rebuke him in severe terms for claiming to have Washington's endorsement. All these political difficulties did not make it easier to manage the economic problem. Most people qualified to judge feel that the Army, so long as it was in control, and, later the State Department and the Economic Co-operation Administration, did an excellent job of assisting Korean agriculture and industry. It was not because of our policies but in spite of them that, when the war began, the Korean *won,* valued at 15 to the dollar in 1945, had fallen to 4,700 to the dollar in the black market.

The most lamentable aspect of American policy was its military sanguineness. Once the military government had accepted the division of Korea as a fact of life it and the Koreans would have to live with it, it began to lend a hand in the work of building, training and equipping an Army for the Republic. When, on June 29, 1949, the last of our troops were withdrawn, this work was continued by the Army's Korean Military Advisory Group, which at no time consisted of less than four hundred men and which stayed on until the invasion. The Russians, of course, had been training a North Korean army from the earliest days of the occupation. When the civil war in China ended, they arranged with Mao Tse-tung to have 20,000 Manchuria-trained Koreans added to the new force, which numbered approximately 200,000, or twice as many as the South Koreans had under arms. The North Korean defense minister was a veteran of the Manchurian armies.

In intention, at least, we did not lag far behind. We set up an infantry school, modeled on Fort Benning, organized a WAC corps, and Americanized everything in sight. We turned over American equipment valued at $110,000,000. We assisted in the operation of small-arms munitions factories in the Republic. The new army, whose enlisted men were getting the equivalent of a penny a month in 1950, was given no airplanes and no tanks. Two reasons have been given for the lack of tanks. One is that our military intelligence had concluded that Korea was very poor terrain for tanks and tanks, therefore, would not be necessary; sauce for the goose is sauce for the gander, so the South Koreans were given no antitank weapons. The other reason is that we feared an invasion of North Korea by South Korea. We had some cause for fear. Syngman Rhee had often expressed an impatience to unify the country by force. "I advocated unification," he once said, "so that we could drive the Russians from the north. . . . We must fight those who are not our friends. As soon as the time comes, I'll instruct you. Then you should be prepared to shed blood. . . . America is our friend. . . . I have already made connections abroad." Yun Chi Yong, a member of Rhee's cabinet, said in 1949, after a session with the United Nations Commission on Korea,

"What was discussed with the UN Commission is that peaceful unification of South and North is nothing more than a political plot. The only way to unify South and North Korea is for the Republic of Korea to regain the lost land in North Korea by force."

American councils of restraint annoyed the South Koreans. "They [the Americans] keep telling us no, no, no, wait. You are not ready," Sihn Sung Mo, the Republic's defense minister said. It is more likely that they told him to forget it than that they told him to wait. At any rate, the agitation for union by force was so great that the United States government, according to a report to the United Nations Commission on Korea, "had informed the government of the Republic that the launching of any attack from South Korea would be immediately followed by the termination of all aid, both military and economic, from the United States." No doubt both reasons applied

But the fact is that we seem to have failed to do well even the inadequate military job we set ourselves. "When the North Koreans invaded South Korea," E. J. Kahn, Jr., reported in the *New Yorker*, "the 96,000 R.O.K. [Republic of Korea] soldiers who opposed them were so far from being fully trained that none had ever taken part in any military maneuver more elaborate than a battalion exercise. By July 25, 50,000 of the 96,000 had become battle casualties, and because of the exigencies of the situation at that time, they had to be replaced by men only four or five days removed from civilian life." Mr. Kahn went on to point out that while the Russians had trained the North Koreans in the kind of guerrilla warfare that was appropriate to the terrain, "The South Koreans have been trained to maintain fixed lines, like American soldiers, and it disconcerts them to have anybody at their rear, with the result that they try, somewhat disastrously, to get to the rear of the people at their rear."

It is an odd but incontrovertible fact that almost the only American official who was alarmed about the possibility of a South Korean collapse in the days before the invasion was the

Secretary of State. He repeatedly importuned Congress for more aid for Korea, painting the situation there in very somber colors; Acheson, who Senator Taft maintained was always blind to communism in Asia, had predicted at a committee hearing on appropriations for the fiscal year of 1950, that the Republic of Korea would "fall within three months" unless a greater American effort were made. He had also warned that the withdrawal of troops in 1948 might in the end turn out to be catastrophic. It was at his insistence that a regimental combat team stayed on until June, 1949.

Military men, however, perceived no serious dangers. Brigadier General William L. Roberts, who, when the invision started, was just returning to this country after the completion of his Korean tour, called the Republic's army "the best doggoned shooting army outside the United States." Six weeks before the invasion, the defense minister of the Republic reported that the North Koreans were massing along the parallel with 185,000 men, 173 tanks, 32 naval vessels, and 197 planes. On May 12, these facts were placed before General Roberts, who told the defense minister that he agreed with the estimates on the size of the force (at least the Republic's Intelligence was working effectively; the figures came very close to representing the actual invading force) but that he did not anticipate an attack.* If one came, he told the defense minister, he was sure the South Koreans could turn it back.

MacArthur's headquarters in Tokyo had been getting the same kind of intelligence reports, but it made light of them. In his testimony before the Joint Committees, the Secretary of State read several intelligence cables from the Commander in Chief,

* The North Koreans had warmed up in border raids and ominous maneuvers on many previous occasions. Also, there had been many false alarms. On December 1, 1948, the chief of police in Seoul had plastered the city walls with a proclamation which informed the citizenry, "North Korea People's Army has already begun its invasion of South Korea. This is a dangerous agitation; from now on, the police will, without hesitation, shoot anybody who scatters handbills or in any way incites people to riot. Citizens are requested not to stand too near these dangerous elements."

Far East, one of which, dated March 10, 1950, announced the receipt of a report that "PA [meaning the North Korean People's Army] will attack South Korea in June, 1950." The comment on this, presumably that of Major General Charles Willoughby, chief of MacArthur's G-2, was that it was really more likely that "the People's Army will be prepared to invade South Korea by fall," but that, even if "further reports bear out the present indications," the Communists "probably will be content to wait a while longer and let South Korea ripen for future harvest." Two weeks later, Willoughby's office told Washington, "It is believed that there will be no civil war in Korea this spring or summer."

No one was very wise about what was to happen. Shortly before the invasion, an American intelligence officer who had been in Korea and who didn't wish his name used told a group of American correspondents that in his judgment the Republic was the "safest place in Asia" because its army was "the best in Asia." In its issue of June 5, 1950, *Time* magazine, looked upon in some quarters as an authoritative journal of Oriental affairs, ran a most complacent report on South Korea. The winter before, it said, the Republic's prospects had been poor, but

> now the Republic of Korea looks like a country on its way to survival . . . [It] has taken its longest step toward recovery in the military field; in two years it trained and equipped a first-rate army . . . U.S. Military advisers . . . recall the failure of U.S.-trained armies in Nationalist China, and have tried to give the Koreans Yankee self-sufficiency as well as Yankee organization and equipment. The policy has paid off . . . Most observers now rate the 100,000-man South Korean Army as the best of its size in Asia. [One wonders what comfort an army can take in being the "best of its size." Wars, after all, aren't run like prizefights, with heavyweights forbidden to take on middleweights and middleweights under instructions to lay off bantams.] Its fast-moving columns have mopped up all but a few of the Communist guerrilla bands. And no one now believes that the Russian-trained North Korean army could pull off a quick, successful invasion of the South without heavy reinforcements. Said a South Korean private manning a foxhole along the 38th Parallel last week: "We expect war to come. But we aren't afraid. For every round they send over, we'll send two back."

On June 13, less than two weeks before the invasion, William C. Foster, at that time deputy administrator of the Economic Co-operation Administration, testified before a congressional committee: "The rigorous training program [in the Republic of Korea] has built up a well-disciplined army of 100,000 soldiers, one that is prepared to meet any challenge by the North Korean forces and one that has cleaned out the guerrilla bands in South Korea in one area after another."

Syngman Rhee had said that the Republic was "strong enough to take Pyongyang [the Communist capital] in three days," adding. "If we had our way, we would, I am sure, have started up already." MacArthur did not address himself directly to the Korean question in the weeks before the invasion (though he had, of course, passed along General Willoughby's sunny estimates) but, taking a large view of Asia in May, he had said: "I don't believe a shooting war is imminent" and he had continued to muse about Japan as "the Switzerland of Asia."

What *Time* called the "best army of its size in Asia" was approaching total disintegration when MacArthur began sending ground units in. The fighting capacities of the South Koreans was to become a hotly disputed and, to say the least, complicated question during the MacArthur controversy; but it was certain from the start that they always fought badly when they lacked equipment and when they lacked training for the kind of operations they were called upon to undertake. It would seem to make sense to assume that their being South Koreans had nothing to do with their speed in moving to the rear, since South Koreans, as General Hodge could have said, are the same breed of cats as North Koreans, and the North Koreans moved steadily, irresistibly forward.

Anyway, the situation was so immediately desperate that MacArthur had to feed in his men in almost in single file. He had hoped to be able to hold the forces that were being flown and shipped to the peninsula behind the Kum River, which was about twenty miles below the front when the movement of troops began, and build up strength for a few days at least. But this could not be. As soon as the men arrived, they had to be sent into action in an effort to stop at least part of the flow through the sieve-like Republican lines. The first American contingent to go in was made up of two rifle companies, one mortar platoon, and four 105-millimeter guns from Japan.

MacArthur had to do what he did not want to do and what all the rules of sound strategy told him not to. Nevertheless, he knew that if the enemy crossed the Han River, which is a big U with Seoul at the left-hand tip, while the Americans were still checking in by the platoon, there might be nothing for the expected reinforcements to reinforce. He wanted to slow down the enemy drive at any cost, and, although the slowing-down was imperceptible to the layman, military observers say that he did what he had to do superbly. He added a little extra muscle to his small American units by drafting such South Korean males as he could lay hands on into the United States army. He stripped down his Japanese occupation forces so rapidly that by September there was not one organized company in the islands. It was not until July 31, when units of the 2nd Infantry Division began to disembark, that any reinforcements came directly from the United States, and it was not until the last week in August that a contingent of troops, a British one, came in from any of the other United Nations. By the time our 2nd Infantry arrived, Chonan, Kumchon, and Taejon had fallen.

At the Senate hearings, MacArthur himself gave a vivid description of his strategy in the early days in Korea:

My directives were to establish a beachhead in the neighborhood of Pusan and to take such steps as I felt I could within the means I possessed to support the Korean government and help maintain the South Koreans.

I was reminded that my resources for the time being were practically limited to what I had and that I must regard the security of Japan as a fundamental and basic policy.

I threw in troops from the 24th Division by air in the hope of developing a loci of resistance around which I could rally the fast retreating South Korean forces.

I also hoped by that arrogant display of strength to fool the enemy into a belief that I had a much greater resource at my disposal than I did.

I managed to throw in a part of two battalions of infantry, who put up a magnificent resistance before they were destroyed—a resistance which resulted, perhaps, in one of the most vital successes that we had.

The enemy undoubtedly could not understand that we would make such an effort with such a small force.

Instead of pushing rapidly forward to Pusan, which he could have reached within a week, without the slightest difficulty, he stopped to deploy his artillery across the Han River.

We had destroyed the bridges.

We gained ten days by that process, before he had deployed in line of battle along the 150 miles front from Suwon as the pivotal point.

By that time, I had brought forward the rest of the 24th Division under General Dean. I gave him orders to delay the advance of the enemy until I could bring the First Cavalry Division and the 25th Division over from Japan.

He fought a very desperate series of isolated combats in which both he and a very large part of that division were destroyed.

By that time we had landed the 25th Division at Pusan, and it was moving forward by rail. And we landed the First Cavalry Division on the East Coast, and they moved over and formed a line of battle. I do not think that the history of the war will show a more magnificent effort against what should have been overwhelming odds than those two divisions displayed.

Taejon was a grisly affair. A verminous shantytown on the banks of the Kum, it had been the headquarters of the Eighth Army. The late Lieutenant General Walton Walker thought that the floodwaters of the Kum would be of great aid to the defenders. So they would have been if they had not eerily and unpredictably subsided when the battle was joined. North Koreans—some in civilian clothes, some in American uniform—walked across the mud flats and entered the city for a great house-to-house battle. The 24th Infantry Division held the city for three days, or one day longer than it had been ordered to, but at the cost of great numbers of its men, including its commander, Major General William F. Dean, who simply vanished in one of the wild street battles. He was last seen setting off to perforate a Russian tank with a bazooka. The engineer of a hospital train which was coming in to take the wounded south was shot at his throttle, and his train did not move again. Neither did most of the wounded. Taejon fell after almost a month of fighting, and the Americans and the R.O.K. troops still had to content themselves with slowing down the advance. By the first week in August, the area they had left to retreat in was a beachhead of four thousand square miles which fanned out around the supply port of Pusan.

On that beachhead, the United Nations forces—for by now they were really becoming United Nations forces, with British, French, Turkish, Australian, Dutch, and Philippine troops, as well as Americans and South Koreans—held for over a month. It was the first of several periods of bloody stalemate, and in that period MacArthur was planning what may well have been the most brilliant operation of his career: the amphibious landings at Inchon which took place on September 15 and led quickly to the first northward sweep of the United Nations armies.

It is pretty clear now that the credit for both the conception and the execution of them belongs to MacArthur. Louis Johnson, who was Secretary of defense until three days before Inchon, implied, when he testified at the Senate hearings, that he was the only man in the Pentagon who endorsed MacArthur's scheme. It is doubtful if his claim to this splendid isolation is entirely valid, but General James Lawton Collins, Chief of Staff of the Army, and Admiral Forrest Sherman, Chief of Naval Operations, thought the plan unworkable and went to Tokyo and tried to talk MacArthur out of it. The rest of the Joint Chiefs had grave doubts, and General Bradley has said that when they finally approved MacArthur's plans, they did so with fingers crossed. MacArthur's own staff was, if anything, more apprehensive. His Tokyo aides knew Inchon as a harbor that offered exceptional hazards even for commercial vessels that could leisurely pick their way through

its silt-filled channels without worrying about fire from shore bat-
teries. Inchon has thirty-one foot tides, which wash over and
constantly rearrange underwater masses of mud. MacArthur and
his staff planners had to reckon with the possibility of at least
some of their ships becoming mud-bound for hours and thus a
set-up for enemy guns ashore. They had to reckon with the possibility of the weather turning in the middle of Operation Chro-
mite, as it was known in the planning stages; a sudden squall
could have deprived them of use of the air in dealing with shore
installations. It was, in brief, a very risky proposition.

But MacArthur carried it off. Two days before the first wave
of General O. P. Smith's Marines went ashore, ten United Nations
warships entered the harbor, shot up floating mines, and went
close to shore to draw enemy fire. Having drawn it, they swung
into position, dropped anchor, and proceeded to blast away at
the port's defenses. The weather was fair, and the shelling from
the harbor was accompanied by a ferocious carrier strike. When
the Marines went in on September 15, the defenders had been
so thoroughly mashed and kneaded ("It was really quivering,"
a marine pilot said, "I thought I was going to roll over and sink")
that it took the Marines only forty minutes to capture Wohli
Island, the key to the harbor's defense system. From Wohli, they
raced over the 1,000-foot causeway to the mainland and into the
battle for Seoul, which was not won until September 27* and the
United Nations troops that came in behind the Marines began
moving north, south and east in great force; they took the heat

---

* These preliminary operations took place on September 13, the 191st anniversary of the Battle of Quebec. MacArthur is said to have found this
gratifying. He has said, in fact, that it was Wolfe's victory on the Plains of
Abraham that emboldened him to go ahead with Inchon. He told his friend
Bascom Timmons that, as Timmons put it in an article in *Collier's*, "The
more he [MacArthur] thought about Quebec, the stronger became his conviction that a landing on Inchon was sound." Timmons quoted MacArthur
directly: "I imagine that Wolfe thought to himself, if his brigadiers and his
admiral believed his plan unfeasible, then General Montcalm must have
reasoned that Wolfe would not try it. And if able American officers think
Inchon impracticable, doubtless the Communists do too."

off the men around Pusan, who began to advance up the peninsula. By October 1, the United Nations forces were in possession
of everything south of the Thirty-eighth Parallel. That is to say,
the Republic of Korea was again in the hands of its friends. And
its friends were ready to liberate and unify all Korea.

FROM INCHON TO THE YALU

MacArthur was in an expansive mood after Inchon—as, indeed,
he had every right to be. He had his command-ship radio wire
ashore his judgment that "the Navy and Marines had never shone
more brightly than this morning." He went ashore, not to announce a personal triumph, but to tell Admirable Struble, "I've
lived a long time and played with the Navy a long time. They've
never failed me." If his relations with the admirals were in good
shape, however, his relations with statesmen and politicians were
not. The conflict with civilian authority that was to bring on a
national crisis in the spring of 1951 had already been under way
for several weeks.

Or perhaps it had been under way for several years. A facile
analyst of motives and compulsions could pick any one of a half-
dozen dates in MacArthur's long career and demonstrate that the
trouble really began way back there. He could, if he wished, go
back beyond MacArthur to the years when the Boy Colonel of
the West was fighting Indians and getting precious little thanks
for it from what Thomas Beer called the Titaness Society. Or he
could bring it up to the early years in Manila, when the elder
MacArthur locked horns with the elder Taft; or to the twenties
and thirties when Douglas MacArthur recoiled from the effete-
ness and decadence he thought he saw in civilian life; or to the
war years when President Roosevelt provoked from him the com-
plaint that Roosevelt "acted as if he were the directing head of
the Army and Navy"; or to his difficulties with the State Department during the occupation of Japan.

It was in that period that several members of the 1951 cast first got into the act. In September 1945, MacArthur gave the reporters in Tokyo a statement about reducing the size of the occupying forces. Washington could not recall having authorized the statement; at a press conference, Dean Acheson, then Acting Secretary of State, explained that the occupation authorities, General MacArthur included, were not the architects of policy but merely "the instruments." It grew to be so bitter a dispute that for some time after it there were no direct communications between MacArthur and the State Department. It has been said that MacArthur never forgave Acheson for this attempt to control him; in any case, Senator Wherry and many of the General's friends in Congress never did. Their anguish and solicitousness dated from this period.

MacArthur was, it is true, more contentious than most members of his profession. Indeed, contentiousness was built into his philosophy. In a conspicuous place on the wall of his office in the Dai-Ichi Building, he had framed a lengthy quotation from Livy which purports to give the view of a Roman general named Lucius Aemilius Paulus, who made war on the Macedonians in 168 B.C. It read in part:

> In every circle, and truly, at every table there are people who lead armies into Macedonia; who know where the camp ought to be placed; what posts ought to be occupied by troops; when and through what pass that territory should be entered; where magazines should be formed; how provisions should be conveyed by land and sea; and when it is proper to engage the enemy, when to lie quiet . . . These are great impediments to those who have the management of affairs . . . I am not one of those who think that commanders ought at no time to receive advice; on the contrary, I should deem that man more proud than wise, who regulated every proceeding by the standard of his own single judgment. What then is my opinion? That Commanders should be counselled chiefly by persons of known talent . . . who are present at the scene of action, who see the country, who see the enemy . . . and who, like people embarked in the same ship, are sharers of the danger. If, therefore, anyone thinks himself qualified to give advice respecting the war which I am to conduct . . . let him

not refuse his assistance to the state but let him come with me into Macedonia. He shall be furnished with a ship, a horse, a tent; even his traveling charges shall be defrayed. But if he thinks this too much trouble, and prefers the repose of a city life . . . let him not . . . assume the office of a pilot. The city in itself furnishes abundance of topics for conversation; let it confine its passion for talking within its own precincts and rest assured that we shall pay no attention to any councils but such as shall be framed within our camp.

Yet it would be misleading to assume that the crisis of 1950 and 1951 was merely the climax of an inevitable and irreconcilable conflict between a headstrong general and long-suffering civil authorities. MacArthur's contentiousness was, in a way, a measure of his abilities. The soldier who never challenges civilian direction may be simply lazy and weak-minded. Whatever can be held against MacArthur, he was never a time-server, and he was only occasionally a buck-passer. Moreover, although the doctrine of Lucius Aemilius Paulus is an extreme one, there is something to be said for the insights—political as well as military—of the professional soldier. To insist on the principle of civilian control is nothing less than to insist on the principle of a free society; to insist on too sharp a distinction between civil and military functions is, however, to misunderstand the problems of a free society. It would be a suspicious circumstance if there were no conflicts between the two spheres, and it would probably be a poor and overcomplacent officer who did not chafe at times under the control of civilians and who failed to criticize their performances on the basis of his special insights.

When MacArthur told the Senate committees that "no more subordinate soldier ever wore the uniform," he was speaking, to be sure, in hyperbole. On the other hand, it would be grossly unfair to say that there was never a more insubordinate soldier. MacArthur's early insubordinations were all pretty much in the line of duty. Nothing in his past suggests that he was being insincere when he wrote, in a 1932 report, "The national strategy of any war . . . must be made by the head of state . . . [It] could not be delegated to any subordinate authority." Nor had there been anything in his recent career to suggest that he was concealing a change in heart or a tongue in cheek when, after having these words recalled to him at the hearings, he observed, "As I look back on my youthful days . . . I am surprised and amazed how wise I was." Temperament unquestionably played a part in the conflict between the General and the President, but by far the larger part was played by policy and principle.

The General never grasped the President's reasons for becoming engaged in Korea. He also misunderstood the corollary action the President took in respect to Formosa, the seat of what was left by 1950 of the government of Nationalist China. Or perhaps he understood it well enough but merely thought it tragically wrong-headed. Either way, he had plenty of company, and it was over this Formosa policy that the first major arguments began.

The role of Formosa in global strategy, like the role of Korea, had been closely studied by American strategists, but they were not nearly as much of one mind on it as they were on Korea. They were all agreed, of course, that it would be helpful to have the island in friendly hands—just as it would be helpful to have most other places in friendly hands. Some of them, however, felt that Formosa in the possession of an enemy would so menace Japan and the Philippines that securing it would be worth anything it cost. If, in the weary idiom of strategists, Korea was "a dagger pointed at the heart of Japan," Formosa was "an unsinkable aircraft carrier" from which massive strikes could be launched against Japan and the Philippines. But the other school, which seems to have been the larger and was unquestionably the more influential, felt that the usefulness of Formosa would not be worth the cost of holding it against a determined invader. It was pointed out that it stood just a hundred miles off the China coast; no one not already in control of the coast could seize the island, and whoever controlled the coast was already in possession of a much larger airbase than Formosa.

Members of this second school argued that we had fought

almost the whole of the last war with Formosa in enemy hands—
and in the hands of an enemy with a far larger fleet and air force
than the Chinese Communists can hope to have in many years.
MacArthur himself, in 1945, had doggedly opposed the Navy view
that Formosa was the key to the conquest of Japan. Three years
before that he had seen no sacrifice of essential military advantage in the neutralization of the Philippines. In 1949, he had
described precisely the same defense perimeter as that described
by Dean Acheson. His 1949 view was the official one up to 1950.
In January 1950, the President announced, "The United States
Government will provide no military aid to the Chinese forces
on Formosa." That was policy.

On June 26, the policy changed. It changed partly for military,
partly for political reasons. The military reasons were simple. The
war in Korea, at least in the early stages, would require a withdrawal of some of our strength from other parts of the Far East.
For the time being, we would have to weaken Japan and the
Philippines and all the other places where we had large invest-
ments of force. To whatever extent we weakened our other out-
posts, to that extent the value of Formosa to an enemy power
would have to be marked up. The political reasons were more
complex. A number of them were domestic. For some time, the
Asia-first bloc in Congress had in fact been a Formosa-first bloc.
Formosa was all that was left of Nationalist China, and all the
friends of Nationalist China thought we should defend it as we
would the gold deposits at Fort Knox.* Almost the whole criticism
of administration foreign policy in the first part of 1951 had turned
on its callous disregard of Formosa as a bastion of freedom. Involving the Republic in a war in Korea, a country which had
about as much reality to most Americans as Dahomey or Leich-

---

* Senator Knowland of California was saying, "If Formosa were in unfriendly
hands . . . our defense line would be driven back to the Pacific coast," as
if Formosa had not been in unfriendly hands from 1941 to 1945. Chiang
carried the magic, of course. If he withdrew to Lars Christenson Land, down
in the Admiral Byrd country, the place would enjoy an immediate upgrading
in strategic importance.

tenstein, the administration simply had to take some account of Formosa, which was under constant threat of attack from the mainland.

But, if strategic and domestic factors suggested one kind of action on Formosa, international factors suggested another. For the security of our line of communications and for the satisfaction of our Republican party, it was necessary to commit ourselves to the defense of Formosa. To maintain our defensive alliances, however, it was necessary to limit that commitment severely. The United States is the only country (China included) which can boast a formidable number of admirers of Chiang Kai-shek. Justly or otherwise, most of our allies in Europe and all our allies in Asia viewed the Nationalist government on Formosa as a distinctly shady proposition. Only Communists, of course, could view the conquest of the island by Communists with satisfaction, but most Europeans and Asians contemplated the possibility (or, as it seemed to them, the certainty) of such conquest with relative indifference. Feeling that Chiang, who had resigned as president in 1949 and reassumed the office on his own authority early in 1950, was very nearly finished anyway, they could not see that much would be lost if the Communists consolidated their conquest of China by taking the last remaining province. Some of them, in fact, felt that since the Communists were already in effective control of China and since the United States was pledged by the Cairo agreement to restore Formosa to the "Republic of China," we had been welshing on a previous commitment by sending, as we did through 1949, a certain amount of military aid to the stricken Nationalists. Great Britain, India, and several other nations recognized the Communist government as the legitimate government of China.

Taking one consideration with another, the administration, at the suggestion of the Secretary of State, decided to "neutralize" Formosa. That is, it decided to protect it from attack by the Communists and at the same time to prevent it from attacking the Communists. "The occupation of Formosa by Communist forces would be a direct threat to the security of the Pacific area," the President said in the June 27 declaration which announced the sending of ships and planes to Korea, "and to the United States forces pursuing their lawful and necessary functions. Accordingly, I have ordered the Seventh Fleet to prevent any attack on Formosa. As a corollary of this action, I am calling upon the Chinese government on Formosa to cease all air and sea operations against the mainland. The Seventh Fleet will see that this is done." It was rather nervy of the President to dictate a course of action for the Nationalist government; for all its infirmities, it was still the government we recognized in China; but it seemed advisable to take some step that would reassure the world, and Asia especially, that our military intervention in Korea was being undertaken to check aggression, not to force Asia back on its distasteful past. Even this reassurance, however, did not satisfy all of our foreign critics. No other nation went along with our Formosa decision; it remains to this day a source of friction with other non-Communist members of the United Nations.*

It became a serious source of friction with MacArthur, whose duty it was, as Commander in Chief of United States Forces in the Far East, to carry out all military aspects of it. Being MacArthur, he construed the military aspects broadly. At the end of July, he flew to Formosa; spent a day and a half conferring with Chiang Kai-shek, whom he had never met before; was photographed gallantly kissing Mme Chiang; and returned to Tokyo

---

* To reduce the friction, the President included the following statement in his message to Congress on July 19: "In order that there may be no doubt in any quarter about our intentions regarding Formosa, I wish to state that the United States has no territorial ambitions whatever concerning that island, nor do we seek for ourselves any special position or privilege on Formosa. The present military neutralization of Formosa is without prejudice to political questions affecting that island. Our desire is that Formosa not become embroiled in hostilities disturbing to the peace of the Pacific and that all questions affecting Formosa are to be settled by peaceful means as envisaged in the Charter of the United Nations. With peace established, even the most complex political questions are susceptible of solution. In the presence of brutal and unprovoked aggression, however, some of these questions may have to be held in abeyance in the interest of the essential security of all."

to await, it was reported at the time, the congratulations of
the President for his contribution to international good will. Mac-
Arthur made only the most noncommittal statements about the
trip, but Chiang, who a few weeks earlier had said in his most
lordly and gratuitous manner that it was not yet too late for his
and President Truman's governments to repair their damaged
friendship and that "no difficulties . . . will arise if United States
relationships are placed in the hands of Douglas MacArthur,"
announced shortly after the visit, "The foundation for Sino-American military co-operation has been laid." He spoke, too, of "final
victory [in] our struggle against communism." In Washington, no
one quite knew what this meant. If Washington had not authorized MacArthur's trip, this was not in itself distressing, since it
was doubtful, in view of MacArthur's assignment, whether authorization was needed: MacArthur was charged with the defense
of Formosa, and there was no reason why he should not confer
with the commander of the friendly troops who held the island.
Nevertheless, the administration was much put out by Chiang's
statement and by the aura of treaty-making which had seemed to
hang over the conference of potentates.

In other capitals, there was great distress. Chiang's statement
was taken to mean exactly what it said—that "Sino-American military co-operation" was in the works and that some kind of agreement had been reached to use Nationalist troops in Korea and
perhaps for an invasion of China. Chiang had made a specific
offer of assistance on June 30,* and had been turned down by the
United States, with MacArthur's concurrence, with the polite
explanation that his troops might better be used to defend the
island. There was nothing disingenuous in the polite explanation
as far as it went, but it was far from the whole explanation. In

---

* The Chinese embassy in Washington informed the State Department that
it could make available "33,000 seasoned troops . . . suitable for operation
in plain or hilly terrain." Also, the "best equipment at China's disposal" including twenty air transports, "a reasonable amount of air cover" and "a
moderate amount of naval escort." This force, it said, could be "ready for
embarkation in five days."

that early stage of the Korean war, it was felt that the Koreans might regard their liberation by Chinese as the beginnings of another Chinese occupation. Whatever the Koreans would make of our use of Chiang's troops, it was certain that it would lose sympathy for our intervention throughout Asia. Quite apart from that, there was the possibility that we would suffer a net loss militarily by such a deal. There would be enormous supply and transport problems for us to shoulder, and the record of Chiang's seasoned troops was not exactly impressive. One hundred and fifty thousand of them had been run off Hainan Island by one-tenth that many Communists. There was a suspicion in the Defense Department that Nationalist troops, when they reached Korea, would either surrender their arms to the Communists or cross the lines and join them.

In any event, MacArthur's visit was a cause of embarrassment; to avoid further embarrassment, the President sent W. Averell Harriman to Tokyo "to brief General MacArthur on what American policy is," as a government spokesman put it, and suggest a little snappier co-ordination of his plans with Washington's.

The briefing trip lasted five days. Harriman returned to explain that MacArthur's visit had been "perfectly natural"—which, considered purely as a tour of inspection, it certainly was—and that the government had really known about it in advance; it had only lacked such data as where MacArthur was going, whom he was to see, and what he was to do. For his part, MacArthur gave out a statement that his talks with Chiang had been "limited entirely to military matters." It seemed to be another case of construing military matters very broadly—particularly on the part of Chiang. In justifying himself, though, MacArthur struck several political notes.

My visit has been maliciously represented to the public by those who invariably in the past have propagandized a policy of defeatism and appeasement in the Pacific . . . I hope the American people will not be misled by the insinuations, speculations, and bold misstatements . . . which tend, if they are not indeed designed, to promote disunity and destroy faith and confidence in the American nations and institutions.

It is impossible to review the history of MacArthur's difficulties with his government without concluding that at some point he embarked on a deliberate course of provocation. This may have begun after the Formosa trip or it may have begun in December 1950, when the insubordinations began to come thick and fast. The early usurpations of the diplomatic function may have been the result of misunderstanding or of excessive zeal. Persuasive arguments can be made to this effect; MacArthur himself has made several of them.*

At some stage, though, he must have become convinced that his government was pursuing a disastrous course in the Far East and that it was his duty as a patriot to bring about a change. He knew, after all, the consequences of insubordination. He may have voted for Billy Mitchell's acquittal, but he knew what happened to Mitchell. He knew where the policy-making power lies in our government. He understood that, as he said in the Senate hearings, "the authority of the President to assign officers is complete and absolute. He does not have to give any reasons therefor or anything else. That is inherent." After his recall, he said that he "hadn't the faintest idea" why he was dismissed, but in fairness to him it has to be assumed that he meant by this that he could not undersand why an American officer should be relieved of his command for advancing a policy calculated, as he saw it, to produce victory for his country's arms.

Still, if MacArthur's provocativeness did not begin until after the Chinese intervention in Korea, it is necessary to attribute to

---

* It was the feeling of those who observed his conduct around the time of the Harriman visits that he was very much in earnest about being a good, subordinate soldier. One of his public statements was rather touching. "It is extraordinarily difficult," he said on August 5, "for me at times to exercise that degree of patience which is unquestionably demanded if the longtime policies which have been decreed are to be successfully accomplished without repercussions which would be detrimental to the well-being of the world, but I am restraining myself to the best of my ability and am generally satisfied with the progress being made."

"Do You Have Much Trouble With Him?"

him a monumental blind spot, something very close to denseness, on the country's Formosa policy. Late in August, when he had had a full three weeks to digest the Harriman lectures, he had SCAP send out the text of a message that was to be read at the annual convention of the Veterans of Foreign Wars, shortly to be held in Chicago. The release date was August 28, but the text was on the desks of editors (but not of the Secretary of Defense) long before then. The message took the view that Formosa was "ideally located to accomplish offensive strategy and at the same time checkmate defensive or counteroffensive by friendly forces based in Okinawa or the Philippines." This was pretty much in line with the military doctrine. "Nothing could be more fallacious," he said, resuming the polemical offensive, "than the threadbare argument . . . that if we defend Formosa we alienate continental Asia. Those who speak thus do not understand the Orient. They do not grasp that it is the pattern of Oriental psychology to respect and follow aggressive, resolute, and dynamic leadership." Eventually this was brought to the President's attention, and the President promptly ordered it withdrawn.

It was not read before the Veterans of Foreign Wars, but the text got widely circulated anyway. One national magazine had it in type before the President knew it existed. It made its appearance at a most inauspicious moment. The United States, through Warren Austin, had just announced at Lake Success that it earnestly wished the United Nations to settle the ultimate fate of Formosa. The American action there, he said, had been taken purely in the interest of preventing aggression.

The General's statement on Formosa led to his first meeting with the President. It took place on October 15 on Wake Island and was in all respects an odd affair. There had been a precedent of a sort for it in a meeting Franklin Roosevelt had with MacArthur in Hawaii in 1944, but Roosevelt then was the leader of a nation conducting a war along a broad oceanic front, and he was in the Pacific to observe the progress of the national effort. He, too, met with MacArthur in order to clear up a few matters growing out of the large question of who gave orders to whom, but there seemed, somehow, to be nothing very much out of the way in the President's journey. For regality of manner, Roosevelt was more than a match for MacArthur.

With Roosevelt's successor, however, the appearance of things was a bit different. Paradoxically, it was not the pomp and circumstance of the occasion but its crude improvisations—the meetings in a hastily cleared-out Quonset hut, the ride over rough roads in a battered Chevrolet—which suggested that two magistrates of mighty power were meeting in some war-scarred neutral zone to fashion a truce and a new alliance. But if surface appearances suggested this, the contrast between the two men suggested something else. MacArthur bore himself with his usual *pukka sahib* air, but the President's manner, which was often very much at variance with his interior strength and resoluteness and doubtless was on this occasion, reminded Anthony Leviero, the New York *Times* correspondent, of "an insurance salesman who has at last signed up an important prospect . . . while the latter appeared dubious over the extent of coverage." When the two could be seen by reporters, the important prospect kept looking at his watch, as if there were more important things on his schedule than dallying with a President. Approached by journalists, MacArthur said, "All comments will have to come from the publicity man of the President."

But appearances can be doubly deceiving. Wake Island was not the scene of a meeting of equals, nor was it the scene of a President's humiliation. There were two meetings—the first, lasting an hour, between the President and the General; the second, also lasting an hour, with the two men and all their advisers present. The records of the meetings, released by the administration during the Senate hearings,* suggest that in the private session

* Thereby achieving transient celebrity for a young woman named Vernice Anderson, secretary to Dr. Philip Jessup, who sat in the shadow of a door that was ajar and took shorthand notes of the group meeting. MacArthur said he was unaware of her existence, to say nothing of her shorthand. The unfortunate young woman became a symbol of the degradation of public morals

the President got rather a handsome apology for the Formosa statement. It was not the President who tried to sell a policy to a balky prospect; it was the President who told the General what policy he would have to buy, and, when the General was told, he informed the President that he regretted any inconveniences his ill-advised statements had caused the government.

In the other session, all manner of things were talked about. For example, the prospects for ending the war in Korea: MacArthur thought they were excellent and that in fact all should be over by Thanksgiving. And the Japanese peace treaty: Truman and MacArthur were eager to have it drawn up as soon as possible, with or without Russian participation. And the post-war reconstruction of poor, battered Korea: some estimates of the cost had run as high as $1,500,000,000, but MacArthur bore the glad tidings that it could be done for about a third this amount. And the prospects for Russian and Chinese intervention: "Very little," MacArthur said. "Had they interfered in the first or second months it would have been decisive. We are no longer fearful of their intervention. We no longer stand hat in hand. The Chinese have 300,000 men in Manchuria. Of these probably not more than one hundred to one hundred and twenty-five thousand are distributed along the Yalu River. Only fifty to sixty thousand could be gotten across the Yalu River. They have no air force. Now that we have bases for our Air Force in Korea, if the Chinese tried to get down to Pyongyang, there would be the greatest

---

in many sections of the American press. Meditating on what might happen if children followed Miss Anderson's practice, George Sokolsky had unsettling visions. "Microphone placing in flower pots," he wrote, "might also help the next generations. They could automatically hear papa and mamma discussing family affairs, but better still it would build the ambitions of a young man. He could perhaps write on his application for a job in the State Department that he placed microphones in his sister's boudoir when he was ten, and tapped the telephone wires in the house by the time he was fourteen. That ought to fit him to be an expert on the Far East, to say nothing of the Middle East and Germany." All sorts of unexpected things happened in the MacArthur controversy, including the emergence of George Sokolsky as an ironist.

slaughter."* MacArthur was so confident that he suggested that the Second Division be transferred from Korea to Europe early in 1951.

No one can say what was in MacArthur's mind when the conference was over. What he authorized the President's "publicity man," the late Charles G. Ross, to say was, "No commander in the history of war has had more complete and admirable support from the agencies in Washington than I have during the Korean operation." (This quotation, anyway, was accurate. Asked about it by Senator Johnson of Texas, MacArthur said, "I am very glad to have the opportunity to reaffirm that. Up to that time, it was certainly so.") Wake Island oozed with magnanimity. The President said, "I've never had a more satisfactory conference since I've been President." He pinned a medal on MacArthur and said he hoped their next meeting would not be long delayed. "Good-bye, sir," the reporters heard MacArthur say, "and happy landings. . . . It's been a real honor to talk to you." Back in Washington the President said of MacArthur, "He is a member of the government of the United States. He is loyal to that government. He is loyal to the President. He is loyal to the President in his foreign policy."

It places no strain on credulity to assume that, at the time of the Wake Island conference MacArthur conceived himself to be the loyal commander the President assured the world he was. Anyway, for the next six weeks there were no more policy state-

---

* This statement was, according to General Bradley, pieced together from notes of participants as well as from the stenographic record. MacArthur refused to accept responsibility for the words and sentiments attributed to him in these records. He had also refused to state in what respects they were misleading; and copies of the record, sent to his headquarters shortly after the meeting, roused no complaints. It is interesting to recall that on November 13, 1950 Stewart Alsop, who had heard something about the Wake Island meeting, reported in his column that MacArthur had assured President Truman that the danger of Chinese intervention had passed. The *Freeman* wired MacArthur asking him to confirm or deny the truth of this report. It received the following reply: "The statement [from Stewart Alsop] quoted in your message of the 13th is entirely without foundation in fact. MacArthur, Tokyo, Japan."

ments from Tokyo. And, if the record, as it was brought out at the Senate hearings, is now complete, there was no more trouble until MacArthur undertook the offensive of November 24—the end-the-war offensive that marked the beginning of what Mac-Arthur called "an entirely new war."

It was not MacArthur's fault that, after Inchon, his troops had been unable to drive across the peninsula and close a vise on the North Koreans. The peninsula was simply too wide—and his forces not numerous enough. But he chased the North Koreans to the Thirty-eighth Parallel and waited there for the United Nations to authorize him to press forward. Technically, he needed no authorization. His mission, as United Nations Commander, was to "restore peace and security in the area," and it was surely evident that there would be no peace and security as long as the North Korean army was intact. Nevertheless, he stayed below the line, allowing only R.O.K. units to make cross-parallel sorties, until October 7, when the General Assembly, "recalling that the essential objective [of its policy] was the establishment of a unified, independent, and democratic Korea" recommended that all appropriate steps be taken to ensure conditions of stability throughout Korea.

To achieve the essential objective, MacArthur pressed the war with his customary vigor and skill.

The United Nations Armies crossed the border in fine shape. Seven United States divisions were in action—as many as the government felt it could spare for the campaign. The last to arrive was the 3rd Infantry, which had fought in North Africa, in Sicily, at Anzio, and in Normandy. It was about the best we had. The South Koreans had reorganized and thrown together six divisions. The magnificent Turks had arrived, and there were reinforcements from England, Australia, and Thailand.

As his troops went over the line, MacArthur was superbly confident. He gave an interview in Tokyo predicting that the first stage of Korean reconstruction would be completed by July of 1951; he announced to the North Koreans that he was giving them their final chance to come to terms with him. "I, as United Nations Commander in Chief," he said, "for the last time call upon you and the forces under your command in whatever part of Korea situated forthwith to lay down your arms and cease hostilities." He put his former Chief of Staff, Major General Edward Almond, in charge of the X Corps and told him to finish up the war in the northeast of Korea. No one at the time had a very clear idea of precisely how and on what terms the war would be finished up, but it was being widely predicted that there would be a surrender shortly after the fall of Pyongyang; it was thought that the North Koreans would be no more eager than we were for a "winter war." (The phrase gained the same kind of currency as "General Mud" during the Polish campaign in 1939, when people thought the Second World War might be called off on account of sloppy weather.) Our Quartermaster Corps was so bemused by the thought of autumn victory that it fell down on the job of supplying troops with cold-weather clothing.

Pyongyang fell on October 20. The First Cavalry had reached the city the day before and found it heavily fortified. But there were no troops to man the fortifications. In contrast to Seoul, where the liberated citizenry had shown little enthusiasm for liberation, the citizens of Pyongyang, were, from all external evidence, overjoyed. They happily joined in sacking the Russian commissary on Stalin Street and the main hotel which Kim Il Sung's government had charmingly renamed the Russian Hotel. On October 20, 1944, MacArthur had come ashore at Leyte and said, "I have returned." Six years later to the day, he landed on the Pyongyang airstrip and said, "Any celebrities here to greet me? Where's Kim Buck Too?"

He was ready to tie up the loose ends and go home. But an unpleasant thing happened. The North Koreans, it turned out, had quite an appetite for cold-weather war. In fact, in early November, as the United Nations forces, spearheaded by the R.O.K. 6th Division moved up beyond the pinched waist of the peninsula, the North Koreans stiffened alarmingly. They let the R.O.K. 6th move ahead, but they cut off the R.O.K. 7th and chopped it up, and began forcing United States troops back on the defensive.

Then came the first hints of Chinese intervention. On October 26 one Chinese prisoner was captured. On October 30, sixteen Communist prisoners taken north of Hamhung were questioned by Lieutenant Reynold Muranaka, a Honolulu Nisei, and found to be Chinese. The next day, X Corps intelligence reported "a Chinese Communist regiment in combat" near the Changjin and Pujon reservoirs. Intelligence reported it had crossed the Yalu by train on October 16. On November 1, some Russian-made MIG-15 jet fighters came over from Manchuria; they engaged some United Nations planes briefly, then flew back over the Yalu. On November 2, the first Cavalry announced that two battalions had been attacked and torn to pieces by Chinese troops. "We don't know whether they represent the Chinese Communist government," a spokesman for the First Cavalry said, but what hit the two battalions was "a massacre, Indian-style, like the one that hit Custer at Little Big Horn." Now there were Chinese everywhere. On November 3, after learning that "the order of the day is full speed ahead to the Yalu River," the 24th Infantry shifted from high into reverse and backed up fourteen miles. The next day the First Cavalry identified five Chinese divisions in its sector; the First Marine Division announced that it had encountered three.

During these several days, MacArthur's headquarters tended to make light of the Chinese; the day that eight divisions were identified in Korea, an intelligence report from Tokyo, as paraphrased in the hearings, said that "while Chinese Communist intervention was a distinct possibility, sufficient evidence [is] not at hand to warrant immediate acceptance." That same day, as it happened, the Peiping radio announced that a journal named *Shih-Shih-Shou-Tse* had described "three views" of the United States which should be developed in every Chinese mind and heart: "Hate the United States for she is the deadly enemy of the Chinese people. . . . Despise the United States, for she is a rotten, imperialist nation, the headquarters of reactionary degeneracy in the whole world. . . . Look with contempt upon the United States, for she is a paper tiger and can fully be defeated."

But the next day Tokyo became greatly agitated. "While the North Korean forces with which we were originally engaged," MacArthur's communiqué of November 6 said, "have been destroyed or rendered impotent . . . a new, fresh army now faces us, backed up by a possibility of large alien reserves and adequate supply within easy reach to the enemy but beyond the limits of our present sphere of military action." In his report to the United Nations of the same day, he summarized some of the findings of the preceding week—adding, from the preceding day, six anti-aircraft volleys from the "privileged sanctuary" across the Yalu—and said that an issue had been raised "which it is incumbent upon me to bring at once to the attention of the United Nations."

He reported that, fortunately, his Eighth Army had withdrawn in time to escape "a possible trap . . . surreptitiously laid" and that there was not, at the time, "any possibility of a great military reverse." Nevertheless, "in the face of the victory of United Nations arms," the Communists committed "one of the most offensive acts of international lawlessness of historic record by moving without any notice of belligerency elements of alien Communist forces across the Yalu River. . . . Whether and to what extent these reserves will be moved forward to reinforce units now committed remains to be seen and is a matter of the gravest significance." He spoke in his report to the United Nations of his own forces being "presently in hostile contact with Chinese military units deployed for action against the forces of the Unified Command."

Now the most bizarre period of the war set in. At Lake Success, MacArthur's news was taken with the utmost gravity. Sir Gladwyn Jebb, the British representative, proposed that the Security Council ask Peiping to send representatives to New York to take part in a discussion of MacArthur's report. There was a general concurrence in Jebb's proposal, though Ambassador Austin, who wanted immediate condemnation of China and a resolution calling upon her to end her aggression, thought that the Peiping representatives should not be "invited" but "summoned" to account for what the United States regarded as a defiance of the world organization thoroughly as reprehensible as the North Korean intervention in June. To this, Mr. Jacob Malik of Russia responded with the observation that "when a colonial power speaks to a colonial slave, it may summon. . . . But in the present case, the term should be 'to invite.'" The point was thought well taken, and, on November 8, the invitation was issued. On November 11, a bit of sweetening was added. A group of nations—among them France, Norway, the United Kingdom, and the United States—presented in the Security Council a resolution calling upon all nations (none was mentioned by name) to refrain from assisting the North Koreans and at the same time affirming that "it is the policy of the United Nations to hold the Chinese frontier with Korea inviolate and fully to protect legitimate Chinese and Korean interests in the frontier zone."

Three days later Peiping replied to the invitation. The Foreign Minister, Chou En-lai, said that the Central People's government could not in all conscience accept the proposal to discuss MacArthur's report, because that report raised far less urgent questions than that of the United States' "aggression" on Taiwan (Formosa) and in Korea. Anticipating a diplomatic victory that was not to come for two weeks (when the Council would adopt an agenda which put discussion of Formosa ahead of discussion of Korea), Peiping, on November 14, dispatched a delegation of fourteen Communist diplomats to New York. They should have arrived on November 15, but they took in the sights of Moscow, Prague, and London along the way and finally arrived on November 24, ready to talk business about Formosa.

It was MacArthur's November 6 reports to Washington and the United Nations that had alerted the world to the Chinese threat. It was not until November 28 that he announced he existence of "an entirely new war," but he had pointed clearly enough to the possibilities in the earlier report. He had said he faced "a new, fresh army." He had described the strategic advantages of the Chinese as accurately as if he had known their intentions. The memory of these warnings was to be so obliterated by the traumatic shock of subsequent events that few people would think it odd when, at the Senate hearings, MacArthur indignantly said, in a discussion of the massing of troops across the Yalu, "That intelligence should have been given to me"—as if it had not been he who gave it to Washington and Lake Success in the first place. On November 6, he had told the Joint Chiefs that the Chinese were massing in such force as "to threaten the ultimate destruction of my command."

There is nothing much to wonder at in the fact that the sequence of events was unclear in the public mind after the Chinese intervention, but there is a great deal to wonder at in MacArthur's behavior in late November.

He seems to have been overcome by an inexplicable euphoria. This was to some extent encouraged by developments at the front. The North Korean and Chinese resistance, which had stiffened in late October and early November, softened once again. The enemy was regrouping, and this was neither the first nor the last time that the regrouping of the enemy, which always took longer than a similar action by western armies, was to be mistaken for something like a collapse. Not everybody made this mistake, though. Joseph Fromm, Tokyo correspondent for *U. S. News*, had interviewed "a high-ranking officer" who had said that "the best the U.N. could hope for was a line across the waist of Korea and that if the Chinese chose to make the necessary commitment they could probably force a U.N. evacuation." Mr. Fromm also said that he had been told by a marine commander that he was "taking all precautions against an overwhelming Chinese counteroffensive which he considered inevitable."

Was MacArthur oblivious to all this? Did he simply forget his own warnings? It hardly seems likely. He had posed for himself a question whose answer he must have sought during those weeks. "Whether and to what extent those . . . alien Communist . . . reserves will be moved forward to reinforce units now committed remains to be seen," he had said on November 5, "and is a matter of the gravest significance." He must have known that when he spoke of "alien Communist" forces he was in fact talking about the 850,000 armed men who, he had been informed by General Willoughby, were at that time quartered in Manchuria. He had signaled the Joint Chiefs that the Chinese were massing in such force as "to threaten the ultimate destruction of my command." Even today, after the long inquest in the Senate, we still do not know on what information or logic he acted when he walked into the Communist trap. A reasonable guess is that he was emboldened by his own belief that "it is the pattern of the Oriental psychology to respect and follow aggressive, resolute, and dynamic leadership." Operating on this doctrine, he could have concluded that the danger of defeat would not be reduced but increased if he hesitated. If he hung back, his weakness would invite Chinese aggression; but, if he showed firmness and marched to the frontier, the Chinese threat would be faced down.

Perhaps he coupled this doctrine with that of Lucius Aemilius Paulus—"rest assured that we shall pay no attention to any councils but such as shall be framed within our camp." Whatever his doctrine, he began disregarding the pilots of the city right and left. For example, on September 27, the day that Seoul fell, he had been told by the Joint Chiefs of Staff that "as a matter of policy, no non-Korean ground forces will be used in the northeast provinces bordering the Soviet Union or in the area along the Manchurian border." He had adhered to this "policy" for a while (explaining in his communiqués that he was using R.O.K.'s for his "deepest northern penetrations"); but on October 24, he instructed his staff in the field to "use any and all ground forces at their commands, as necessary, in order to capture all of North

Korea." The Joint Chiefs didn't take this as too serious an infraction at first; MacArthur at that time still had quite a distance to go to the borders; but when he explained that he had acted from "military necessity," having just about run out of South Koreans for his "deepest northern penetrations," they explained to him that they would like to be informed of his decisions before he put them into effect. As General Collins paraphrased their reply, the Joint Chiefs said that, although they realized that "CINCFE [Commander in Chief, Far East] undoubtedly had sound reasons . . . they would like information of these reasons, since the action . . . was a matter of concern to them."

For a while, the Joint Chiefs got their information. MacArthur pulled back his non-Korean advance units, and the Joint Chiefs wrote off the affair. But by November 23, MacArthur had non-Korean units dispersed all over North Korea, and Joint Chiefs had to call him down for it again. On November 24, the day of the offensive, the Joint Chiefs informed him of "the growing concern of other members of the United Nations over the possibility of bringing on a general conflict if the United Nations forces advanced and seized the entire North Korean area at the boundary between Korea and Manchuria and the U.S.S.R." It was suggested that "CINCFE . . . hold his forces in terrain dominating the approaches to the valley of the Yalu. These forces should be principally R.O.K. troops. Other United Nations forces should be grouped in positions of readiness."*

They got a rather debonair reply. MacArthur took the position

* Word of the existence of such a message leaked out shortly afterward, and James Reston reported in the New York *Times* that instructions to stop short of the Yalu had been sent to MacArthur. Arthur Krock of the same newspaper wired the General asking if he had received any such instructions. MacArthur replied on November 29, 1950: "I have received no suggestion from any authoritative source that in the execution of its mission, the command should stop at the Thirty-eighth Parallel, at Pyongyang, or at any other line short of the international boundary." It is possible that he did not regard the Joint Chiefs as "authoritative sources," since they were merely four office workers in Washington, D.C. At the hearings, he said that he had received the document in question.

that the United Nations really had no cause for concern. According to the Joint Chiefs:

In CINCFE's reply . . . he indicated that the suggested approaches would, in all probability, not only fail to achieve the desired result, but would be provocative of the very consequence we were seeking to avoid. CINCFE felt that it would be utterly impossible for the United Nations forces to stop on the commanding terrain south of the Yalu, as suggested . . . CINCFE stated that his plan was to consolidate positions along the Yalu River as soon as he was able to and then to replace, as far as possible, American forces with those of the Republic of Korea. He would then announce his plans, which would include

A. The return of the American forces to Japan.

B. The parole of all prisoners of war to their homes; and

C. Leaving the matter of the unification of Korea and of the restoration of the civil processes of government to the people, with the advice and assistance of United Nations authorities.

He felt that as soon as United Nations military objectives had been reached prompt implementation of his plan would effectively appeal to the reason in the Chinese mind.

It must be made clear that it was not the actual presence of non-Korean troops on the Yalu that upset the Joint Chiefs. Hardly any of them ever got that far. What they considered outrageous were MacArthur's orders, which called for the use of any troops anywhere in Korea and his deployment of troops so that, in the event the United Nations armies did pull up at the frontiers, non-Koreans would occupy the advanced positions. This was pointed up in the following exchange at the hearings.

SENATOR MORSE: [Do] you believe that General MacArthur could have stopped some distance this side of the Yalu and adequately protected his troops?

GENERAL COLLINS: Yes, sir. But in fairness to General MacArthur now, I should say that we would have had to have gone further than he was at the time the Chinese made their mass attack on the 24th [26th] of November.

In any event, he framed his own advice and made his own appeal to the Chinese mind. He marched. The offensive was planned for the day after Thanksgiving. Thanksgiving Day 1950 in Korea must be put down as some kind of landmark in the history of American enterprise and imagination. American troops, sitting on the cold, high ground above the Yalu and about to walk into a valley of death, were served, chiefly by air drop, huge turkey dinners, with cranberry sauce, buttered squash, Waldorf salad, mince pie, after-dinner mints, and just about everything else they could have destroyed a five-dollar bill for in any Knott or Statler on the mainland. MacArthur stayed in Tokyo on the holiday.

On November 24, in the middle of the Korean morning, he put down on the advanced American airstrip near Sinanju to watch the big push that had been rolling for some hours. He told correspondents that it was a "general offensive" to "win the war." Someone asked if he had any idea how many Chinese were then in Korea. He was quick with an answer. About 30,000 regulars, he said, and 30,000 volunteers. (The next day, Saturday, the 25, his headquarters said there were 80,000; the following Tuesday MacArthur said 200,000.) On the morning of the 23rd he told Major General John B. Coulter to tell the troops, "They will eat Christmas dinner at home." In his communiqué, he announced:

The United Nations massive comprehension envelopment in North Korea against the new Red armies operating there is now approaching its decisive effort . . . If successful, this should for all practical purposes end the war, restore peace and unity to Korea, enable the prompt withdrawal of United Nations military forces,* and permit the complete assumption of Korea of full sovereignty and international equality. It is that for which we fight.

---

* This talk about "prompt withdrawal" suggests the lengths to which his enthusiasm had carried him. It did not take an alarmist or a pessimist to realize, long before the Chinese came in, that prompt withdrawal from Korea was far too much for anyone to hope for. Washington had for months been grappling with the problem of how peace, if and when it came, could be maintained in Korea. The Defense Department had hoped it would be possible to withdraw most U.S. troops, but it had not been very sanguine about the chances of doing so. Neither, except for the General, was anyone else.

In his special report to the United Nations, he said:

The giant U.N. pincer moved according to schedule. The Air Forces in full strength completely interdicted the rear areas, and an air reconnaissance behind the enemy line, and along the entire length of the Yalu River border showed little sign of hostile military activity [sic]. The left wing of the envelopment advanced against stubborn and failing resistance. The right wing, gallantly supported by naval air and surface action continued to exploit its commanding position. Our losses were extraordinarily light. The logistic situation is fully geared to sustain offensive operations. The justice of our course and promise of early completion of our mission is reflected in the morale of troops and commanders alike.

The offensive was two days old when it was crushed by 200,000 Chinese. They drove a flying wedge through the central sector, which had been held by the R.O.K. II Corps. "If the Chinese tried to get down to Pyongyang, there would be the greatest slaughter," MacArthur was said to have said at Wake Island. Indeed there was! The South Koreans melted away; the U.S. First Cavalry and some British and Turkish units were rushed in behind them. The Americans, British, and Turks didn't melt, but they fell back. They fell back 30 miles from Tokchon, where the R.O.K.'s had been, to Sinchang, lost that city, and kept on going back as fast as their transport could take them. They shot as they went, and the Turks, having run out of ammunition, began carving Chinese Communists with scimitars.

Eventually, when the Chinese had torn off about 40 miles through the center, they abandoned the pursuit, temporarily, and swung east and west. The X Corps in the east and the Eighth Army in the west had been split clean apart. Communications were completely disrupted. The invading Chinese linked up with Korean guerrilla bands to isolate the X Corps. The mountainous weight of Chinese manpower caved in the right flank of the Eighth Army.

Way up in the northwest, the First Marine Division, which had been about forty miles ahead of the rest of MacArthur's forces, made a try at going around behind the Chinese attacking the Eighth Army and setting upon the invaders from the rear. The Chinese were ready for a second front. The lone marine division found itself attacked and soon surrounded by ten divisions of Chinese infantry. In fourteen days of magnificent fighting, the Marines joined now by the 3rd and 7th Infantry Divisions and the R.O.K. Capital Division cut their way through walls of Chinese fire to the port of Hungnam, from which they were evacuated. One particularly dazzling feat of American ingenuity aided their getaway—the deposit of a whole suspension bridge from the flying boxcars of the Combat Cargo Command.

On November 28th, MacArthur reported the "entirely new war," which he said,

has shattered the high hopes we had entertained that the intervention of the Chinese was only of a token nature on a volunteer and individual basis as publicly announced [What a curious refuge the public announcements of a Communist state make for an American commander!] and therefore the war in Korea could be brought to a rapid close by our movement of the international boundary and the prompt withdrawal thereafter of U.N. forces, leaving Korean problems for settlement by the Koreans themselves.

Of what had happened in the field there were, broadly speaking, two divergent views. One was vigorously expressed by Homer Bigart, who was then covering the war for the New York *Herald Tribune:*

The harsh and unassailable fact of the Korean campaign is that a fine American Army, powerfully supported by Air Force and Navy, was defeated by an enemy that had no navy, virtually no air force, and scarcely any armor or artillery. The defeat was delivered by masses of Chinese Communist infantry so lightly equipped that they could cross the mountains of North Korea on foot trails and strike undetected at exposed flanks of the United Nations troops . . . Unsound deployment of United Nations forces and a momentous blunder by General MacArthur helped insure the success of the enemy's strategy.

The other view was stated by General Charles Willoughby in an article for *Stars and Stripes* on December 17, 1950:

It was only too evident that the potential of "invasion" on the large scale was always present . . . The decision on the highest level was beyond ordinary intelligence channels. One could watch the Chinese corps around Antung within 50 or 60 miles of the nearest United Nations bases in Sinanju; but the secret inner councils of Mao Tse-tung were behind the Iron Curtain. . . .

This did not explain how it was that "the air reconnaissance behind the enemy line," which MacArthur had reported, "showed little sign of hostile military activity." But that perhaps was unimportant in view of MacArthur's explanation given at the Senate hearings:

The concept that our forces withdrew in disorder or were badly defeated is one of the most violent prevarications of truth that ever was made . . . It was a planned withdrawal from the beginning . . . Those forces withdrew in magnificent order and shape . . . The whole reversal of the movement was a strategic one.

FROM DAI-ICHI TO THE WALDORF

It is ironical that after the Chinese intervention, when MacArthur's strategy was as vulnerable as his statesmanship, the commonest complaints against him dated back to the period when he was on his best behavior. It was, and for that matter still is, almost impossible to put down belief that his crossing the Parallel and his attempt to occupy all Korea were in violation of the orders under which he fought. Even so imposing an authority as Herbert Morrison has had a hand in spreading the legend that MacArthur went into North Korea on no authority but his own. Yet no one has ever claimed that the General Assembly resolution of October 7 was a forgery. It called for action "to ensure stability . . . throughout Korea." It may be that the resolution got rather casual consideration in the United Nations. The Security Council did not even discuss it; the General Assembly debate was not up to its usual standards. Still, the resolution did pass, and MacArthur got specific authorization for the crossing from General Marshall, a legal agent of the United Nations.

Was it the crossing of the Parallel, authorized or not, that brought the Chinese Communists into the war? Or did they come in because the Soviet Union, cheated by our intervention of the easy victory it had expected in Korea, decided to turn our presence there to its advantage and use the Chinese Communist armies to hold us in Asia as long as the ratio of American to Communist losses made this worth its while? Senator McCarthy of Wisconsin, a legislator with a passion for archives, proposed that we learn the answer to such questions by marching to Moscow and Peiping and opening their files. It would be the costliest quest for primary sources ever undertaken, but there is no doubt that without undertaking it we cannot go very far beyond conjecture.

Those who are now persuaded that the Chinese would not have come in if we had limited the war to South Korea support their view by pointing to the fact that the United Nations and Washington had been warned that what *did* happen *would* happen. On October 3, 1950, Peiping's Foreign Minister, Chou En-lai, told the Indian ambassador, Sardar K. M. Panikkar, that, as Mr. Acheson rephrased a message that must have reached him only after several rephrasings, "if the U.S. or U.N. forces crossed the Thirty-eighth Parallel, China would send troops to the Korean frontier to defend North Korea. . . . He said that this action would not be taken if only South Korean troops crossed the Parallel."

So far as is known, this warning was delivered to the Indian ambassador orally. Mr. Panikkar transmitted it to Mr. Nehru in New Delhi, who in turn transmitted it to his government's representatives in Washington and New York. It was from them that our government learned of its issuance. Whether Chou En-lai's original statement was cast in language substantially the same as that used by Mr. Acheson in his Senate testimony is unknown.

In any case, a warning that what *did* happen *would* happen was received both in Washington and New York. Speaking of Washington's reaction, the Secretary of State said, "We all reached the conclusion that it was more likely that they would not come in than that they would." Of course, Washington might have urged the crossing even if it had been certain that Chou meant business. The risk of encountering Chinese or Russian armies in Korea had always been part of our calculations.

Obviously, though, we would have arranged certain matters differently if the warning had not been heavily discounted. The State Department thought it had good reason for discounting it, and it is still inclined to doubt that anxiety over China's territorial integrity had very much to do with the intervention.

For one thing, the timing of the warning suggested that it was chiefly a political maneuver. It was issued on October 3; the resolution on Korean unification was then pending in the Political Committee of the General Assembly. The vote was to be on October 4. Furthermore, the bearer of the warning, Mr. Panikkar, had been making the walls of Peiping ring with cries of "Wolf!" He had on previous occasions warned that a Chinese attack on Formosa would come at an early date unless the United States abandoned its plan to defend the island.* In some quarters,

---

* Mr. Panikkar is a curious figure in world affairs. He is regarded by as shrewd an observer as Walter Lippmann as perhaps the ablest diplomat in the world. He may well be that, although the failure of his elaborate efforts to talk Peiping out of the annexation of Tibet suggests that, where there is a will to resist his charms, a way can be found. Some people think him spectacularly inept. Considering the number of times he had sounded false alarms on Formosa, the Alsop brothers were constrained to remark that he was at least aptly named. Nevertheless, he was one of the few diplomats from a non-Communist country who was *persona grata* in Peiping, and our State Department made use of his good offices on a few occasions. In August 1950, for example, he called to Chou En-lai's attention the President's statement of July 19—the one in which it was explained that our action in neutralizing Formosa was taken "without prejudice to political questions affecting that island." He also transmitted messages assuring the Chinese that we had no intention of violating China's rights on the borders of Manchuria or anywhere else. How the Foreign Office—or, for that matter, its distinguished visitor—reacted to these declarations of benign American intent is not known.

there was a feeling that what Mr. Panikkar was reporting about Communist China might be colored somewhat by his known sympathies for Chinese communism. It is worth noting that when Sir Benegal Rau, the Indian delegate to the United Nations, conveyed his government's apprehension, which was based on the warning from Chou En-lai, to the General Assembly, he did it in language that was anything but categorical. India, he said, "fears that the result [of the resolution] may be to prolong North Korean resistance, and even to extend the area of conflict. Our fears may turn out to be wrong, but each government had to judge the situation upon its best information and act accordingly. Thus we view with the greatest misgivings the particular recommendation I have just mentioned."

Sir Benegal pleaded for a twenty-four-hour delay in the voting. But most governments felt there had been enough temporizing already. Even New Delhi was not certain enough of the dangerous consequences of the resolution to vote against it. Sir Benegal abstained.

To sustain the theory that the crossing of the Parallel provoked Chinese intervention, it is necessary to ignore the fact that Peiping had previously issued warnings in far more comprehensive terms than those of the message which the Secretary of State said had been given the Indian ambassador. From the very start of the war, Peiping, like Moscow, had denounced the United States as an aggressor both in Korea and in Formosa. When Chou En-lai said in September that the Chinese would not "supinely tolerate seeing their neighbors savagely invaded by imperialists," he did not specify North Koreans as the neighbors he had in mind. For months he had been saying that the United States was "the most dangerous foe of the Chinese people." Indeed, both Peiping and Moscow recognized the North Korean government as the legitimate government of all Korea.

Even totalitarians have to justify their wars in terms of national interest. If we had proceeded more cautiously in North Korea, we might have deprived Peiping of an argument, and we would certainly have deprived ourselves of a first-class defeat. But there is still no good reason to suppose that we would have deprived her of motive (as distinct from a rationalization) for entering the war. For the fact is that Peiping announced its intention to make war on us while we still had our backs to the sea on the Pusan beachhead. On August 25, Chou En-lai addressed himself not orally to a single ambassador but in black and white to the United Nations with the announcement that "the people of China . . . are determined to liberate from the tentacles of the United States aggressors Taiwan and all other territories belonging to China." In a telegram to the President of the Security Council, the Communist Foreign Minister accused us of having made "an open encroachment on the territory of the People's Republic of China" and of a "criminal act [of] armed invasion," for which, he said, the Security Council should condemn this country. If there was genuine anxiety in Peiping, it seems far more likely that it was caused by our Formosa policy than by our Korea policy. (This, of course, would not make a valid American argument against the Formosa action, since allaying Communist anxieties is not the basic purpose of American foreign policy.) If the anxiety was faked for propaganda reasons, then Peiping already had its case for entering the war.

In moving north of the Parallel and north of Pyongyang, MacArthur was not violating policy but putting it into effect. Both the State and the Defense Departments favored the occupation of all Korea, the only reservation being that the last few miles below the Chinese and Russian borders be assigned to Republic of Korea troops. But it was implicit both in the United Nations resolution and in the Joint Chiefs' directive of September 27, which laid down this policy, that United Nations troops occupy the entire country. This directive was issued almost a month before there was any sign of Chinese intervention, and as a matter of fact it sprang, in all probability, more from a concern over the possibility of trouble on the Russian frontier in the northeast than over the possibility of Chinese intervention as they drew close to the Manchurian border.* And as a matter of fact, MacArthur himself shared these feelings. Shortly after the Inchon landings, it was explained in Tokyo that one of the chief reasons for hoping that United Nations forces could drive straight across the peninsula and contain the war in the territory of the Republic was that it would keep the Russians from nourishing their neurotic fears of encirclement.

Dean Acheson and most members of the State Department (George Kennan, not then on active service, being a notable exception) stood firmly behind MacArthur's operations in North Korea. The Department made it clear that it was pained by many of MacArthur's views, but it took the position, in justification of the drive to the Yalu, that the responsibility of the United Nations, and particularly of the United States, for reconstructing Korea after the war made it essential that the whole country be liberated. State Department people were then in the habit of pointing out that putting Korea on its feet would be a hopeless task if Communists, either Chinese or North Korean, remained in

---

* After the Chinese came in, this aspect of things, too, was almost forgotten. In the summer of 1950, there had been much concern over the possibility of China entering the war, but the general feeling then was that she would come into it not by way of Korea but by way of Formosa or Indo-China. One of us, reporting to *The New Yorker* from Washington on August 25, 1950, wrote that "for two or three weeks now the fear that has haunted Washington has been the fear not of defeat in Korea or even of an early war with Russia but of an unimaginably long, profitless, and perhaps inconclusive war with Communist China." Formosa, the report continued, was thought by most people in Washington "to be the most likely spot for war to start." The survey of opinion went on to say that the chance of war over Formosa had made many people take a second look at our commitment to the island. "At the time it was made, it was judged in most critical circles to be a crafty political move, since it seemed apt to neutralize not only Formosa . . . but also Chiang Kai-shek and that confederation of his admirers that has come to be known in Washington as the China lobby. . . . Uneasiness over [the policy] is apparent in both the State and Defense Departments. . . . State Department people usually explain that it was mostly a military decision. . . . Defense Department people, while admitting the strategic value of Formosa, say they understand that the primary reason for the decision to neutralize it was diplomatic."

sole control of the dams and power stations* along the Yalu. For those power stations provided electricity for Korean as well as for Manchurian industry. Moreover, if we had cut off a strip of North Korea and given it to China, a solution widely recommended, the Communists could have turned out the lights all over Korea any time the fancy took them. Knowing Communists, the Department said, the fancy would take them often.

The real case against MacArthur in October and November was not that he provoked Chinese aggression but that he failed to prepare for it. That case is overwhelming. More than two weeks after he had warned the United Nations that he faced an army which threatened "the destruction of my command," he challenged that army with forces he knew to be vastly inferior in numbers. He attacked along a three-hundred-mile front with a force that had previously had a difficult time holding a seventy-five-mile front. He walked straight into a Communist trap and led American arms to one of the most ignominious defeats in American history.

At one point, while the Senate hearings were going on, the President said at a press conference that he had been thinking of dismissing MacArthur for about a year. Reminded that if that were really the case, he must have been considering the recall of his commander in Korea before the war there started. Joseph Short, the President's press secretary, explained that Mr. Truman had of course miscalculated. But he left the impression that as early as August, after MacArthur's unauthorized release of his unauthorized message on Formosa, the thought had occurred to

* Senator Cain of Washington claimed that the failure to destroy these installations was "a tragic example of political control, resulting in the needless death of American boys." He thought Communist sympathizers in the State Department were responsible. In fact, the policy, which may have been penny-wise and pound-foolish, was intended to save the money of the American taxpayer, who would eventually have to pick up the check for building new power stations.

Mr. Truman that he might have to find a new general for the Korean war. And it occurred to him again after the November 24 offensive miscarried so disastrously. Other members of his administration have said that he thought long and hard about it then and that he came very close to doing it. Much consideration, it is said, was given to keeping MacArthur as Supreme Commander of the Allied Powers in Japan while giving the Korean commands to General Bradley, but in the end MacArthur stayed on.

He stayed on not only to conduct his "planned withdrawal" and re-form the United Nations lines but to step up the power of his verbal offensive against United States and United Nations policy. He released a bewildering barrage of special messages, exclusive interviews, and replies to editorial inquiries. It was a poor editor who could not come up with an exclusive transpacific interview, a feeble organization which could not elicit a congratulatory cable from Tokyo. "Within the space of four days," the New York *Post* observed on December 3, "MacArthur has found time to 1) reply to an (exclusive) cable from Ray Henle, a lesser known radio commentator, 2) answer an (exclusive) inquiry from Arthur Krock, New York *Times* Washington correspondent, 3) tell all (exclusively) to Hugh Baillie, President of the United Press, and 4) grant an exclusive cabled interview to *United States News and World Report.*"

The burden of these messages was that all his troubles flowed from his being ordered to limit the war to Korea. It was not faulty intelligence or faulty evaluation that forced the retreat from the Yalu but the "extraordinary inhibitions" which kept him from pursuing Chinese planes across the Manchurian borders*

* On November 13, the United States government had sounded out six countries with troops in Korea on the question of "hot pursuit"–that is, giving chase into Manchuria of Manchuria-based planes. According to the testimony of the Secretary of State, everyone in our government had favored doing this. But the six countries whose views were solicited were opposed, so the matter was dropped. The Joint Chiefs of Staff felt that while "hot pursuit" was fully justified, it was not a critical matter. Its chief value, General Bradley said, would be in lifting the morale of the airmen.

and from bombing supply bases there. The interview in *United States News* was fairly typical of what he was saying:

Q. Are the limitations which prevent unlimited pursuit of Chinese large forces and unlimited attack on their bases regarded by you as a handicap to effective military operations?
A. An enormous handicap, without precedent in military history.
Q. What accounts for the fact that an enemy without air power can make effective progress against forces possessing considerable air power?
A. The limitations aforementioned, plus the type of maneuver which renders air support of ground operations extremely difficult and the curtailment of the strategic potentiality of the air because of the sanctuary of neutrality immediately behind the battle area.
Q. Is there a significant lesson in this for U.S. planning?
A. Yes.

He was ominously unresponsive to two questions about the atom bomb.

Q. Can anything be said as to the effectiveness or ineffectiveness of the bomb in the type of operations in which you are now engaged?
A. My comment at this time would be inappropriate.
Q. In the type of warfare now going on in Korea, are there large enough concentrations of enemy troops in any one area to make the bomb effective?
A. My comment at this time would be inappropriate.

And so it went. If MacArthur had been merely a source of friction with some of our allies in the period before the Chinese entered the war, he made the whole conduct of American diplomacy extraordinarily difficult in the dangerous months that followed. To be sure, things would have been hard enough without him. The President and the State Department had to steer a course that would be acceptable to their necessary allies both in the world at large and in the United States. They had to pilot the country through the channel, broad enough but full of hidden perils, that lay between the congressional warhawks who wanted to carry the fight to China right away and those members of the United Nations who, as Richard P. Stebbins put it in the

1950 *United States in World Affairs,* "now seemed to consider restraint of Communist China less important than restraint of the United States."

It can be said that, if MacArthur had not existed, anti-Americanism would have had to invent him. Nevertheless, he did exist, and if no one paid much attention to Vishinsky's outbursts against him as "a maniac, the principal culprit, the evil genius," a great many people were impressed with the contention of the Indians and of the *New Statesman* group in England that because of MacArthur the Chinese Communists were justified in moving, as Sir Benegal Rau blandly put it, "toward a kind of Monroe Doctrine for China." Even those who saw the irrationality in this, and who were aware that MacArthur was not making American policy but challenging it, were provoked to their own moderate irrationalities. "To treat General MacArthur as the main enemy," R. H. S. Crossman, a Labour M.P. and a *New Statesman* dissident, wrote, "or even . . . as a threat to peace as dangerous as Soviet policy, is to neglect everything which has happened both in the U.S.A. and in the U.S.S.R. since 1930." Still, he went on, if MacArthur and other bellicose generals were allowed "to usurp the functions of the State Department in order to organize an anti-Cominform in Europe or to smash Communism in China, the case for European neutrality would become unanswerable."

On December 6, after the *U. S. News* interview appeared, MacArthur received, via the Joint Chiefs, two directives from the President. One was addressed to just about every member of the Executive branch outside the Fish and Wild Life Service. It said that "until further written notice from me . . . no speech, press release, or other public statement concerning foreign policy should be released until it has received clearance from the Department of State." The second was a polite but unmistakable this-means-you:

Officials overseas, including military commanders and diplomatic representatives, should be ordered to exercise extreme caution in public statements, to clear all but routine statements with their departments, and to refrain from direct communication on miliary or foreign policy with newspapers, magazines, or other publicity media in the United States.

"The above," the Joint Chiefs added, "is transmitted to you for guidance and appropriate action."

MacArthur responded playfully to this directive. He submitted the text of his next headquarters communiqué for the State Department's approval. On December 8, however, after he had been notified by Erle Cocke, Jr., national commander of the American Legion, that four veterans organizations had joined to demand that the President authorize the bombing of Manchuria, he wired his "profound thanks" to Cocke. Of course, Cocke was not a newspaper or a magazine or even a medium, but the American press is full of cunning, and somehow or other it learned of the message.

December 1950 was a month that must be without parallel in the history of American foreign policy. It was at once momentous and zany. In the course of it, the President declared a national emergency; asked Congress for new appropriations of money and manpower; and sent General Eisenhower to Europe as Supreme Commander. House and Senate Republicans demanded the immediate resignation of the Secretary of State. In New York, General Wu Hsiu-Chuan and his thirteen aides from Peking were ensconced in the Waldorf, leaving it only to scream at Lake Success about the "blood debt" they owed America and to purchase job lots of Mixmasters, nylons, and books on atomic energy in New York department stores. In Washington, Senator Wiley asked the State Department to find out if anything could be done about placing Andrei Vishinsky under arrest.

While General Wu was in New York, Clement Atlee was in Washington. He had flown over from London because garbled press reports had said that the President was ready to atom bomb the Chinese. In what seems to have been the most pointless conference of its sort ever held, the President assured the Prime Minister that the reports were false and that America would not renege on its European commitments. In Charlottesville, Virginia, however, a former ambassador to England, Joseph P. Kennedy, was urging us to "mind our own business and interfere only when someone threatens our . . . homes," and in New York, Herbert Hoover addressed the country with a proposal to cut Western Europe off without troops or money until its own armies were "of such large numbers as would erect a sure dam against the Red flood." At that point, presumably, we could start hauling coals to Newcastle. In Montana, a draft board refused to call another man until MacArthur had been authorized to use the atom bomb as he saw fit in China.

In Korea, United Nations armies spent the month in a kind of mobile reorganization. After the first couple of weeks of disarray, the retreat was conducted in an orderly fashion, and the United Nations rearguard made the Chinese pay heavily for the territory they were getting. The troops that had been evacuated from Hungnam were ferried south and brought back into combat to stiffen the Eighth Army, of which the X Corps, with its one Marine, two Army, and two R.O.K. divisions, was now made a part. On December 22, the day that Eisenhower went to Europe, General Matthew Bunker Ridgway was put in command of the Eighth Army, whose former commander, General Walker, had been killed in a jeep accident.

Ridgway, who also became MacArthur's over-all ground commander in Korea, turned out to be an inspired choice. It was no secret that the morale of the American troops was very low; "bugout fever"—the urge to break contact and move south—was a widespread affliction; and even where this malady had not caught hold, the thought of going back to Pusan and beginning the long grind up the peninsula all over had a deeply dispiriting effect. By shaking up almost the whole top level of the command, by ordering the abandonment of some of the heavy gear that had hampered American troops throughout the long months of largely unmechanized warfare, and by constant lecturing, Ridgway braced the faltering resolution of his men. He was shrewd enough to see that the presence of the Chinese in Korea would cause a change in our war aims—that our goal henceforth, provided we could hang on in Korea at all, would be not to push the enemy the whole way back but rather to engage him in areas where our firepower could deplete his manpower. "Real estate is, here, incidental," he said. This new military policy, which was, in a way, to become the new political policy in Korea, was communicated through proper channels to the troops, who found it far more palatable than the prospect of a hike back to the Yalu.

Still, it was anything but certain that we could hang on. The Chinese offensive slowed down, but it never let up. Moreover, the North Koreans came back into the war. Their armies, torn apart in November, had been reassembled under Chinese supervision in December. On New Year's Eve, when almost all United Nations forces were trying to stabilize a line above Seoul and Wonju and south of the Parallel, the Chinese, with the support of the regrouped and refreshed North Koreans, loosed a blow more powerful than their November 24 offensive. There had been some hope, particularly among those who subscribed to the Monroe Doctrine theory of Chinese policy, that Mao Tse-tung would set a good example and order *his* commanders to stop at the Thirty-eighth Parallel. But the hope was not well-founded. As the Chinese army stormed over the line into the Republic, Radio Peking announced that their aim was "to liberate Korea . . . crush the imperialist aggression." It announced that it would "drive Warmonger MacArthur into the sea."

Apparently, MacArthur was not so sure that the boast wouldn't be made good. At the hearings, it was his best recollection that he had not known a moment of defeatism in Korea; he had always been stout in the faith that the United Nations could hold, even though, as he had said in one of his January communiqués, "the entire military might of China is available against this relatively small command." "The Joint Chiefs of Staff," he said at the hearings, "were not sure we could stick in Korea. It was my opinion that we could." But Generals Bradley and Marshall recalled a gloomy message from MacArthur in which he had prophesied that, while he would go down fighting, he would go down. The message was dated January 10, and in General Bradley's paraphrase it stated that

> . . . In view of the self-evident fact that as presently constituted my command is of strength insufficient to hold a position in Korea and protect simultaneously Japan against external assault, strategic dispositions taken in the present situation must be based upon overriding political policy in establishing the relativity of American interests in the Far East. That a beachhead line can be held by our resisting forces for a limited time in Korea, there is no doubt, but this could not be accomplished without losses. Whether or not such losses were regarded as "severe" would to a certain extent depend upon the connotation one gives the term. . . .
>
> Under the extraordinary limitations and conditions imposed upon the command in Korea, as I have pointed out, its military position is untenable, but it can hold, if overriding political considerations so dictate, for any length of time up to its complete destruction.

It may be that he exaggerated the bleakness of the prospect because he was so thoroughly convinced that he knew a way of bringing the war to a quick victory. It was the way he had talked about from the moment the Chinese had come into the war and that he was still talking about when he barnstormed the country after his recall. It was simply to remove the "extraordinary inhibitions" which the President and the Joint Chiefs had imposed upon him in order to prevent the extension of the war into China or Russia or both. As he told the Joint Chiefs on December 29, in reply to a request they had made as to what he thought might be done if the Chinese forced us to evacuate, he felt we should

> Blockade . . . the coast of China.
> Destroy through naval gunfire and air bombardment China's industrial capacity to wage war.
> Secure appropriate reinforcements from the Nationalist garrison on Formosa.

Release existing restrictions upon the Formosan garrison for diversionary action against the vulnerable areas of China's mainland.*

Now this was clearly a counter-proposal on MacArthur's part. He had been asked, as General Marshall said, to tell what course we might take "if we found ourselves forced into a withdrawal from Korea." He replied with a plan that, in his view, would avert any need for withdrawal. After being told, on January 9, that "the Joint Chiefs of Staff, with the approval of the Secretary of Defense and the President" had decided that "the retaliatory measures suggested . . . could not be permitted" at that time, he replied that "as presently constituted my command is of strength insufficient to hold a position in Korea." He was then directed to continue his withdrawal "inflicting maximum to hostile forces . . . subject to the primary consideration of the safety . . . of troops and [the] basic mission of protecting Japan." In General Marshall's words, he was told that "should it become evident . . . that evacuation was essential to avoid severe losses of men and material, he was at that time to withdraw from Korea to Japan."

His four points, rejected as measures to be taken so long as there was a chance of holding in Korea, were not, however, thrown into the discard. In Washington, the Joint Chiefs, alarmed by MacArthur's dark appraisal, were working on a plan of operations to be put into effect in the event that we were either forced to withdraw to Japan or confined, with no hope of breaking out, on the Pusan perimeter. The plan they drew up contained sixteen proposals, including all four of MacArthur's and

---

* This text is taken from General Marshall's testimony. He was presumably reading from MacArthur's first formal communication of his own program. But it should be noticed that these four points are not quite the same as the four he listed in his speech to Congress and on which he took his stand during the hearings. In his speech he spoke of "air reconnaisance of China's coastal area and Manchuria" but said nothing about bombardment. The third point above—reinforcements from Formosa—was missing altogether. It was replaced by a provision for "intensification of our economic blockade against China."

twelve others. Not all of the twelve were made public at the hearings, but those that were provided for air and naval strikes on the Chinese in Korea and for diplomatic and economic sanctions against the Chinese. Naturally, they were at this stage tentative proposals; they could not have been put into effect, at least as United Nations actions, without United Nations approval. They were sent to MacArthur for his reactions on January 12. The next day they were supplemented by the President's message on the political objectives we had sought all along in Korea. In explaining the reasoning behind the proposals of the Joint Chiefs, the President said:

> Our courses of action at this time should be such as to consolidate the great majority of the United Nations. This majority is not merely part of the organization but . . . also the nations whom we would desperately need to count on as allies in the event the Soviet Union moves against us.
>
> Further, pending the buildup of our national strength, we must act with great prudence in so far as extending the area of hostilities is concerned. Steps which might in themselves be justified and which might lend some assistance in the campaign in Korea would not be beneficial if they thereby involved Japan or Western Europe in large-scale hostilities.
>
> We recognize of course that continued resistence might not be militarily possible with the limited forces with which you are being called upon to meet large Chinese armies. Further, in the present world situation, your forces must be preserved as an effective instrument for the defense of Japan and elsewhere. However, some of the important purposes mentioned above might be supported if you should think it practicable and advisable by continued resistance from offshore islands of Korea, particularly from Cheju-do, if it becomes impracticable to hold an important portion of Korea itself . . . It would be important that if we must withdraw from Korea, it be clear to the world that that course is forced upon us by military necessity and that we shall not accept the result politically or militarily until the aggression has been rectified.

It was surely plumbing the depths of ill fortune to picture the power of the United States, and with it the hopes of peace and

"We've Been Using More of a Roundish One"

justice invested in the United Nations, thrown back on a flyspeck island in the East China Sea named Cheju-do. Yet that was what seemed in view at the moment; a valedictory note ran through the whole of the President's message, which concluded with an assurance to MacArthur that "the entire nation is grateful for your splendid leadership in the difficult struggle in Korea and for the superb performance of your forces under the most difficult circumstances."

But the dark appraisals which had been the cause of these exchanges were being undermined, even as they were being made, by General Ridgway's rallying of his forces. By January 10, the day of MacArthur's most despairing message, the Chinese offensive that had begun on New Year's Eve was coming to a stop on the banks of the Han. The Eighth Army, dug in temporarily about thirty miles south of the Seoul-Wonju line it had earlier hoped to hold, and expecting to be pushed further south at any moment, suddenly found that the enemy was unable to strike his fierce, ponderous blows as effectively as he had further north. It was the Communist communications that were now attenuated and highly vulnerable to our air power.

The change in the situation was witnessed by two of the Joint Chiefs. Early in January, Generals Collins and Vandenberg, along with General Walter Bedell Smith, head of the Central Intelligence Agency, and several aides—had flown to Korea "to report back to us" General Marshall said, "with regard to the morale of our forces and the possibility of our having to evacuate Korea." They stayed on until January 17. They were assured by General Ridgway that "there is no shadow of doubt that the Eighth Army can look after itself"; they saw tank-led infantry teams of the 3rd Division recapture Osan, the last town that had fallen before the Communist push, and advance twelve miles northeast; they joined in planning the limited offensive the United Nations was to launch on January 26. The word they brought back was that "bugout fever" was no longer epidemic. There was no danger of disintegration. The Communists, in the view of Collins and Van-

denberg, had dealt us the worst they had to offer, and they agreed
with Ridgway that there need no longer be any thought of evacuation.

In these happily altered circumstances, most of the steps Mac-
Arthur had urged, and the supplementary ones put forward by
the Joint Chiefs, received very little further consideration.* They
had been planned for an extremity; the extremity was averted. It
would have been one thing to strike at the mainland by air and
from Cheju-do, where we would have no other means of retaliation against the Communist armies, but as long as we could hold
in Korea there was plenty of employment for all the force we
wished to commit to Asia. For, if it became plain in January that
we could stay in Korea, it also became plain that, short of devot-
ing all our resources to the peripheral battle, we could not hope
to do a great deal more than stay. It had been hard enough to
achieve a deadlock in Korea. "Taking on Red China," General
Bradley was to say at the hearings, would have led us only "to a
larger deadlock at greater expense." "So long," General Bradley
said, "as we regarded the Soviet Union as the main antagonist
and Western Europe as the main prize," the strategy advanced
by MacArthur, "would involve us in the wrong war at the wrong
place at the wrong time and with the wrong enemy."

Attrition was the new policy in Korea—not because it was the
noblest or the best but because it was judged the only feasible
policy. The larger deadlock could not be conceived as a desirable alternative to the smaller deadlock. Even if the Bradley estimate was a defeatist one, the MacArthur policy could never have
commanded the support of our European allies, some of them
no less than forty-five minutes from the Red Army and most of
them firm in the belief that total war against China, in however
good a cause, would be a war that would turn, in the minds of
the masses of Asia, on issues of race and color and economic ex-

---

* Some of the economic and diplomatic ones were put into effect. Our economic blockade was intensified, and the United Nations, after MacArthur's
recall, did vote an economic embargo.

ploitation. Breaking the back of a Communist army bent on aggression, an army whose masters rejected negotiated settlement, was quite a different matter. That seemed to be within the power of the United States and its allies and within the spirit of the United Nations Charter.

The new policy did not sit well with MacArthur; it was alien to his temperament,* to his mode of operation, and to the absolutist tenor of his thinking—"In war there is no substitute for victory . . . war's very object is victory, not prolonged indecision." It was so alien, indeed, that he appears never to have taken in the fact that a new policy had been forced on us and was already in operation. In his speech to Congress—and, later, in his testimony—he insisted that his views were shared "by practically every military leader concerned with the Korean campaign, including our own Joint Chiefs of Staff," a striking contention which it became the Joint Chiefs' unpleasant duty to deny categorically.

MacArthur in Tokyo was, apparently, never able to believe that his program had been rejected by military men on military grounds, not just by political men on political grounds. He seems to have become possessed by the idea that he was a victim of the egregious folly of statesmen. At any rate there is no way of interpreting his conduct in the weeks that followed except as that of a man determined at whatever cost, even at the cost of his command and a political crisis in his country, to get that folly undone. If Acheson and Truman, those tiresome meddlers, those city men who had not even looked in on the hard life in Macedonia,

---

* In this respect, MacArthur is a true native son. Americans in general are poorly equipped for campaigns of attrition. The British grew restless in the course of Wellington's nine-year Peninsular campaign, but it is hard to imagine what would have happened in this country if we had been asked to endure that much inactivity. MacArthur was by no means the only American officer who found our Korean policy hard to take. Major General Emmet O'Donnell, Jr. came back from Korea at one stage to say that he could see no sense in applying "Marquis of Queensbury rules . . . to 300,000 Chinks" who had attacked us. "There are several good targets in China which would be suitable for attack by atomic bombs; we could deliver those attacks," he said. MacArthur never went quite that far.

could not be brought to understand what evil they were doing, then he would have to tell them; and if telling them led to his dismissal, as he must certainly have appreciated that it would, then he would have to appeal to the higher authority.* He would have to explain to his bamboozled countrymen what a ruinous course their civilian leaders had chosen. His behavior in the late winter and spring of 1951 allows only one of two constructions to be put upon it: this one, in which the motivation would be patriotic; or some far more sordid one, in which the motivation would be a desire to evade the responsibilities of his command or, as some of his most bitter detractors have held, to move himself into a favorable position for the Republican presidential nomination of 1952. The more honorable construction seems the more likely.

At all odds, he took his case before the country and the world. He did it when his armies (they were in fact becoming General Ridgway's armies; the Joint Chiefs were now, in most cases, dealing directly with the field command) were making small but steady gains in the area below the Parallel; they recaptured the initiative in the latter part of January and held it throughout February. Pressing slowly toward the Seoul-Wonju line from which they had been thrown back at the turn of the year, they were, by early March, only a short distance below the Parallel. On March 7, MacArthur, after an inspection of the front lines, dictated to reporters a brisk, contemptuous challenge to American and United Nations diplomacy.

"There should be no illusions in this matter," he said. Unless there were "major additions" to his forces, there was no hope of achieving anything but prolonged indecision. He predicted that "the battle lines in the end will reach a point of theoretical stalemate" after which the world, as he saw it, would be treated to the

* In February and March the Truman administration, harried by the Kefauver and Fulbright investigations, was at a low point. It may well have seemed in Tokyo that the administration, already on the ropes and apparently on the verge of collapse, would not dare to compound its difficulties by taking on General MacArthur.

spectacle of unceasing "savage slaughter" by an army that displays "a complete contempt for the sanctity of human life." He called for "decisions" which he, as "the military commander," could not make but which were urgently needed to "provide on the highest international levels an answer to the obscurities [of] Red China's undeclared war in Korea." This was the most moderate of his challenges.

The second, which the President was later to say proved to his satisfaction that either he or MacArthur had to go, came on March 25. It followed by a few days a notification from the Joint Chiefs that the President was soon to make a stab at reopening diplomatic channels. "Strong U.N. feeling persists," the message stated, "that further diplomatic effort toward settlement should be made before any advance with major forces north of Thirty-eighth Parallel. Time will be required to determine diplomatic reactions and permit new negotiations that may develop." The message did not say what the Joint Chiefs and MacArthur and almost everyone else knew—that Peking, at that stage of the game, would be as eager to make a decent settlement in Korea as Moscow would be to arrive at an accommodation with the Polish democrats. The purpose of the President's plan was to demonstrate this very fact to the world.

The President never got the chance. The State Department was only part way along on the job of determining "diplomatic reactions" when, on March 25 MacArthur undercut the whole plan of the President with an extraordinary MacArthur plan that was in almost every respect at variance with the administration's. It began with a military estimate:

Operations continue according to schedule and plan. We have now substantially cleared South Korea of organized Communist forces. It is becoming increasingly evident that the heavy destruction along the enemy's lines of supply caused by our round-the-clock massive air and naval bombardment, has left his troops in the forward battle area deficient in requirements to sustain his operations. This weakness is being brilliantly exploited by our ground forces. The enemy's human-wave tactics definitely failed him as our own forces became seasoned to this form of warfare; his tactics of infiltration are but contributing to his piecemeal losses, and he is showing less stamina than our own troops under rigors of climate, terrain, and battle.

This was a reasonable summary of the state of affairs on the battlefield. But he went on, in this message which was to conclude with an offer to accept the enemy's surrender in the field, to tell Peking that he might shortly find himself invested with the authority to bring about its early downfall. He said that the Korean campaign had provided "the clear revelation that this new enemy, Red China, of such exaggerated and vaunted military power, lacks the industrial capacity to provide adequately many critical items essential to the conduct of modern war" and that "even under inhibitions which now restrict activity of the United Nations forces and of the corresponding military advantages which accrue to Red China, it [Red China] has shown its complete inability to accomplish by force of arms the conquest of Korea." Therefore the enemy must by now be painfully aware that a decision of the United Nations to depart from its "tolerant effort to contain the war to the area of Korea through expansion of our military operations to his coastal areas and interior bases would doom Red China to the risk of imminent military collapse."

Here was pressure exerted simultaneously on Washington, Lake Success, and Peking. Washington and Lake Success had already refused to depart from the tolerant effort to contain the war in Korea; and Peking, of course, knew this. Besides, as Walter Lippmann was to say, "Regimes do not negotiate about their survival. There is nothing to negotiate about."

But the threat was only a basis for a modest proposal. The "basic facts" of China's imminent danger "being established," MacArthur went on

there should be no insuperable difficulty arriving at decisions on the Korean problem if the issues are resolved on their own merits without being burdened by extraneous matters not directly related to Korea, such as Formosa and China's seat in the United Nations.

The Korean nation and people which have been so cruelly ravaged must not be sacrificed. That is the paramount concern. Apart from the military area of the problem where the issues are resolved in the course of combat, the fundamental questions continue to be political in nature and must find their answer in the diplomatic sphere.

Within the area of my authority as military commander, however, it should be needless to say I stand ready at any time to confer in the field with the commander in chief of the enemy forces in an earnest effort to find any military means whereby the realization of the political objectives of the United Nations in Korea, to which no nation may justly take exceptions, might be accomplished without further bloodshed.

The challenge, too, was now direct, unequivocal, outspoken. By "political objectives" MacArthur meant, of course, the unification of Korea. That had been a United Nations objective since 1948 and a United States objective since the Cairo conference in 1943. But the purpose of the United Nations, in fact the purpose of all diplomacy, is to achieve political ends without the use of military means. ·

Peking's reaction was the predictable one. "Warmonger Mac-Arthur made a fanatical but shameless statement," the government radio said, "with the intention of engineering the Anglo-American aggressors to extend the war of aggression into China. . . . MacArthur's shameless tricks . . . will meet with failure . . . The people of China must raise their sense of vigilance by doubling their effort for the sacred struggle." In Europe, even in the quarters untainted by neutralism, the general response was outrage. "An Asiatic war," said *Franc Tireur,* an anti-Communist newspaper in Paris, adapting a famous remark of Clemenceau's, "is too serious to be left in the hands of a military man whose years exasperate his turbulence." The London *Economist,* if anything more sympathetic to American policy than to that of its own government, regarded it as a piece of unmitigated "mischief."

It was to be the last challenge but one. As soon as the President learned of it, he decided the challenge had to be met by dismissal. He anticipated procedural difficulties, however, and did not, so far as is known, announce the decision, even to his advisers, for some time. Meanwhile, to cover the intervening period, he directed the Joint Chiefs to get off a crisp note to MacArthur and remind him that earlier orders still stood:

In view of the information given you 20 March 1951—any further statements by you must be co-ordinated as prescribed in the order of 6 December. The President has also directed that in the event Communist military leaders request an armistice in the field, you immediately report that fact to the J.C.S. for instructions.

In the final episode, MacArthur had an accomplice: Joseph W. Martin, Jr. of Massachusetts, the minority leader of the House of Representatives and a congressman with an unusual gift for self-caricature. Sometime in March, Martin had communicated to MacArthur his belief that it was sheer madness not to make use of the Chinese Nationalist troops. Always ready to defer to genuine authority, however, he wished to know if the Supreme Commander shared this outlook. "I would deem it a great help," he said, "if I could have your views on this point, either on a confidential basis or otherwise. Your admirers are legion, and the respect you command is enormous." He got back the following reply, under date of March 20 and with no indication as to whether it was on a confidential basis or otherwise:

I am most grateful for your note of the eighth forwarding me a copy of your address of Feb. 12. The latter I have read with much interest, and find that with the passage of years you have certainly lost none of your old time punch.

My views and recommendations with respect to the situation created by Red China's entry into war against us in Korea have been submitted to Washington in most complete detail. Generally these views are well known and clearly understood, as they follow the conventional pattern of meeting force with maximum counterforce as we have never failed to do in the past. Your view with respect to the utilization of the Chinese forces on Formosa is in conflict with neither logic nor this tradition.

It seems strangely difficult for some to realize that here in Asia is where the Communist conspirators have elected to make their play for global conquest, and that we have joined the issue thus raised on the battlefield; that here we fight Europe's war with arms while the diplomats there still fight it with words; that if we lose the war to communism in Asia the fall of Europe is inevitable, win it and Europe most probably would avoid war and yet preserve freedom. As you point out, we must win. There is no substitute for victory.

With renewed thanks and expressions of most cordial regard, I am. . . .

Martin read the letter on the floor of the House on April 5. He said that for ten days he had waited for some indication that MacArthur wished the letter withheld. He finally decided that he "owed it to the American people to tell them the information I had from a great and reliable source."

The President of the United States is a man whose manner leads both his friends and his enemies to underestimate him. Joseph Stalin, Thomas E. Dewey, James F. Byrnes, Louis W. Johnson—a society at least as distinguished as the Mennen After-Shave Club could be formed among statesmen and politicians who have made the fatal mistake of supposing that the President could be subjected to unlimited heat without coming to a boil. In the White House news room at one A.M. on April 11, 1951, the reporters who had been summoned for a "special announcement" were agreed that one of two things must have happened: either the President had died or another war had been declared. They were to learn that the President was much alive and that no new wars were immediately in the offing. They were handed three announcements, of which the first read:

With deep regret I have concluded that General of the Army Douglas MacArthur is unable to give his wholehearted support to the policies of the United States government and of the United Nations in matters pertaining to his official duties. In view of the specific responsibilities imposed upon me by the Constitution of the United States and the added responsibility which has been entrusted to me by the United Nations, I have decided that I must make a change of command in the Far East. I have, therefore, relieved General MacArthur of his commands and have designated Lieutenant General Matthew B. Ridgway as his successor.

Full and vigorous debate on matters of national policy is a vital element in the constitutional system of our free democracy. It is fundamental, however, that military commanders must be governed by the policies and directives issued to them in the manner provided by our laws and Constitution. In time of crisis, this consideration is particularly compelling.

General MacArthur's place in history is fully established. The Nation owes him a debt of gratitude for the distinguished and exceptional service which he has rendered his country in posts of great responsibility. For that reason I repeat my regret at the necessity for the action I feel compelled to take in his case.

The second was addressed to the General:

Order to General MacArthur from the President

I deeply regret that it becomes my duty as President and Commander-in-Chief of the United States military forces to replace you as Supreme Commander, Allied Powers; Commander-in-Chief, United Nations command; Commander-in-Chief, Far East; and Commanding General, U.S. Army, Far East.

You will turn over your commands, effective at once, to Lieutenant General Matthew B. Ridgway. You are authorized to have issued such orders as are necessary to complete desired travel to such place as you select.

My reasons for your replacement will be made public concurrently with the delivery to you of the foregoing order.

And the third was simply a formal notification to General Ridgway of his increased responsibilities.

Along with these statements, the White House released a series of relevant documents—the December 6 order; the March 20 notification of the President's plan to attempt the reopening of diplomatic channels; the MacArthur peace plan; the reprimand that followed it; the Martin letter; and two rather baffling documents about the arming of South Koreans. These last required a certain amount of exegesis. The story behind them was this:

On January 4, the Joint Chiefs of Staff cabled MacArthur that they were considering a program to arm units of the South Korean Army. MacArthur replied on January 6 that "the over-all interests of the United States will be better served by making these weapons available to increase the security of Japan rather than arming additional ROK forces." This was all very well; the Joint Chiefs accepted his judgment. But, subsequently, the indefatigable *Freeman,* hearing that the South Koreans were going unarmed, asked MacArthur, "Why do we fail or refuse arms to 400,000 South Korean draftees?" MacArthur's response was prompt and imperturable. "The issue is one determined by the Republic of Korea and the United States Government," he said, "and involves basic decisions beyond my authority."

On the streets of Washington, as the news was being given out in the White House, trucks were picking up unsold copies of the April 10 Washington *Post* and delivering the April 11 edition. The *Post,* which for weeks had demanded recall, had by now abandoned all hope. The April 10 headline read: "MAC-ARTHUR RECALL RULED OUT BY PRESIDENT, 'HILL' HEARS—Reprimand Is Seen Still Possible." The April 11 edition had a cartoon which suggested that the country was suffering a widespread loss of prestige for no better reason than that the President— who was shown pathetically quivering in his sleep on an army cot in front of which was the foot-locker of "Capt. Harry Truman"—was unable to overcome the awe of generals instilled in him thirty-four years ago and face up manfully to the responsibilities imposed upon him by the Constitution. Close to it was an editorial headed "Bring MacArthur Home!" It did not, however, press the President to bring MacArthur home by the direct means the President had already chosen. It took it for granted that Capt. Truman lacked the courage to play it that way. "In default of President Truman grasping the nettle in the manner of Lincoln and Polk," it said, "the way to get General MacArthur here is through the Joint Chiefs of Staff. Recall for report is the general practice with the diplomats and military chieftains of all countries."

The President *had* grasped the nettle, two weeks back. But he had expected that the firm command from the Joint Chiefs of

Staff would silence MacArthur for at least a few weeks. (Mac-
Arthur wrote the letter to Martin before receiving the order and
then, according to his testimony, forgot all about it. He said that
if the order had reached him earlier "it might have had some influence.") The release of the Martin correspondence with Mac-
Arthur forced the President to speed the action. He called in the
Joint Chiefs, the Secretaries of State and Defense, and his special adviser on foreign affairs, Mr. Harriman, for consultation.
The exchange of views at these meetings was one of the few
things left pretty much unrevealed by the Senate hearings, though
the Joint Chiefs testified that they all felt the action had to be
taken and the President in a press conference said that the Secretary of State, anticipating the domestic reaction, advised caution. General Marshall testified that for a while it was thought
that MacArthur could be relieved only of his Korean command:

There was a specific discussion as to whether or not it would be
desirable to retain General MacArthur in his role in relation to Japan
only . . . That was set aside on the ground that it would put Ridgway
in an almost impossible position because Japan was his base, and there
would be a divided authority there that might make it very difficult
to conduct affairs. [Ridgway was] intimately familiar with every stage
of the military fight in that region. In fact, he was largely the director
of it . . . If it had been . . . somebody other than General Ridgway . . .
it would have been quite different.

The dramatic midnight announcement was not part of the original
plan. Again General Marshall:

Originally, it was decided to transmit the notification to General Mac-
Arthur . . . on Wednesday April the 11. Secretary of Army Frank
Pace, then in Korea, was instructed to make the delivery of the messages to General MacArthur at his residence. However, late on Tuesday, April the 10, there were indications that the action to be taken
had become known publicly, and it was then decided by the President
to accelerate the transmission of the official notification to General
MacArthur by approximately twenty hours.

The Chicago *Tribune,* either because it did not underestimate
the President or because it had received a good tip, already had

a wire open to Tokyo in anticipation of the breaking of a big story. As it happened, General Marshall testified, Mr. Pace never did receive his instructions—"due to a breakdown in a power unit in Pusan." The Secretary of the Army had originally been sent to Tokyo to provide additional insurance against further outbursts by MacArthur during the period in which his relief was being planned. "Sending Secretary Pace to contain this raging egoist," said Harold Ickes, who knew about speaking out of turn from both sides of the fence, "was like commissioning a canary to bell the cat." The job was one for a President.

There were elements of pathos in the scene in Tokyo. MacArthur was lunching with Senator Warren Magnuson of Washington when an aide brought him a note—the announcement from the White House as received by radio. The aide who heard the broadcast had first broken the news to Mrs. MacArthur, then delivered it to the General; it was 3:00 P.M., Tokyo time. The General said nothing, but abruptly terminated the luncheon. It was not until twenty minutes later that the official notification reached him. The procedure the President had adopted did not allow MacArthur time for that prized prerogative of generals, the farewell address—nor for the formal ceremonies of turning over the command to General Ridgway. As of the moment he received the official message, he was a general without a command. He was still, however, a general with a great army of followers.

IV

In the Senate Office Building

ROOM 318

The MacArthur controversy was many things: it was the investigation conducted by the Senate Armed Services and Foreign Relations committees; it was the debate in the regular sessions of the House and Senate; it was thousands of newspaper editorials; it was Henry Luce bugling a "Tattoo for a Warrior" in *Life;* it was the music business turning a fast buck with recordings of "Old Soldiers Never Die"; it was General Eisenhower in Paris saying he hoped there wouldn't be any controversy; it was Winston Churchill paying his respects to MacArthur—"that great soldier and great statesman"—and advising Europe to be discreet, which in general it was; it was Senator Wherry asking the public to compare the "monumental record of General MacArthur with that of his accusers—with the record of moral decay, greed, corruption, and confusion"; it was Norman Thomas saying that "if MacArthur had his way not one Asian would have believed the United States had civilian government"; it was the burning in effigy of the President and the telegrams demanding impeachment; it was the Seattle drinker shoving his companion's head in a bucket of beer and three senators exchanging oaths and laborious blows outside a Washington radio station.

But the center—the controversy proper, so to speak—was the

177

2,045,000 words spoken and transcribed in the Senate Office Building between May 3 and June 25, 1951. The plans for this overpowering cascade of talk were begun before dawn broke on April 11. A half-hour after the White House announcement, Representative Martin was out of bed and hard at work. By noon, he had accomplished many things; he had talked with Tokyo and received the most reliable assurances that General MacArthur would be agreeable to addressing a joint session of Congress; he had presided over a conference of party leaders and worked out much of the strategy for the hearings, as well as some of the details of stage management for the General's return; he had also alerted the press to the "possibility of impeachments"—meaning, it was generally presumed, the Secretary of State and perhaps the Secretary of Defense as well as the President.

There were several preliminary exchanges and debates. Senator Russell of Georgia, chairman of the Senate Military Affairs Committee, wished to have MacArthur testify immediately at a closed session. This did not suit MacArthur. In response to Russell's invitation, he made a counter-suggestion that was in line with Martin's plans:

> I am advised resolutions are pending in Congress inviting me to address a joint session as was done in the cases of Generals Eisenhower and Clay and others when they first came from abroad and that until action has been taken on such resolutions I would deem it inappropriate to make any other plans. If such resolutions are approved, I would regard it a great honor and distinction to address the Congress in general terms.

There was broad agreement on doing it this way. There was some wrangling, though, over whether the General should address a joint "session" of both Houses or a joint "meeting." The Democrats did not for a moment resist the plan to have the General speak in the Capitol. To have done so would have been not only ungenerous but politically masochistic. With the encouragement of the President, who was later to give government employees a half-holiday so that they could witness the conqueror's return, they joined with the Republicans in sponsoring the invitation. Some of the unregenerate among them, however, insisted that out of respect for the office of the presidency, if not for the man who held it, the event should be described as a "meeting" rather than as a "session." They also tried to load the invitation. Representative Adolph Sabath of Illinois announced that the Rules Committee, of which he is chairman, was going to "consider the concurrent resolution giving General of the Army Douglas MacArthur an opportunity to address a joint meeting of the Senate and House to explain and give his reasons for failure to comply with the orders of his superiors and in disregarding the instructions of the President, the Commander in Chief." That was not at all what Martin had in mind, and Sabath was heavily sat upon. But the Democrats stuck to their point about the "meeting." They wished the world to regard the occasion as less a function of state than a voluntary gathering—a kind of lecture, as it were, at which attendance was purely a matter of individual choice. Eventually, the Republicans were won over on what they regarded—quite properly, since it is doubtful if anyone but parliamentarians ever noticed the distinction—as a small point.

The arrangements for the hearings were the cause of hotter dispute. The Republicans wanted a special committee appointed —with equal representation. The Democrats wanted to use the standing committees' on Military Affairs and Foreign Relations. The Republicans, to a man, wanted the investigation open: not only open but broadcast, newsreeled, and televised. Almost to a man, the Democrats wished them closed. They were anxious, *Time* reported, "to keep General MacArthur's thundering rhetoric out of earshot of the microphones and his dramatic profile off the screens of twelve million television sets." No doubt *Time*'s political insight was sound, but the case for keeping out television cameras and nameless strangers did not rest entirely on the audio-visual delights of General MacArthur. It rested on approximately the same kind of logic which holds that jewels should be kept in a safe. "We are entering doors that have been barred,"

Senator Russell, who acted as chairman of the joint committees said at a time when the hearings were being conducted under a compromise procedure designed to keep the public informed and spies uninformed. "We are unlocking secrets that have been protected in steel safes. Even the public record has carried some material which strikes me as dangerous."

It took some time to work out the compromise. The Republicans gave ground on the matter of the committees. In a last-minute vote, the fifth one taken, the Democrats yielded on procedure to the extent that the hearings could be attended by all members of the Senate (though questioning was limited to committee members) and that, while there would be no broadcasting or televising, and no correspondents in the hearing room, an effort would be made to give the press whatever parts of the testimony the Defense Department could, in good conscience, release. It was felt on all sides, particularly on the press side, that this procedure would be unbearably clumsy and that its clumsiness would result in inadequate and colorless newspaper coverage, but it led, astonishingly, to the most thorough and accurate coverage there has been of any congressional hearing within memory. Usually, correspondents have to base their stories of hearings on notes they have taken in the midst of many distractions and, in most cases, in a rudimentary shorthand of their own invention; no two accounts of what was said are likely to agree except, on occasion, in substance. Under the ground rules at the MacArthur hearings,* they were not merely able to select

* Censored transcripts of the testimony were in the Senate Office Building press room within about an hour after the testimony had been given. Whenever the stenotypist in the hearing room had a few hundred words, his ribbon was taken to the mimeograph room, where the text was cut on a stencil. The stencil was then submitted to Admiral Arthur C. Davis, the Defense Department censor who, with the advice of Adrian Fisher of the State Department, cut out with a razor blade the material that would endanger security. Thus mutilated, the stencil was put on an electric duplicating machine, which, sheet by sheet, fed duplicates practically into the hands of the correspondents, who had arranged to purchase them. The fee was twelve and a half cents a sheet, and for a time there was a brisk second-hand market at three cents a sheet. All told, there were 8,000 sheets.

"It's Fine for You, But It Sure Kicks Hell Out
of My Stories That They're Warmongers"

what they wanted from the transcript but, more important, to quote verbatim, and at far greater length than is the case under normal procedures. Indeed, a surprisingly large number of newspapers began publishing the complete text of the testimony, and this not only proved to be surprisingly well received by the readers but tended to induce fairness in editors. The papers that began by printing the full text of General MacArthur's testimony went on, in most cases, to give the whole of General Marshall's rebuttal and in most cases a relatively full, and therefore relatively fair summary of the testimony of the others.

To serve the public well meant, of course, to serve the Russians well. Censorship could keep out the kind of details that could be turned to immediate advantage in the Korean fighting; it could not hope to keep out the large concepts of strategy that were really the heart of the controversy nor could it keep out the broad estimates of our ability to fulfill our role in the world. These were the facts that would be needed for judgment, not only by the senators but by the public—from whom, in reality, both sides were asking a verdict. And these facts did come out: as the New York *Times* was to observe, when the hearings had been going on for three weeks, "Our friends and adversaries all over the world have been able to listen to an exposition of our military and diplomatic strategy such as has never been put on the record before by any other nation in history." For five cents a day, the Russians were able to get items—like the transcript of the Wake Island conference—for which they would have paid their agents vastly larger sums a few weeks before. The Russians learned, as the *Times* said, not only what they wanted to know about us but, equally important, what we did and did not know about them. At the same time that we described to them under what circumstances we would take the ultimate risk of war, we revealed that the tolerances in our own policy were determined in part by our inability to obtain a clear knowledge of the considerations which moved them. "Before God," Senator

Tobey of New Hampshire said, "the picture makes me stand aghast."

To be sure, the bare announcement that these hearings were to be held—that American generals were to debate matters of public policy, that there was to be a political controversy between General MacArthur and the Joint Chiefs of Staff—constituted the delivery of a piece of information of immeasurable value to the Politbureau and the Red Army General Staff. No matter how alert the censors were, no matter, in fact, if the hearings had been closed altogether, they were fraught with peril. And in the view of many people, they were fraught with peril not only to our grand strategy but to our institutions. "We see now," Walter Lippmann wrote on April 30, four days before the hearings began, "the beginnings of an altogether intolerable thing in a republic: namely a schism within the armed forces between the generals of the Democratic Party and the generals of the Republican Party." It did not matter that it was clear from evidence already in that the schism grew not from previously established party affinities but, on both sides, from independent judgments that happened to correspond to party doctrines. It was, really, less the fact that generals, being human, differed that was so distressing than the fact that their views chanced to lend themselves so neatly to political exploitation.

Then there was a clearly perceptible threat to the relation between a President and all his confidential advisers. The senators who wished either to justify what they saw as the admirable course of the administration or to expose what they saw as its derelictions were bustling about, long before the hearings opened, for the documents that would support their views. Although they would accept Admiral Davis' judgment of what should and should not be published, they took upon themselves the right to judge what should and should not be subpoenaed for their private inspection. Walter Lippmann described this danger with his customary eloquence:

We must ask ourselves what is going to happen to the Joint Chiefs of Staff. They face the fact that there is now to be published an only somewhat expurgated version of their most secret papers. When they wrote or approved these papers they believed that [they] would not be published—that they would be confidential for themselves, their lawful superiors and the commanders in the field to whom they issued instructions.

There is no need to guess now about what the publication of these papers is going to prove about the best way to conduct the Korean war. But one does not have to be a prophet to see what the precedent now being set is going to do to the conduct of the United States government. . . .

It is being done, some say, in the name of the sacred right of the people to know all the facts. They are, I believe, profoundly mistaken. If this theory goes unchallenged, if what is about to be done is accepted as a precedent, as one of the legitimate usages of our constitutional system, the effect will not be to give the people access to the truth. The effect will be to conceal, to disguise, to falsify the truth that is given to the President and to the Congress and to the people. . . .

Those who think that the right of the people to know can be met by destroying the rules of confidence and publishing anything and everything should ask themselves why they think it right, why they believe it to be part of the very substance of liberty, that some relations shall be privileged and not opened to publicity: the relations of husband and wife, of lawyer and client, of doctor and patient, of priest and his charges. Why do we protect these relationships? Is it not in order to protect our liberties? In government the relationship between the civil power and the military, between the President and his lawful military advisers, the Joint Chiefs, is as sensitive and as critical as any of the private relations that we protect. On the integrity of the relation between the President and his advisers may depend the life of the Nation. That relation must be destroyed, it will be destroyed, if the privilege of confidence is taken away.

The hearings began on Thursday morning, May 3, with MacArthur as the first of the thirteen witnesses. He and General Whitney had flown down from New York in the *Bataan*,* and

* He commuted by plane to New York during the three days in which he testified, which seemed rather a tribute to the felicities of life in the Waldorf, where he and Mrs. MacArthur were by now well settled in their $130-a-day suite. The *Bataan* was, of course, Government Issue. It was one of the anom-

at 10:18 they arrived together at Room 318, the Senate Caucus Room and the scene of all Grade A Senate hearings.

MacArthur was unspectacularly dressed. He wore dark slacks and a battlejacket undecorated except for the emblem of rank. Almost the entire Senate was there—the committee members and the committee staffs at the committee tables and the others in the section generally given over to the public. The phoographers and reporters were quickly shooed out, and Senator Russell began a lengthy opening statement.

Gentlemen of the Committee on Armed Services and the Committee on Foreign Relations, today we are opening hearings on momentous questions. These questions affect not only the lives of every citizen, but they are vital to the security of our country and the maintenance of our institutions of free government.

We shall attempt to obtain the facts which are necessary to permit the Congress to discharge its proper functions and make direct decisions on the problems of war and peace in the Far East and indeed throughout the world.

General of the Army Douglas MacArthur has consented to be the first witness at these hearings. I am sure it is unnecessary for me to attempt to recount in detail the deeds and services which have endeared General MacArthur to the American people.

On the permanent pages of our history are inscribed his achievements as one of the great captains of history through three armed conflicts; but he is not only a great military leader, his broad understanding and knowledge of the science of politics has enabled him to restore and stabilize a conquered country and to win for himself and for his country the respect and affection of a people who were once our bitterest enemies.

The General is here today to counsel with our Committees and to help us in the fulfillment of our legislative responsibilities . . . con-

---

alies of his position that, though stripped of his command and very much at odds with his Commander in Chief, he was not, and never could be, a private citizen. A General of the Army cannot be retired. He is subject to re-summoning at any time and, theoretically, to discipline. Moreover, he remains on full salary—in MacArthur's case, $18,761 a year—and enjoys all perquisites, such as the *Bataan* and General Whitney. Soon after his testimony, MacArthur returned the *Bataan* to the government. General Whitney put in for retirement.

ducted with the single purpose of serving the national interest in this hour of crisis. . . .

The guiding light here today, and in the days to follow, must be the national interest, for the national interest transcends, in importance, the fortunes of any individual, or group of individuals.

If we are to exercise one of the highest legislative functions, we must see that the American people are brought the truth, and the whole truth, without the color of prejudice or partisanship, and with no thought as to personalities.

If we do less, we will thwart the proper working of the processes upon which the success of our form of government depends.

He outlined the security precautions to be taken and gave the additional warning that "many outsiders, particularly gentlemen of the fourth estate, are skillful in piecing together a series of separate and apparently unrelated comments, that they get from different members of Congress, into stories that could be very damaging." After the caution of restraint, Russell swore the witness and invited him to open his testimony. MacArthur had no prepared statement. "My comments were made fully," he explained, "when I was so signally honored by the Congress in inviting me to appear before them. I appear today not as a voluntary witness at all but in response to the request of the committee, and I am entirely in the hands of the committee."

His presence was involuntary but his performance was most co-operative. As Chief of Staff, he had had more experience than he relished in placing himself in the hands of congressional committees; if he had found it bitter then, he now—from the evidence of the transcript—found it pleasant, even relaxing and refreshing. To some extent, obviously, he had the President to thank for this. Recall had made him a man who could say exactly what was on his mind—and say it in full. His direct responsibilities now were to his country and his conscience. At any rate, he was an exceptionally agreeable witness and, beyond that, the kind of witness in whose testimony, even on the printed page, one finds the stamp of the man and his mind. In the testimony of General Marshall, of the Joint Chiefs, of Secretary Acheson, not only caution and responsibility but native economies and restraints blur the human images. They were responsive to the questions asked, but that was all. They did not indulge in the kind of free association that would lead MacArthur on for ten or fifteen minutes at a time and from which, at an early stage of the endless Q. and A., the image of the man rose sharp and clear.

The first matter to be explored was whether or not he and the Joint Chiefs had actually been at odds. The Joint Chiefs had already announced, and were later to testify under oath, that the differences ran deep, but MacArthur still would not have it so. He was perfectly willing to agree that he, on the one hand, and Truman and Acheson, on the other, were in profound disagreement, but he insisted in the face of the Joint Chiefs' advance statements of their concurrence in the President's reasons for the discharge that "nothing I can recall" suggested disagreement and that their views as he had understood them in Korea "coincided almost identically with my own beliefs in the matter. And I may say that every responsible military authority . . . not only in my own command but in the foreign commanders who are there . . . agreed with [me]. . . . I don't know a single exception." He grasped at an opportunity to pay his respects to the Joint Chiefs: "I want to say that the relationships between the Joint Chiefs of Staff and myself have been admirable. All members are personal friends of mine. I hold them individually and collectively in the greatest esteem. If there has been friction between us, I am not aware of it."

What, then, did he make of the Joint Chiefs' own assertions to the contrary? What had led him to assume that they did support his view? Nothing, apparently, but the sixteen points—including his four—which the Joint Chiefs had recommended as possible courses of action when Cheju-do seemed likely to become our last stronghold. That plan, it would appear, and, the inability of his mind to conceive reasoned military disagreement:

SENATOR JOHNSON: Has there been any other indication, other than the document of January 12, to the effect that the Joint Chiefs support the program you advocate?
MACARTHUR: Nothing in writing that I know of.
JOHNSON: Anything orally?
MACARTHUR: Nothing that I know of.

Still, he was not once to admit in the course of his twenty-two hours on the stand that his comrades-in-arms, his professional colleagues did or could have anything to do either with the persecution of him or with what he regarded as the unconscionable political interference in Korea. It was the so-called policy makers, Truman and Acheson, who had not allowed him to bring the whole thing to a quick, victorious end ("Had I been permitted to use my air when those Chinese forces came in there, I haven't the faintest doubt that we could have thrown them back") and who even in removing him had mishandled the job so as to endanger the Republic ("I don't think there is any question that the interest of the United States was jeopardized in such a summary mode of turning over great responsibilities which involve the security of the country").

Only the politicians in the White House and the cookie-pushers in the State Department could have insisted on running a war in that absurd way and in relieving an officer so clumsily. Did he acknowledge his disagreements with them?

MCMAHON: General, there are some fundamental basic differences between the Government and yourself. . . .
MACARTHUR: Naturally.

But were they "fundamental basic" differences of *policy*? Not to MacArthur's way of thinking. They were the differences between a man with a policy and a man without one. "The inertia that exists!" MacArthur said. "There is no policy! There is nothing, I tell you, no plan, no anything." It was this fervent conviction that made it possible for him to maintain that the reasons given in the President's announcement of the recall were "completely invalid." They were invalid because no man can fail to support a policy that doesn't exist: "I was operating in what I call a vacuum. I could hardly be said to be in opposition to policies which I was not even aware of. I don't know what the policy is now." And again:

Now, when you say I have enunciated my recommendations, they are plain and clear. The only reason that you can logically say that I would disagree was the concept that something else than what I recommended was going to be done.

But that concept, he thought, was false. "There is no policy." Leaving aside the question of whether the administration had a policy, was there any merit in its criticism of his program? No, because it was entirely in the realm of speculation: "There is no certainty that Russia will come in. There is no certainty that she will not come in. There is no certainty that anything that happens in Korea will influence her. That is speculative. . . . All I know is that our men are going by the thousand every month, and if you keep this thing on indefinitely, nothing could happen that would be worse than that."

Prolonged indecision was the worst thing of all. Once he said that it was even worse than losing the war:

Now there are only three ways that I can see of, as I said this morning: Either to pursue it to victory; to surrender to the enemy and end it on his terms; or what I think is the worst of all choices—to go on indefinitely and indefinitely, neither to win or lose, in that stalemate; because what we are doing is sacrificing thousands of men while we are doing it.

Gradually, in all of this, the clear fact emerged that whatever might be said of the consequences of his views, the man who talked was not the bellicose, sabre-rattling MacArthur of the Indian and British imagination. That MacArthur did not really exist. It could be argued that an application of his views would increase and prolong bloodshed in Asia, that what he was advocating was really a form of preventive war. If there was, as the Joint Chiefs seemed to feel, a grand and fatal illogic in his contentions, it had at least to be said that the grand illogic rested on a grand illusion. MacArthur hated war; he hated war in general and in particular. He hated the particular war from which he had so recently returned. "I have never seen such devastation," he said. And then he told of a reaction to it that the Indians must have found hard to credit. "I have seen, I guess, as much blood and disaster as any living man, and it just curdled my stomach the last time I was there. After I looked at that wreckage, and those thousands of women and children and everything, I vomited." The man who had seen so much of war and who once, long ago, had found peace so distasteful, now said, "I shrink—I shrink with a horror that I cannot express in words." He spoke of the war in Korea as "this savage and terrific conflict, the most savage I ever fought in." "The only thing I am trying to do, Senator," he told Brien McMahon, "is to settle the thing in Korea, to bring it to a decisive end without the calamity of a third world war. I believe if you let it go on indefinitely in Korea, you invite a third world war. I believe the chances of the terrible conflict that you so rightly dread—and all the rest of us dread with you—would be much more probable if we practice appeasement in one area even though we resist to our capacity all along the line. That is all I am saying. I am saying it with the acute consciousness of the dreadful slaughter that is going on in Korea today."

So the thing to do was to take the uncalculated risk (uncalculated, because calculation never really helps) and try to bring the fighting to a quick, victorious conclusion: bomb Manchuria, blockade China, sick Chiang's troops on the Communists. That way lay at least a hope of ending the prolonged indecision, "the insensate slaughter."

Broadly speaking, MacArthur made three challenges to American policy: in an ascending order of importance they were, first, the challenge to our policy (or non-policy as he would have it) in Korea; second, to our policy in China from the end of the last war down to the present; and third, to the grand strategy in which both Korea and China have subordinate parts. Because the

public was struck by his assertion that he and the Joint Chiefs
were in substantial agreement on Korea, a great deal of time was
spent in taking testimony on this matter. The result was that, on
the record anyway, MacArthur was in error. General Bradley felt
that almost everything was wrong with MacArthur's strategy—
time, place, war, enemy. Speaking for the airmen, General Vandenberg characterized MacArthur's bombing strategy as "peck-
ing at the periphery." To commit the Air Force to China "would
fix it so that, should we have to operate in any other area with
full power . . . we would not be able to." General Collins, his
most extreme critic among the Joint Chiefs, thought that his actual
deployment of troops had threatened our strategy. Admiral Sherman said that he had wanted no part of a naval blockade which
his Navy alone would have to conduct; this was, of course, the
only kind of blockade in prospect.

The fact that the Joint Chiefs were not in agreement with Mac-
Arthur was, however, important but not really fundamental. The
President's case against the General would have been just the
same—just as strong or just as weak—if the Joint Chiefs had agreed
with MacArthur. In that event, he would simply have had to consider the removal of all of them—assuming, naturally, that he had
reconsidered his own program in the face of such estimable
critics.

Whatever he might have done, he would have been left with
the three challenges. And although it quickly enough became
apparent that no one of them could be considered alone, it was
one of the assumptions of the whole investigation that the Korean
problem had to be thought of in the light of our policy toward
that China whose legions had six months earlier reopened the
Korean question just as it seemed about to be neatly disposed of.
MacArthur laid it on the line:

It is my own personal opinion that the greatest political mistake we
made in a hundred years in the Pacific, was in allowing the Communists to grow in power in China. I think, at one stroke, we undid
everything, starting from John Hay, through Taft, Leonard Wood,

Woodrow Wilson, Henry Stimson, and all those great architects of our Pacific policy. I believe it was fundamental, and I believe we will pay for it, for a century.

THE CHINESE PUZZLE

In the case of the Far East, MacArthur's challenge galvanized a deep and spreading national bafflement and discontent. This had been whipped up in part, no doubt, by the Luce publications and the Scripps-Howard press, but it sprang basically from something far more important—that is, from a direct reaction to the Chinese catastrophe itself. After all, Chiang Kai-shek, the George Washington of China, the repository of the democratic hope in Asia, had survived weary years of war with Japan to win his great victory; then suddenly, inexplicably, his victory was shot out from under him, and his regime went into a hopeless collapse. Moreover, as his position grew worse, the American government, which a few years before had pronounced China to be a great power, one of the Big Four which would guarantee the peace, now declined to hold out a helping hand—or, rather, offered to help only in a manner so brusque and churlish that the hurt was greater than the help. These calamities, and particularly the American attitude toward them, required explanation. Was the State Department immobilized by the theory that the Chinese Communists were but a fellowship of "agrarian reformers," a latter-day and Oriental Non-Partisan League or Granger movement? And had this view been systematically propagated by Communist agents working inside the government? (It could not be overlooked that Alger Hiss had served as special assistant to the director of the Office of Far Eastern Affairs, and that other State Department names had been involved in the *Amerasia* case.)

In this atmosphere of confusion, MacArthur spoke out with authority. Not only was he himself a figure of immense certitude, but he had a remarkable, almost unique, experience of the mysterious East. At the hearings in May 1951, people turned to him as an oracle, not just on the Korean war, but on Far Eastern policy in general. "Do you know of any man in America that has had the vast experience that you have had in the Orient?" Senator Wiley asked the General to his face ". . . Do you know of any other man that has lived there so long, or known the various factors and various backgrounds of the peoples, and their philosophy, as yourself?" To which the General, after a nod to decorum ("That is a very flattering estimate you make, Senator"), could truthfully reply, "I think I have probably lived in the Far East as long as anybody that I know of, in an official position in the United States."

MacArthur had not always pressed his views on China. When Senator McMahon asked the General whether he did not regard his present information on China as more extensive than it had been two or three years back, the General responded, "I thought I was pretty well informed at both times"; but it developed that McMahon had in his hands a letter which MacArthur had sent in March 1948 to the House Foreign Affairs Committee, in which he had carefully explained how meager his knowledge of China was. "With this background," MacArthur had written, "you will readily perceive I am not in a position to render authoritative advice." ("The Chinese problem," MacArthur had continued, "is part of a global situation which should be considered in its entirety in the orientation of American policy. Fragmentary decisions in disconnected sectors of the world will not bring an integrated solution.")

Yet these were but public expressions. In private he had been less restrained. Congressman Walter Judd of Minnesota could recall MacArthur saying to him in 1947, "For the first time in our relations with Asia, we have endangered the paramount interests of the United States by confusing them with an internal purification problem in China"—a penetrating statement on a complex situation. And, whether or not MacArthur knew very much about

China,* there were, after all, few enough Americans who could claim to know more. MacArthur himself, in any case, in a letter of June 1951 released in the midst of the hearings, voiced with special conciseness certain premises which lay behind one American attitude toward the collapse of China and thus toward the administration's foreign policy.

This letter was provoked when Secretary Acheson, without making much of a point of it, dug out of his briefcase a proposal of December 7, 1945, that American aid to China "be made available as a basis for negotiation by the American ambassador to bring together and effect a compromise between the major opposing groups in order to promote a limited democratic China." The proposal was commonplace enough that year; what was remarkable about this one was that it had been made by General MacArthur, along with General Albert C. Wedemeyer and Admiral Raymond A. Spruance. MacArthur had already gone over this period a bit briskly in the hearings. He had said that "allowing" the Communists to grow in power in China was "the greatest political mistake we made in a hundred years in the Pacific." When asked whether he would have tried to bring the Nationalists and Communists together, he had scornfully replied that there was as much chance of doing this as of mixing oil and water. One senator meticulously asked, "That was your idea at that time, too; was it not?" MacArthur flatly replied, "It would have been then, and always."

It was thus incumbent upon MacArthur to explain away the recommendations he had made jointly with Wedemeyer and Spruance. He promptly did so, arguing—in terms which undoubt-

---

* Some of his admirers must have been shaken when, in his address to Congress, he declared in a cursory review of Chinese history, "At the turn of the century under the regime of Chang Tso-lin efforts toward a greater homogeneity produced the spark of a nationalist urge." Chang Tso-lin was an inconspicuous youth at the turn of the century. Some twenty years later he became a leading Chinese warlord and succeeded in consolidating a position of his own in Manchuria. At no time was China as a whole ever ruled by anything which could be described as "the regime of Chang Tso-lin."

edly summed up and confirmed the suppositions of many thousands of Americans—that the Chinese Communists were "but a nebulous threat at the time," constituting "only one of many factions."* Now if the Chinese Communists were indeed but "a nebulous threat" in 1945, only one of many minor tongs contending in the Chinese arena, then their dizzy rise to power in the next four years does require explanation—both positive, as to how they could do it, and negative, as to why they were not stopped. Such explanation, given the disproportion between start and finish, might well be cast in terms, not of natural process, but of betrayal, perfidy and treason. For many Americans, who carelessly assumed the theory of Communist nebulosity, treachery has seemed the simplest explanation.

Yet that theory of Communist nebulosity does not seem to have been widely held in informed circles, outside, perhaps, the Dai-Ichi Building, even so early as December 1945. Wedemeyer did not hold it: on November 20, 1945, he had reported that, while with thoroughgoing social reform Chiang might be able to stabilize the situation in South China, "he will be unable to stabilize the situation in North China for months or perhaps even years unless a satisfactory settlement with the Chinese Communists is achieved." The War Department in Washington did not hold it: on July 5, 1945, the Intelligence Division had issued a secret

---

* There has been a complicated controversy over what the December 1945 recommendation meant. MacArthur said in 1951 that all he had wanted then was to "effect a sound basis for political unity through the call for a convention reasonably representative of all segments of the people." Presumably he did not regard the Communists as being one of the "major" opposing groups. This effort, MacArthur added vigorously, if a trifle inscrutably, was the "exact opposite" of General Marshall's later attempt to effect a sound basis for political unity through the call of a convention reasonably representative of all segments of the people. Wedemeyer in 1951 similarly rejected the notion that he ever thought a coalition government would work, while conceding that anyone reading the 1945 message "would be justified" in thinking that this is precisely what the writers were contending. Spruance restated the aim in 1951 quite candidly: "The idea was to get the Communist armies incorporated into the Nationalist armies, and perhaps, to allow some Communists in the Nationalist government." The line between the MacArthur-Wedemeyer-Spruance recommendations and the Marshall mission seems very thin.

report entitled "The Chinese Communist Movement" which crisply declared, "The Chinese Communists are the best-led and most vigorous of present-day organizations in China." Major General Claire L. Chennault, the valorous leader of the American Air Forces in China and a strong supporter of Chiang, did not hold it: on September 21, 1944, he had written to President Roosevelt that if there should be, as he anticipated, a civil war in China, "The Yenan regime has an excellent chance of emerging victorious, with or without Russian aid." The State Department certainly did not regard the Communists as nebulous; throughout the war, foreign service officers had filed despatch after despatch emphasizing their strength, organization and morale.

Nor did Chiang himself regard the Communists as small fry. He knew Communism well; in the early twenties he had collaborated with the Kremlin, making a pilgrimage to Moscow, becoming an honorary member of the Comintern and sending his son to Moscow for the usual treatment. He had even been himself an issue in the Kremlin's internecine warfare. Trotsky opposed him, insisting that the U.S.S.R. should base its China policy upon the Chinese Communists, while Stalin defended the Chiang connection. Trotsky won the argument when Chiang turned on the Chinese Communists in 1927, but Stalin soon won a larger argument over Trotsky and was able successfully to blame the loss of China on the shenanigans of Trotskyites in the Soviet Foreign Office acting as secret agents of western imperialism. (This was a plausible pattern of explanation; given reverse English, it would come in useful in America a quarter of a century later.)

Chiang thus became the first Tito (as he would end by being the second Mihailovich). He knew all too well in 1945 that the Communists, whom he had spent nearly two decades in trying to subdue, were not "one of many factions" offering only a vague and feckless threat to a well-entrenched regime. The Chinese Civil War, indeed, far from just beginning in 1945, was then entering its final phase. The common war against Japan had only interrupted it without stopping it. And in the bitter course of this struggle the Chinese Communists had developed one advantage which they would press until it became decisive: they had mobilized the peasants. The need for the redistribution of land has been for centuries part of the systole and diastole of Chinese history; by the nineteen forties the organic process had been too long delayed. While the Kuomintang had done great things in uniting and modernizing China, it was unwilling or unable to do anything effective to organize the rural poor. It came to rely on the landlords rather than the peasants; it held the cities, but it lost the country. Chiang's gestures in their direction, largely the result of American pressure, were nominal and meaningless. "Compared with the Generalissimo," Dr. Karl A. Wittfogel has said, "Tsar Nicholas and his minister Stolypin were farsighted and daring." Just as the Japanese were eventually submerged in China, isolated in walled cities while the Chinese guerrillas ruled the countryside around them, so, in the end, the Kuomintang achieved the same isolation, and the same defeat.

The Chinese Communist Party in these years had a great appeal —the appeal of great epics of personal heroism, of thrilling experiments in social organization, above all, the appeal of organizing the downtrodden and oppressed. Its leaders were earnest, attractive and disarming. Communist and fellow-traveler journalists certainly helped spread the theory that the Eighth Route Army would be the salvation of China, but their contribution was not decisive. Many non-Communists, especially those who knew communism only in China, came to the same conclusions. War sharpened the contrast between the luxury and squalor, the imbecility, vice and corruption of Chungking and the dedication and zeal of Yenan.

If it is hard today to reconstruct that contrast, no one can doubt the power a decade ago of the Yenan spell. The Chinese Communist Party, Freda Utley wrote in 1939,

long ago abandoned the dream of establishing its own dictatorship . . . Its aim has genuinely become social and political reform along capitalist and democratic lines. The Chinese Communists have become radicals in the English nineteenth-century meaning of the word.

Now Freda Utley was no babe in the woods; she had lived wretched years in Stalin's Russia; her husband had vanished in a Communist purge. If such a person, with her grim firsthand experience of Communist dictatorship, thought that the Chinese Communists were liberty-loving British radicals, who is to blame the young newspapermen and foreign service officers and soldiers in Chungking, reacting against the decadence of the Koumintang, for thinking that the Chinese Communists were agrarian reformers? (The weird answer is: Freda Utley.)

As the Communists gained power, the Kuomintang retracted, turning increasingly narrow and autocratic. War placed a terrible strain on the administrative capacities of Chiang's government; the uncontrollable—or, at least, uncontrolled—inflation played havoc with income and distribution. American aid, arriving in increasing quantities after 1940, offered extreme temptations. There were brave and devoted men in the Kuomintang. But as a whole the party was too much in the thrall of corrupt officials, whose jobs were their fortunes; it would do nothing to offend the bankers, the tax collectors or the landlords; it moved farther and farther from any foundation in popular confidence. As Chiang's political position grew increasingly shaky, as the intellectuals, in particular, began to criticize the regime, he turned more and more to rely on fraud and force to maintain his power. Conveniently fraud was embodied for him in his entourage in the person of Dr. H. H. Kung and force in the persons of General Ho Ying-Chin and of the Chen brothers, the notorious C-C clique: it was to such men that Chiang looked increasingly for advice and support.

Chiang was always an ambiguous and, in the end, a tragic figure, drawn toward both past and future, in touch both with Confucius and the twentieth century, at home with neither. If he was not the George Washington Americans believed him to be in 1940, he certainly was not the shabby scoundrel people saw a decade later. He had great potentialities—greater than any other Chinese—for national leadership. The failure of American policy was the failure to encourage those potentialities. The crucial phase of that failure took place during the Second World War. Its chief agent was the tough, rugged, tormented figure, General Joseph W. Stilwell. The result was to make Chiang irrevocably a figure of the past; it was to deliver the Kuomintang to its most inflexible leaders.

Joe Stilwell had evidently developed something of a scunner against the Kuomintang during a tour of duty as military attaché in Nanking before the war. But he had also learned Chinese, and this made him a logical choice for the American command in China. His mission was to strengthen the Chinese contribution to the war against Japan. Few more difficult missions would have been imagined, because Chungking, by 1943, had lost most of its will to fight. Convinced that the United States could be counted on to defeat Japan, many Kuomintang leaders wanted to hoard their arms and men for a post-war settlement with the Communists. It was Stilwell's job to win their confidence, get their armies into the field, and strike at the outstretched antennae of Japanese power.

If it is hard to imagine a more complicated and delicate mission, it is harder still to think of anyone less suited for it than Vinegar Joe. He had many fine qualities; he was brave and frank, an admirable person and an excellent field commander. But he had little patience, little charity, little understanding of the higher politics or even of the higher strategy. He quarreled with Chennault and by-passed and ignored Clarence B. Gauss, the able American ambassador. He began by doing his best to help Chiang; but he soon came to hate him with a virulent hatred. He called Chiang the "Peanut," harangued him, scolded him, fought with him and plotted against him. After one angry scene with the Generalissimo, he came home and noted in his diary that the interview with the Generalissimo had been "like kicking an old lady in the stomach." Roosevelt quickly developed an uneasy feeling that Stilwell was not the man for the job. As early as September 1942, he wanted to fire him; but then, as on subsequent occasions, Marshall intervened to save him.

The effect of Stilwell was to orient United States policy against the Kuomintang as a whole. Yet, if the only alternative to the Kuomintang was the Communist Party, was it not perhaps necessary to do everything possible to urge reform on Chiang and to strengthen his more modern-minded, Americanized advisers—men like T. V. Soong and General Chen Cheng? And the Communist alternative, as General Chennault wisely observed, had to be excluded. "I need not point out," he pointed out to Roosevelt in 1944, "the extent to which the establishment of a government in China, closely tied to Moscow, would upset the balance of power in the Pacific, or what this might mean to us in the future." Some observers—Joseph Alsop, for example, who was there as an aide to Chennault—consequently sought out and wished to back a "modernist" wing of the Kuomintang as against the "reactionaries" of the C-C clique.

Stilwell rejected the theory that capability must somehow be developed within the Kuomintang and ignored the implications of Communist victory. He did not like Chennault; they had argued about strategy as well as politics. The two men had a good deal in common. Both were narrow, resourceful, fearless, hardy—far too direct for the great, complex, remorseless country which absorbed and destroyed them. Both, in the end, would be reshaped by almost the worst elements in the camps which attracted them—Stilwell writing about his desire to "shoulder a rifle with Chu Teh," the Communist general, and Chennault becoming a prosperous member of the inner ring of the Nationalists. The irony was that, as Stilwell was substantially correct in his analysis of the Chiang regime, so Chennault was substantially correct in his analysis of the Communists. They cancelled each other out.

So Stilwell discarded the notion that there were salvageable elements in the Kuomintang. For him the immediate military goal always dominated: get as many Chinese divisions as possible, no matter what their politics, into action against the Japanese. Since his assignment was Chiang, it was Chiang who most regularly seemed to obstruct this mission. His stock of conventional American Jeffersonian ideas was inadequate to the unfathomable depths of Chinese politics. His interventions into palace intrigues were often disastrous: he even at times sought alliances with the reactionaries—Madame Kung, Madame Chiang, General Ho—in order to break the power of the moderates, when the moderates seemed to be opposing him. And, in his recoil against the excesses of the Kuomintang, he began to nourish a genuine sympathy for the Chinese Communists.

Ambassador Gauss shared Stilwell's impatience with Chiang; and Stilwell's bright young State Department advisers encouraged him in the rejection of the Kuomintang. "The Kuomintang, once an expression of genuine nationalist feeling," John Davies, Jr., wrote in late 1943, "is now an uncertain equibrium of decadent, competing factions, with neither dynamic principles nor a popular base." It had lost its revolutionary drive; above all, it had lost the peasants, and it could not hope to regain them. The State Department men were convinced—and they were very probably right—that Soong would be no more capable of launching basic social reform than Kung; the Kuomintang, whether modernist or reactionary, seemed to them beyond redemption.

The only hope was a gamble—a gamble that magnanimity and support might wean the Chinese Communists away from Russia, that Mao might be induced to do what Chiang had done twenty years earlier. The young men from the State Department preached the possibility of Titoism two years before Tito. It is necessary to emphasize this point, because it goes to the root of the question whether the China policy was invented by Communists in the State Department. Stilwell and his political advisers—Davies, John S. Service, Raymond Ludden—began by hoping to build up Chiang. They gave up on Chiang because they felt that commitment to him would not advance American interests. They looked to taking the Chinese Communists into the American camp as a means of advancing American interests, not of advancing Communist interests.

This is not to deny the existence in the Stilwell circle of burgeoning sympathies for the Yenan regime. What hit Freda Utley in 1939 hit many Americans in Chungking in 1944. "One enters an area like this," one diplomat wrote after six days in Yenan in 1944,

concerning which one has heard so many entirely good but secondhand reports, with a conscious determination not to be swept off one's feet. The feeling is that things cannot possibly be as good as they have been pictured, and that there must be a "catch" somewhere. It is interesting, therefore, that my own first impressions . . . have been extremely favorable . . . All of our party have had the same feeling . . . The general atmosphere at Yenan can be compared to that of a rather small, sectarian college—or a religious summer conference . . . smugness, self-righteousness and conscious fellowship . . . The spell of the Chinese Communists still seems to work.

For those who believed—as most people then believed—that the alliance of war would survive the coming of peace, Yenan could not but exert a spell after Chungking. And certainly, if Yenan were dynamic and Chungking feeble, there was little security for American interests in backing the past against the future. This view was mistaken—perhaps terribly mistaken;* it was not disloyal. Wedemeyer, who inherited Stilwell's advisers when he replaced Stilwell in 1944, and Alsop, who had many arguments with them at the time, have testified since to their conviction of the entire loyalty and patriotism of Davies, Service and the rest.†

* Even this is not too certain: Joseph Alsop, for example, wrote in 1951: "If Davies' recommendations had been followed, I now believe he would have been proven right." Yet this supposes that it is possible to wean Communists away from Moscow, while experience suggests that weaning will do nothing until Moscow itself does something decisive to alienate the national party. Thus, in effect, Britain and the United States followed the Davies policy toward Tito in 1943 and 1944; but it was of no avail until Moscow broke with Belgrade in 1948. [From the perspective of 1965, Davies and Alsop seem to us more prescient than they did in 1951.]
† While there is no evidence that the Far East Division of the State Department harbored Communists (except for Hiss), there is clear evidence that General MacArthur's SCAP did. Richard L-G Deverall, presently the Amer-

There is even less evidence of design in Washington. Roosevelt was never happy about the China situation but never had time to develop a clear policy about it; Harry Hopkins supported Chennault against Stilwell, as did many other New Dealers, mobilized by Thomas G. Corcoran; and Stilwell's decisive backing came, not from the State Department or from New Dealers, but from Marshall and Stimson in the Pentagon.

This, then, was the situation at the Japanese surrender. China, after long years of war, was battered and exhausted. In the north the Communist armies were in control; in the center were the Japanese armies; in the southwest corner were the armies of Chiang Kai-shek. American policy was uncertain: it was deeply suspicious of Chiang and wary of the Communists, though the euphoria of victory and Wedemeyer's moderate and constructive handling of his Chungking relations had somewhat raised Chiang's stock. The problem, as Acheson put it in the MacArthur hearings, was out of this confusion to create a nation. There were three courses for the United States: to abandon China altogether, or to move into China in force, or to assist China to recover stability. The first was inconceivable; the second, in the year of the Great Demobilization, was equally inconceivable (and from the viewpoint of Americans who fear open-end commitments on the Asian mainland, inconceivable in any circumstances).

The third therefore seemed the sensible course. The immediate requirement was to restore the power of Chiang in as much of

---

ican Federation of Labor representative in India and, before that, MacArthur's Chief of Labor Education, has written, "A group of Communists and pro-Communists in MacArthur's headquarters played a dramatic part during the early days of the Occupation, in turning over press, radio and movie facilities in Japan to native Communist elements. . . . Those of us who combated this plot against America inside MacArthur's own headquarters were forced to resign 'because you are too anti-Communist.' " In 1948 a leading State Department official remonstrated with MacArthur about the Communists in SCAP. MacArthur replied, as one man of the world to another, "Of course we have Communists in SCAP. They have them in the Defense Department. You have them in the State Department. But they don't matter. We can take care of them."

China as possible. This was achieved through a tremendous and little-known airlift operation which carried the Nationalist armies from the southwest corner to take over territory from the surrendering Japanese. In a short time American planes dropped three Nationalist armies from the skies to occupy big cities in East and North China, including Shanghai, Nanking and Peiping. In some cases American Marines held ports and railroads until the Nationalists could arrive. Without this operation it seems unlikely that Chiang could have got into North China at all.*

The next step was to seek some formula by which civil war could be avoided and national unity attained. This was no new idea. As early as 1937, Chiang himself had spoken of the need for a "political" solution of the Communist problem. By 1944 he was thinking in terms of a national political convention as a first move toward such a solution. In the background lay the idea of a coalition government, in which the Communists would sit as members of Chiang's cabinet. This idea struck Chiang with much less horror than it struck members of the Senate during the hearing.† Conceiving himself the spider, he was happy to invite the flies into his parlor. The main threat to him was the Red Army; the best way, he believed, to end that threat was to incorporate it into a national army under Nationalist command; and to achieve that objective, he would be more than willing to throw the Communists a few seats in his cabinet. Coalition was not a one-way street.

In view of the fact that practically no one today—operating, as Senator McMahon well put it in the hearings, with "20-20 hind-

---

* General Wedemeyer wished to extend the operation into Manchuria, but lacked the troops. When he applied to MacArthur for enough troops to enable him to do the job, MacArthur, as Wedemeyer testified at the hearings, "refused to make them available to me."

† Senator Wiley voiced a familiar misconception in the hearings, "Is it not a fact that in every government in which the Communists have been a component part, sooner or later, they have taken over the same, lock, stock and barrel?"—to which Secretary Acheson properly answered that it was not a fact, citing Italy, France, Belgium and the Netherlands (to which he might have added Greece, Chile and other nations).

sight"—will admit to have favored a coalition in China in 1945, it is all the more curious to discover that practically no one opposed the idea in 1945. After all, there were coalitions all over Europe at that time—and in Western Europe they served the exceedingly useful purpose of neutralizing the Communists during the first crucial months of reconstruction. In China coalition seemed the logical solution. Even the warmest partisans of Chiang thought he would do better by coalition than by civil war. "There is only one way out now, as I see it," wrote Chennault in 1944. "That is for us to sponsor thorough political reconstruction at Chungking, followed by true unification between Chungking and Yenan." Joseph C. Grew, head of the Office of Far Eastern Affairs in Washington, favored the effort; so did Clarence Gauss and John Carter Vincent in Chungking; so did Henry Wallace, Donald Nelson and other presidential envoys; so (at least, according to the plain meaning of their recommendation of December 1945) did Wedemeyer, Spruance and MacArthur.

So above all did Major General Patrick J. Hurley, who appeared in China in 1944 as Roosevelt's personal representative, stayed on as ambassador and became the most vociferous advocate of the theory that the Chinese Communists were not Communists and that all the boys should get together. Hurley, a dashing and colorful figure, had been Hoover's Secretary of War (where he had ordered Douglas MacArthur to drive the Bonus Marchers out of Washington). Roosevelt, with his weakness for adventurous Irishmen, gave him a series of missions during the Pacific War, culminating with the Chinese assignment. In his way, Hurley was almost as improbable a choice as Stilwell—a second bull in the China shop.

One reason perhaps for sending Hurley to China was the theory that he got along well with the Russians. Certainly Hurley cultivated that theory himself. In moments of Great Plains exuberance he would claim to have taught Stalin an Oklahoma warwhoop. At Teheran, according to another Hurley story, he coached Stalin to say in English "What-the-hell-is-going-on-here" whenever he saw Roosevelt and Churchill conferring together. In any case, proceeding to Chungking by way of Moscow, Hurley stopped off for a significant chat with Molotov, the Soviet Foreign Minister. Molotov made it very clear that, so far as the Soviet Union was concerned, the United States was conceded to have the primary interest in China. "The Soviets would be glad," Molotov indicated, "if the United States aided the Chinese in unifying their country, in improving their military and economic condition and in choosing for this task their best people." As for the so-called Communists, it is true, Molotov said, that there were desperately impoverished people in China, "some of whom called themselves Communists but were related to communism in no way at all. It was merely a way of expressing dissatisfaction with their economic condition. . . . The Soviet government should not be associated with these 'communist' elements."

The second part of the Molotov statement—the implication that the Chinese Communists were merely agrarian reformers—was the standard Communist eyewash.* But—reaffirmed by Stalin himself to Hurley the next April—the assertion of primary American interest in China was probably honest enough for the time. The Russians were already sufficiently involved in the European War. Moreover, they were thinking generally in sphere-of-influence terms; they had just reached an informal agreement with the British dividing the Balkans, in which the British were to get Greece and a half-interest in Yugoslavia. They evidently placed China in the same category with Greece: while they would not call off the native Communists, they would do nothing to save them if they got in trouble. Stalin, moreover, must have regarded

* It is difficult (apart from the Hurley case) to document the fashionable thesis that the State Department regarded the Chinese Communists as mere agrarian reformers. Secretary Acheson repeatedly challenged his critics to produce a single statement to this effect by any foreign service officer. After prolonged research, someone came up with an ambiguous interview given by a minor State Department official to a Philadelphia paper. Aside from General Hurley, the main advocates of the William Jennings Bryan theory of Chinese communism were journalists and soldiers, like Brigadier General Evans Carlson.

the whole problem of Chinese communism with personal distaste. He had blundered there badly in backing Chiang in 1927; he had blundered again in insisting that the Chinese Communist Party be based on the city working classes, not, as Mao Tse-tung had contended, on the peasantry. In 1936, when the pro-Soviet Chang Hsueh-liang kidnapped Chiang and took him to Sian, Soviet intervention (according to later claims of Molotov) procured his release. In 1945 Stalin evidently took the Henry R. Luce view of Chiang: he spoke favorably of him to Hurley, calling him "selfless" and "a patriot."

Hurley went gaily about his mission. "The only difference between Chinese Communists and Oklahoma Republicans," he told newspapermen, "is that Oklahoma Republicans aren't armed." By December 1944 he could brag of having convinced Chiang that "the Communist Party in China is not an agent of the Soviet Government." Then, in February 1945, the Yalta conference introduced new factors into the situation. From the American and British viewpoint, a prime purpose of the Crimean meeting was to get the Soviet Union into the Pacific War. The American Joint Chiefs, Wedemeyer and MacArthur all held this view; so did millions of less well-informed Americans. As Senator Wiley himself, so waspish a critic of the Joint Chiefs in the 1951 hearings, put it as late as July 25, 1945:

In millions of American homes, mothers, fathers and sweethearts are waiting anxiously for news of Russia's intentions . . . Countless American lives are at stake in Russia's decisions . . . Why should we follow the lead of the 'nice Nellies' of our State Department who have been more concerned with diplomatic niceties than with the preservation of American interests and lives? Let no one say that we are meddling in Russia's business when we tell them that we want them to carry their load in the Far East . . . We will not easily forget Russia's contribution in the Far East if she pitches in with us and will not easily forgive her shirking of her responsibility if she remains on the side lines.

The feeling in official circles had been all the more intense the February preceding, before the Japanese peace feelers and before the successful testing of the atomic bomb. The "nice Nellies" of the State Department were determined to do what was necessary to preserve American interests and lives.

So, not out of Communist duplicity or liberal wooliness but out of hardboiled military calculation, Roosevelt was urged to pay what the market demanded for the guarantee of Russian participation. The price he paid was the return of southern Sakhalin and the transfer of the Kuriles to Russia; the internationalization of Dairen in Manchuria and the leasing to Russia of Port Arthur as a naval base; and the joint Soviet-Chinese operation of the Manchurian railroads. In exchange, the Soviet Union agreed to enter the war and to conclude a pact of friendship and alliance with the Nationalist regime.

This military attitude toward Russian participation was no passing mood. Quite some time after Yalta, President Truman and Edward R. Stettinius, Jr., were subject to the same pleadings. In his memoirs, Stettinius wrote:

At a top-level policy meeting in the White House, just before the San Francisco Conference opened on April 25, President Truman, the military leaders, and I discussed the failure of the Soviet Union to abide by the Yalta agreement on the Balkans. At this meeting the United States military representatives pleaded for patience with the Soviet Union because they feared that a crackdown would endanger Russian entry into the Far Eastern war.

In the military mind, moreover, the case for buying Russian participation would not necessarily have been weakened by the knowledge that the main islands of Japan were on the verge of defeat. According to Stettinius:

Even as late as the Potsdam conference, after the first atomic bomb had exploded at Los Alamos on July 16, the military insisted that the Soviet Union had to be brought into the Far Eastern war. At both Yalta and Potsdam, the military staffs were particularly concerned with the Japanese troops in Manchuria. Described as the cream of the Japanese army, this self-contained force, with its own autonomous command, and industrial base, was believed capable of prolonging the war even after the islands of Japan had been subdued, unless Russia should enter the war and engage this army. With this belief, the President's military advisers urgently desired Russian entry into the war. Our casualties would be far smaller if the Japanese had to divert forces to meet Russia in the north.

It has been charged in recent years that through the Yalta agreement Roosevelt and Churchill sold Nationalist China down the river; that the conference doomed Chiang and sealed the victory of the Communists. In the feverish atmosphere of the late forties, such charges gained considerable currency. On cool examination in the light of day, however, it is hard not to share Senator McMahon's skepticism over "the proposition that the concessions, so-called, made at Yalta of a couple of ports and a half-interest in a railroad are what caused the defeat of Chiang." To blame the Russian occupation of Manchuria, for example, on Yalta is somewhat to overestimate the capacity of paper agreements to stop marching armies. Russia would have taken those areas in any circumstances; what Yalta sought to do was to yield what was inevitable in advance and try to get something in exchange. What Roosevelt and Churchill got in exchange was something Chiang very much wanted, and the possession of which would continue for some time to give him vocal pleasure—that is, a treaty with Stalin. This treaty, with its full recognition of Chiang as the ruler of China, promised to ratify Stalin's writing down of the Chinese Communists. By this means, Roosevelt hoped to obtain for Chiang his great opportunity to create a true national state.*

Hurley showed no signs, at the time, of disapproving Yalta. Before the conference, indeed, as he later wrote, "I suggested to President Roosevelt a plan to force the National government to make more liberal political concessions in order to make possible

---

* Cf. *Life* magazine, September 10, 1945: "The Moscow Treaties Give China Her First Real Chance to Complete an Old Revolution. . . . The Soong-Stalin treaties contain less pessimism than any diplomatic event in the last twenty years," etc., etc.

a settlement with the Communists. The President did not approve the suggestion." Yalta itself gave Hurley's mission new significance. It was up to him now, not just to complete unification within China, but to lay the groundwork for the Soviet-Chinese treaty. He threw himself into the job with immense zest, with coalition still the essential first step. The Communists, he remarked the month after Yalta, "are not in fact Communists, they are striving for democratic principles." In June he described himself as "the best friend the Communists had in Chungking."

Hurley freely uttered these and a dozen other similar aphorisms at the time; but when Senator McMahon pitilessly brought them up, the handsome, white-haired general responded with an outburst of righteous indignation. He also came up with the story that Roosevelt had told him before his death to ameliorate or set aside the Yalta agreement and had sent him in this cause to Churchill and Stalin in the spring of 1945.† Roosevelt doubtless did tell him that the success of the Yalta agreements on the Far East would depend on the nature of the Soviet-Chinese pact, but Hurley's more dramatic claim probably belongs in the same gallery with his story that he taught Stalin to give a warwhoop. His 1945 interview with Stalin, as fully reported by Hurley himself and reproduced in the State Department White Paper, seemed a meeting of true souls concerned with clearing the way for a unified government in China under Chiang's leadership. "The Marshal was pleased," Hurley joyfully told Washington, "and expressed his concurrence and . . . agreed unqualifiedly to America's policy in China as outlined to him during the conversation."

Hurley emerged from the Stalin talk aglow with enthusiasm. But Averell Harriman, then Ambassador to Moscow, who had been present with Hurley, came out considerably less enthusiastic.

† Hurley had two appointments with Roosevelt after Yalta. The appointment on March 8 was requested by Hurley for himself; it hardly seems likely that this would have been an occasion for Roosevelt's alleged new orders on Yalta. During the second interview, on March 24, General Wedemeyer was present; he has nothing to substantiate Hurley's story.

Both he and George Kennan, then chargé d'affaires, were quick to inform Washington that Hurley's estimate of Soviet policy seemed to them wildly naïve and optimistic. But the treaty remained in the future, and much might still be done. When it was finally negotiated in July and August, however, the Nationalist government made concessions to the Soviet Union which exceeded anything required by Yalta—and which were opposed by Averell Harriman and the State Department. Chiang, Hurley and Henry Luce expressed themselves well satisfied with the results. Only the killjoys Harriman and Kennan registered doubts.

Thus Stalin stood aside to give Chiang his opportunity to organize China. The standing aside seems to have been genuine enough, if not very long-lived: when Russia in late 1945 looted Manchuria of Japanese-owned factories to the value of nearly a billion dollars, it was hardly acting as if it expected Mao and the Communists to take over this area in the near future.* The question for Chiang now was whether the contest between the Nationalists and the Communists would take the form of politics or war. Hurley, to the end of his stay in China, continued to encourage negotiations between the opposing factions. But he was also having increasing trouble with his State Department advisers, partly for personal reasons and partly because they did not share his faith in Chiang and were more persevering than he about doing business with the Communists. In November 1945 Hurley resigned with a blast at the foreign service. The next day Truman announced the appointment of George C. Marshall as his special representative in China.

Marshall continued the unification mission. But he found himself dealing with an impossible situation. Neither side believed in unification, except in the sense of the spider and the fly, and both backed and filled whenever unification proposals threatened to

* Joseph Alsop was shown in Belgrade what he regards as "indisputable proofs," dating from the days of Yugoslav membership in the Communist family, that Stalin ordered the Chinese Communists to enter a coalition and accept the primacy of Chiang.

cramp their own freedom of action. Marshall tried to paper over the gap with various proposals; but none of them got very far— particularly in the face of Chiang's growing conviction that he could solve the problem permanently by force. The statistics in this respect, indeed, were overwhelmingly in Chiang's favor. At the end of 1946, he had about 2,600,000 men under arms as against slightly over a million Communists; in rifle firepower, he had superiority of three or four to one. The temptation was too great to resist.

Once the fighting began, the Nationalist armies were able at first to make stirring advances across a broad sweep of territory. When Marshall warned him that he was overextending himself and heading for trouble, Chiang paid no attention. But after a time his soldiers, far outrunning his civil administration, found themselves walled up in the cities they captured; his armies thus became immobilized; and maneuver and initiative were left to the Communists. In time the balance began to change. The Communists, sustained by a fighting faith, aided by the sympathy of the countryside and the increasing hatred of the Nationalist government, began to win victories; and, as they won victories, they captured arms and attracted deserters. By mid-1948 Chiang was in retreat.

Could Chiang have been saved in 1947? In July of that year General Marshall, by now Secretary of State, sent General Wedemeyer on a fact-finding tour. The spreading incompetence and corruption in the Nationalist regime shocked Wedemeyer; in one speech he told Chiang and his government to their faces that their own wretched performance was to blame for the failure to contain the Communists. Yet Wedemeyer also felt the absolute necessity of opposing the spread of communism. "The only working basis on which national Chinese resistance to Soviet aims can be revitalized," he told Truman on his return, "is through the presently corrupt, reactionary and inefficient Chinese National government." His recommendations were not clear-cut. On the one hand, he favored giving Chiang "sufficient and prompt military assistance, . . . ground, sea and air" to save him: on the other, he also believed that "until drastic political and economic reforms are undertaken United States aid cannot accomplish its purpose"; and, while still convinced that Chiang was personally sincere, "I am not certain," Wedemyer confessed, "that he has today sufficient determination [to carry through reforms] if this requires absolute overruling of the political and military cliques surrounding him."

The Wedemeyer report had no easy panacea for the Chinese situation.* But it was at least a call for positive action. It produced very little—partly because nothing had changed the State Department's conviction that the Chiang regime offered no realistic basis for action; partly because the dimensions of the action suggested by Wedemeyer were so staggering as to alarm a government already committed to the vast job of stabilizing Europe. Wedemeyer told Marshall that his plans would require at the start about ten thousand officers and others to direct the various operations. There were at that time but one and a third divisions in the entire United States; so Marshall and the Joint Chiefs agreed that the Wedemeyer proposal could not be considered.

It hardly seems likely, looking back to 1947, that the American Congress, which a few months before had to be whipped into a sense of impending doom before it would vote to loan $300,000,-000 to stop a similar but far less immense situation in Greece, would have welcomed the quite fantastic commitment which Wedemeyer proposed for China. Even those who weep for the Wedemeyer plan most today showed no signs at the time of desiring any such massive United States intervention on the main-

---

* One of the great phoney issues in the whole China debate was the alleged "suppression" of the Wedemeyer report. Presidents and Secretaries of State have been sending out representatives for years without immediately making their reports public on their return. The expectation of publication, indeed, would destroy the very confidential character required by such a report if it is to serve its purpose. In this case, moreover, the report contained scathing criticisms of Chiang Kai-shek and also a proposal to place Manchuria under United Nations trusteeship with the Soviet Union as one of the trustees.

land of Asia. As Senator Vandenberg summed up the Republican view in submitting the China Aid Act of 1948, "We cannot underwrite the destiny of China." The Foreign Relations Committee, Vandenberg added, favored the bill because they felt it would strengthen the Nationalist position "without, at the same time, involving the United States in any additional commitments of a military nature." Senator McMahon, searching the records of the Foreign Relations Committee from 1947 to 1949, was unable to find "a single, solitary suggestion" for "a change of policy"; no disagreement with the China policy, he said was recorded "by any member of the committee," Republicans included.

Some Republicans, it is true, beginning with Governor Thomas E. Dewey, did assail the administration for inadequate aid to Chiang; but they did it in terms which suggested that this was more an issue in American domestic politics than in the international field; certain of them, indeed, attacked the administration at the same time for giving aid to the rather more stable governments of Europe, a process they characterized as "pouring the taxpayers' money down a rathole." And many Republicans clearly wanted to wash their hands of the whole business. During a trip to the Far East in November 1947, Colonel Robert R. McCormick, owner of the Chicago *Tribune* and the Washington *Times-Herald,* stated his opinion of China for the Associated Press: "The Chiang Kai-shek government cannot put down an insurrection which is falsely called a Communist insurrection. Although Communist-backed, it is still a bona fide insurrection against a government which is little more than an agency of the Soong family."

The Wedemeyer plan was remote from any political reality of 1947 or 1948. Yet it seems equally true that nothing short of the Wedemeyer proposals, which in their ultimate implications meant an all-out American adoption and control of the Nationalist regime, would have saved it against the Communist revolution. Certainly the provision of more arms and more money would not have done the job. All responsible American officers agree that the Nationalists were in 1947 far better equipped than the Communists. When Marshall was asked in the hearings whether he thought substantially increased American military aid could have changed the picture, he replied that he thought not: "The question was one of leadership. . . . What was basically lacking was the support of the army by the people." When Wedemeyer was asked what caused Chiang's defeat, he answered even more sharply, "Lack of spirit, primarily lack of spirit. It was not lack of equipment. In my judgment they could have defended the Yangtze with broomsticks if they had the will to do it." Major General David Barr, head of the United States Military Mission to China, spent many patient months trying to cope with the "grandiose planning" of the Chinese generals, with their "unsound strategy and faulty tactics," with their "wall psychology." In November 1948 he reported to Washington:

I am convinced that the military situation has deteriorated where only the active participation of United States troops could effect a remedy. No battle has been lost since my arrival due to lack of ammunition or equipment. Their military debacle, in my opinion, can all be attributed to the world's worst leadership and many other morale-destroying factors that led to a complete loss of the will to fight.

The diagnoses were all reminiscent of Winston Churchill's regretful epitaph on the Russian Whites, who he hoped would win but had the wisdom to recognize could not: "It was not want of material means, but of comradeship, will-power, and rugged steadfastness that lost the struggle."*

* Vice Admiral Oscar C. Badger, former naval commander in the Far East, declared in the hearings that a five-month delay in sending American arms to Nationalist forces in North China led to the surrender of General Fu Tso-yi and the collapse of Nationalist resistance in the north. He also made the point that, while the Nationalists might never have lost a battle for want of equipment, this might, in certain cases, have restrained them from making the decision to join battle. General Barr in his testimony vigorously disputed Badger's citation of the Fu Tso-yi case, ascribing the delay to the Admiral's own action in altering the original requirements and adding that in any case no amount of weapons could have saved Fu. This controversy, like the larger controversy over the actual amount of American aid sent to Chiang, is not susceptible of easy resolution. The White Paper puts the amount of American aid at around two billion; the case against this figure is put by Freda

Such an analysis required not only Churchill's magnaminity, but also his understanding of history—an understanding which reached back beyond commercial civilization to the days when blood, sweat, and tears were the negotiable currency. We think too easily in bourgeois culture that economic aid—or diplomatic agreement—can govern the great flow of history. The fashionable parallel to the economic fallacy in the China story is the theory that the current world mess is all the result of a bad contract at Yalta. "The unauthorized agreements made at Yalta," Senator Robert A. Taft remarked in January 1951, ". . . set up Soviet Russia in a position where it dominates Europe and Asia today"—as if a different set of agreements might have forced the Red Army back to the Urals.

In fact, Yalta yielded the Russians no territory (except probably the Kuriles) that they would not have gained in any case by the natural advance of the Red Army. Had the Yalta engagements been kept, both in Europe and Asia, Russian power would have been closely confined. The fact that Stalin never intended to honor the engagements should certainly have been more clearly understood by our leaders. But, even had they understood it with total clarity, this would not have eliminated the need for Yalta. The people of the world had to be convinced of the aggressive nature of Soviet purposes before they could be mobilized against Soviet aggression; thus there had to be agreements if only so the Communists could break them before the world. "The strength of our moral position today," Averell Harriman has well said, "rests upon the fact that we made every effort to reach an agreement with the Soviet Union." The fatal mistake of the West, indeed, was not Yalta; the fatal mistake was the Great Demobilization

---

Utley in *The China Story* where effective American aid is estimated at about two hundred and twenty-five million. Her account is based on an analysis by Colonel L. B. Moody, published in part in *The Freeman,* July 10, 1951, under the title "Help Chiang Did Not Get." But, however much actual American aid the Nationalists received, no one has disputed General Barr's statement that after the fall of Weihsien and Tsinan in 1948, "the Communists had more of our equipment than the Nationalists did."

which invited Stalin to ignore Yalta; yet would there have been the will in the West to keep its vast armies intact in advance of any clear demonstration by the Soviet Union of hostile intent?

The fallacy of thinking that parchment governs history has been matched in American thinking by the rise of the egocentrism which afflicts all nations, as they grow mighty and powerful. A few Washington clerks, we tend to believe, writing memoranda and drafting documents, can switch about great historical movements on remote continents, like railroad cars in a marshalling yard. If the Red Star has risen over China, it cannot, this theory contends, be due to long pent-up demands for social change, to feebleness and incompetence on the part of the Nationalists, to demoralization and loss of faith in the regime, to the crusading drive and military skill of the Communists; it must be due, not to actions in China, but to actions in Washington—to fellow-travelers in the State Department who publish white papers attacking Chiang and leak scandalous stories about him to newspapermen.

General Wedemeyer is right in a sense when he criticizes the State Department for not going all-out for the Nationalist regime in 1947 and 1948; there can be no question that the Department, having soured on Chiang and seeing no future in the Communists, was at times less than half-hearted in its support of the Nationalists.* Yet Wedemeyer admitted his own doubt as to whether his grand project could have worked in any case. General Marshall, as Secretary of State, and President Truman were required to weigh the costs of the Wedemeyer plan against the urgent necessities in Europe. They chose Europe, which they desperately needed and had a good chance to save, over China, which they needed far less and where their chances were hardly discernible to the naked eye.

* Thus the ECA program—one of the most successful of American ventures in China—was forced upon the administration by Congressman Judd and a pro-Chiang bloc in the House. Still, the State Department could have replied, no amount of ECA would have saved Nationalist China without a new policy and a new will on the part of the Nationalist leaders.

The State Department wrote off Chiang Kai-shek too soon and too placidly;* but it did not destroy him—any more than a different posture on the part of Britain could have altered the outcome of the American Civil War. The Kuomintang destroyed itself. Chiang failed to create a nation, not because he lacked ammunition for his rifles or because a State Department official showed secret documents to the editor of a Communist magazine in the United States or because the Big Three agreed on x rather than y at Yalta, but because he and his followers did not have within them the capacity to rise to a great historic challenge. "What is needed," wrote John Leighton Stuart in March 1948 (the last American ambassador to China, he watched Chiang's final days with compassion), "is inspired leadership, of which so far the Generalissimo seems incapable." The view is not "infrequently expressed," Stuart cabled in December 1948, "that he is best asset Communists have."

The Communist victory in China remains an historical cataclysm. It appears likely that nothing, short of the commitment of American troops in force, could have averted it; nor would this have saved Chiang for very long unless he began to display at least the intelligence of Tsar Nicholas and Stolypin (and this was not enough to save the Romanovs).

And so Chiang fled to Formosa, tragic in defeat; Acheson waited for the dust to settle; and, in the spring and summer of 1951, Americans reconsidered the question of Far Eastern policy. The return of MacArthur precipitated a debate which should have been held, at the very latest, three years earlier. If the recommendations of the Wedemeyer report had been openly canvassed, Secretary Acheson would have been spared much subsequent trouble. Yet there was good reason why the issues of China policy

---

* There is a disagreeable complacency to at least the second clause in Dean Acheson's letter of transmittal for the White Paper: "Nothing that this country did or could have done within the reasonable limits of its capabilities could have changed that result; nothing that was left undone by this country has contributed to it."

were never joined. The administration needed Republican votes for the Marshall Plan and later for the North Atlantic Pact; to get these votes, it was prepared to pass over points which seemed less essential. It never effectively responded (until Acheson spoke out at the MacArthur hearings) to the attacks on Yalta or on the Chiang policy lest such response alienate support needed for pending measures of policy. The result was to smother the issues and maximize the public confusion—the very confusion which would make men turn convulsively to Douglas MacArthur in the April and May of 1951.

So far as the future was concerned, MacArthur and the administration differed sharply on two points. One was the question of Chiang Kai-shek, whom MacArthur thought to have still the potential for the anti-Communist leadership of China, if not, indeed, of all Asia. The other was the question of the relationship between Communist China and the Soviet Union. In his address to Congress MacArthur had painted a fearsome picture of China as an aggressive and militarized nationalist state whose "interests are at present parallel with those of the Soviet" but whose aggressiveness came from its own "lust for the expansion of power."* This analysis placed MacArthur, oddly enough in the same camp with such old China hands as Owen Lattimore, who have long contended for the Titoist theory of Mao Tse-tung. MacArthur stuck firmly to this view in the hearings. "The degree of control and influence that the Kremlin may have in China," he said, "is quite problematical." When Senator Fulbright politely inquired whether it was not true that Mao Tse-tung had been trained in Moscow and had close relations there, MacArthur replied, "How would I know, Senator?" Fulbright observed that that, at least, was what he had read in the papers, to which MacArthur made

* Few people reflected on the irony of Douglas MacArthur telling an applauding joint session of Congress less than ten years after Pearl Harbor that the Chinese people were "militarized in their concepts and in their ideals" and were possessed by "increasingly dominant aggressive tendencies" while the Japanese were serene, orderly, industrious, peace-loving and overflowing with a desire for constructive service in the advance of the human race.

the enigmatic reply: "My advice to you, Senator, is—if you listen to advice from a fellow Arkansas man—not to believe everything you see in the press."

The administration would agree, that on the whole, some form of Titoism is ultimately likely in China, simply because two hundred million people cannot indefinitely push around four hundred million, particularly when the four hundred million are infected by an especially rambunctious form of nationalism. Yet, in the short run, as General Marshall put it, "I have gone on the assumption that she was operating not only in conjunction with but literally under the direction of the Soviet Union."

The hearing did not clear up these issues, but at least it ventilated them. It did not clear up the question of American policy in the Far East, but at least it brought light and air into a murky and obscure tangle. The MacArthur challenge did not overthrow the Far Eastern policy nor did it even deepen the discredit into which it had already fallen. It did demonstrate beyond any doubt that the situation was so uncertain and confused that there was no sure footing, nor obvious path out of the morass. In the confusion, the administration path seemed no more hopeless or idiotic or wicked than any of the others; it made more sense, perhaps, than most.

THE NEW ISOLATIONISM

From the challenge to Far Eastern policy, MacArthur moved on to a basic attack on the whole theory of American foreign policy— the theory to which the United States is still committed and with which it has been able to mobilize the free world. "It is not just a difference of method which is now under examination," Dean Acheson said in the hearings. "What is challenged is the bedrock purpose of our foreign policy."

In developing this challenge—in his address to Congress at the hearings, in his speeches before state legislatures, and in his letters and his interviews—MacArthur placed only a moderate emphasis on what had originally seemed the key issue: that is, the question whether the Communist threat is to be countered principally in Europe or in Asia. In his letter to Martin he had given forcible expression to a series of propositions about the relationship of Europe and Asia, arguing "that here in Asia . . . the Communist conspirators have elected to make their play for global conquest . . . that here we fight Europe's war with arms while the diplomats there still fight it with words; that if we lose the war to communism in Asia, the fall of Europe is inevitable." He continued to defend all these propositions in the Senate hearings. But it became clear that the priority he assigned to Asia was simply the priority of circumstance: there, as he saw it, the war had begun. The priority was not absolute; he asserted no necessity in any and all circumstances for preferring Asia to Europe, MacArthur, indeed, reaffirmed his support of the program of sending American troops to Europe (the divisions promised at Wake Island, alas, had never arrived). So far was he from the Gibraltarism of his Herbert Hoover that he even contended for a policy of universal containment. "I believe we should defend every place from communism," he said. "I believe we can. I believe we are able to. I have confidence in us. I don't believe we should write off anything and accept the defeat that is involved in it. . . . I don't admit that we can't hold communism wherever it shows its head."*

With such statements the Asia-Europe argument receded into the background. It soon became evident that two other questions far transcended it in importance. One was whether in the world today, East or West, the United States needs allies. The other was whether the United States is wise in its pursuit of a foreign policy

* "There are those," MacArthur also said, "who claim our strength is inadequate to protect us on two fronts. I can think of no greater expression of defeatism." Most people, though perhaps not MacArthur himself, would construe this as a reference to Herbert Hoover, who had said, "We must not overcommit this country. . . . There is a definite limit to what we can do." In another mood, however, MacArthur could out-Hoover Hoover. Three months after he declared for universal containment, he reversed himself and denounced at Boston "the dangerous illusion that our wealth [can] be limitlessly shared with others."

which, though accepting war as more than a possibility and pre-paring for it, is nevertheless founded on the hope of an eventual settlement by means short of war.

To the first of these questions MacArthur addressed himself with a clarity that was rare in the great turbulence of words he had loosed since his return. The theme emerged sharply on the first day of the hearings. Senator Green, the game old Rhode Island octogenarian, propounded a question, which, as he said, "seems to me to go to the basis of the whole difference that has been developed." The question was whether the MacArthur thesis about the Korean war did not suggest that "we would proceed alone and not with any help from the other United Nations." MacArthur, at first, did not appear much interested in the question.

MACARTHUR: I can give you no testimony about the United Nations, Senator.
GREEN: What would be your expectation?
MACARTHUR: My hope would be of course that the United Nations would see the wisdom and utility of that course, but if they did not, I still believe that the interest of the United States being the predomi-nant one in Korea, would require our action.
GREEN: Alone?
MACARTHUR: Alone, if necessary. If the other nations of the world haven't got enough sense to see where appeasement leads after the appeasement which led to the Second World War in Europe, if they can't see exactly the road that they are following in Asia, why then we had better protect ourselves and go it alone.

"Alone, if necessary" was a recurring motif in his speeches and his testimony. He conceded that allies can be helpful on occasion; he was ready to patronize the United Nations as a noble experi-ment; he even went so far as to say that the troops of other na-tions in Korea, as distinct from the governments which sent them, had been useful to him. "The actual commands there," as he put it, "have been splendid in every respect. . . . The only criticism I would have of them: There are not enough of them." As for the governments behind the commands, MacArthur had little else to say, beyond dark references to unspecified but sinister pressures from overseas. (Our national policy, he said in Texas, is "now largely influenced, if not indeed in some instances dictated, from abroad.")

When he did say something specific about allies, it sometimes seemed calculated to hurt. At one point during the hearings he read a report supposedly from the American consul general in Hongkong listing the strategic materials which had passed through Hongkong on their way to Communist China. It was not at all a creditable list, and MacArthur read it implacably: "Ball and roller bearings . . . aluminum scrap . . . microscopes . . . diesel oils, fuel oils, gasoline." But what he neglected to note were the facts first that the report came, not from the American consul but from the Hongkong government itself, and second that the entries in the row opposite many of these items, such as oil, read "*nil*" or "virtually *nil*." This omission was not calculated to reassure the British about MacArthur's attitude toward them; his action, said the ordinarily restrained *Economist*, was "the extreme of ignorance or unscrupulousness."*

The impression soon emerged from the hearings that MacArthur fundamentally felt that winning and keeping allies was hardly worth the trouble. The question of the grand coalition obviously bored him when it did not irritate him; he would dis-

* Even more anomalous was the fact that Japan under MacArthur's proconsulship itself carried on a thriving trade with Communist China. In 1950 Japan exported over nineteen million and one half million dollars worth of materials to China, of which seventeen million dollars—85 per cent—was iron and steel sheet, machine tools, precision instruments and the like; the larger part of these strategic materials was exported *after* the Chinese intervention in Korea. Even in 1951, when the United States embargo on shipments of strategic materials to China cut down on Japanese exports, Japan still managed to send China during the first quarter the not inconsiderable amount of $2,400,000 worth of textiles, bicycles, sewing machines and similar innocuous objects. The reason for this trade, like the reason for the trade through Hongkong, is plain enough: both Japan and Hongkong have been traditionally dependent on China for certain necessary imports—Hongkong, in fact, for substantially all its food and water. Why it was wicked for Hongkong to do what MacArthur considered it necessary for Japan to do is another matter.

cuss it only when it was pressed upon him, and often not even then. When Senator McMahon, his sharpest and most searching interrogator, asked him, "General, do you believe in the concept of collective security?" MacArthur replied, "What do you mean by 'collective security' Senator?" An exasperated exchange followed.

MCMAHON: Do you believe in the concept of collective security upon which our foreign policy is based?
MACARTHUR: What do you mean by 'collective security'?
MCMAHON: I mean the attempt to weld together a military alliance to keep the peace such as we have attempted to do in the North Atlantic Pact.
MACARTHUR: I have only a superficial knowledge of the North Atlantic Pact, Senator. I am not prepared to discuss it in any way, shape, or manner.

Nor was he any more prepared to discuss the United Nations itself; indeed, in his public addresses after his return he barely mentioned the organization which had honored him by making him the first commander of the first command of its kind in world history. Of course, regarding allies as a nuisance is one thing; even strong supporters of the coalition principle may succumb to moments of exasperation. Believing in the ability of the United States to go it alone is quite another. By some reasoning whose inner processes he did not choose to explain, he seems to have convinced himself that it would be not only possible but fairly simple, all things considered, for the United States, acting on its own initiative and drawing only on its own resources, to rid the world of the threat of communism.

On the second great question—whether there is any longer any sense in seeking to avoid war—MacArthur took the negative position, but in phrases so muffled and equivocal that it sometimes became difficult to decipher their true meaning. Indeed, with his testimony as a whole, it takes a good deal of probing and fishing around before one can be certain one is representing MacArthur correctly. At one point, for instance, he said, "I believe the Soviet has so often repeated the incorrect statement that we are planning to attack him that he has finally begun to believe it himself." Not five minutes later he said: "He knows just as well as you and I know that we are not going to attack him." Still, after one had done a decent amount of probing and fishing, one could hardly avoid the conclusion that MacArthur felt war to be so nearly inevitable that he had become an advocate of a species of preventive war—the species which might better be called the provocative war.

His definition of the enemy was significant in this respect. When Senator McMahon asked him who the enemy was, the General replied, "Communism, in my opinion." Did this mean communism as evidenced in Red China or the Kremlin? "I mean all over the world," MacArthur replied, "including the interior of many of the fine democratic countries of the world."

MACMAHON: General, where is the source and brains of this conspiracy?
MACARTHUR: How would I know?
MACMAHON: Would you think that the Kremlin was the place that might be the loci?
MACARTHUR: I might say that is one of the loci.
MCMAHON (later in the testimony): It is obvious that we agree they are our main enemy—that the Soviet Union is.
MACARTHUR: I didn't agree to it. I said that communism throughout the world was our main enemy.

This colloquy sorely troubled Senator Fulbright, who, when his turn came up, reopened McMahon's question. He had not himself thought, Fulbright explained to MacArthur, of our enemy as being communism; he had thought of it as being primarily an imperialist Russia. He didn't like communism, he said, but it seemed to him to become a subject of international concern only when it disturbed international order by aggression and imperialism: it was this, and not communism, which we were fighting. "In that concept, Senator," snapped the General, "I disagree with you completely."

The implications of this view were manifold. Evidently believing in what Fulbright later called a "modern ideological crusade against communism," MacArthur presumably would never tolerate any Communist state, no matter how small or how well housebroken. Like those on the left who regard fascism as a threat to the world *per se*, whether in powerful countries like Germany or in weak countries like Portugal, so MacArthur implied that he regarded communism *per se*, whether in Russia, in Yugoslavia, or in the microscopic state of San Marino, as a threat to be countered. And not to be countered simply by passive containment, but by the application of counterforce. The General made it perfectly clear that he did not want a preventive war against the Soviet Union (which is, after all, no more important a center of the Communist conspiracy than Peiping, East Berlin, Warsaw, Prague or even, perhaps, Belgrade); this was not the point. The point was that, when overtly challenged, we must respond with unconditional vigor to that challenge: we cannot permit ourselves to be constrained by too close a calculation of the countermoves of the enemy.

To MacArthur, as his testimony unfolded, this self-restraint was obviously the unpardonable sin, the almost treasonous heresy. "War never before in the history of the world," he said, "has been applied in a piecemeal way, that you make half-war, and not whole war. . . . That is a new concept in war. That is not war—that is appeasement." The basic wisdom, he repeated again and again, lies in "meeting force with maximum counterforce." If counterforce is to bring Russia or anyone else into the war, so be it, and if the war should then spread to Europe or any other part of the world, again, so be it. Fate, not policy, must determine such matters; if those were risks, they "should have been discounted when we entered the war in Korea." Once that decision was made, it is "appeasement," MacArthur said, "to think that when you use force, you can limit that force." When Senator McMahon suggested that we might be stronger two years from now, MacArthur observed, "You assume, of course, that relatively your strength is going up much more than the enemy's. That is a doubtful assumption, Senator." Thus we are already at war with communism; it is just as well that we are; and "in war there is no substitute for victory." For MacArthur, victory means "victory over the nation and men who without provocation or justification have warred against us."

To be sure, MacArthur sometimes seemed to be advocating the limited-force heresy himself, as when he said that only a lunatic would wish to use American ground forces in China. Sometimes he seemed to be denying his own doctrine of accept-no-substitute-for-victory, as when he said, "Our only objective is to force the Chinese to stop their attacks in Korea on our troops." But the belief that it is folly and near-cowardice to continue working toward an eventual diplomatic settlement of the world's conflicts was a black thread running through everything he said after his triumphal return. If communism everywhere was the enemy, and if there were no substitute for victory, then the logical conclusion must be that victory could not be achieved until communism everywhere had been eradicated. The conclusion was not spoken by MacArthur; but it pervaded the atmosphere of his speeches; and in its context his rhetoric acquired an ominous significance. "Never before have we geared national policy to timidity and fear. . . . There can be no compromise with atheistic communism—no half-way in the preservation of freedom and religion. It must be all or nothing."

Alone-if-necessary, maximum counterforce, and, less strongly, Asia-first: these were not only MacArthur's themes but those of that mid-century isolationism with which MacArthur made so warm and dramatic a political alliance. That alliance has many perplexing as well as many readily understandable elements. It would seem, offhand, as if it would have accorded better with MacArthur's temperament, with his poetic vision and his sense of manifest destiny, personal and national, to take the largest possible view of events—a global, even a cosmic view. He was not, nor had he ever seemed to be, a narrow nationalist. He liked broad vistas of time and space; he enjoyed playing, as he did in his speech to Congress, with bold and sweeping historical generalizations; he prided himself on his understanding of aspirations different from his own; he cherished his project for the abolition of war. In view of all this, one might suppose that the command of a planetary army, making the first concerted efforts to outlaw aggression, would have had an immense appeal to him. It is hard, somehow, to reconcile the man who fondled fancy geopolitical words like "epicenter" and rolled phrases like "the chancelleries of the world" from his tongue at every opportunity with the man who could write a letter congratulating that most complacent of isolationists and most pedestrian of standpatters, Joseph Martin, for "having lost none of your old-time punch." Douglas MacArthur and Joe Martin, who is caparisoned in gems unseen if caparisoned at all, made as peculiar a team as Winston Churchill and Sir Waldron Smithers would have made—or, in another realm, Rudyard Kipling and Edgar Guest.

In justice to MacArthur, he and Mr. Martin were not precisely arm-in-arm. Early in the controversy, MacArthur said several things that set his views somewhat apart from those of Martin and the old-fashioned isolationists. Not only did he agree that the commitment to the defense of Europe served the national interest; but he gave no sympathy to Senator Wherry's campaign to tie the government's hands on the disposition of American troops; he rejected "strait jacket or academic formulas" developed by the legislative branch to restrict the executive conduct of foreign policy. The military theory of the isolationists had reposed entire faith in the infallibility of airpower in the face of all conceivable strategic threats; here, too, MacArthur took a stand against the air-power extremists. He also refused to join the isolationist attacks on the Joint Chiefs of Staff, saying that he had "complete confidence" in the institution itself and in its present membership. Without mentioning the fatal words "Point Four," he even endorsed in principle the notion of a program through which this country would undertake to share its technological culture with Asia, a program which customarily draws nothing but dyspeptic groans from Representative Martin and Senator Wherry and which Senator Jenner believes to have been invented by Earl Browder. Finally, he did say that "to consider the problems of one sector [of the world] oblivious to those of another is but to court disaster for the whole."

Yet these differences in view did nothing to diminish the ardor with which the isolationist leaders embraced MacArthur, nor the ardor with which he returned the embrace. The plainly discernible—indeed, the widely advertised—truth was that, despite their differences, MacArthur was a member of the same political family as Martin and Wherry and Robert A. Taft and Herbert Hoover and Colonel McCormick and William Randolph Hearst. He was their hero and in 1951 their most powerful spokesman; they were his press agents and partisans and camp followers, his political managers and political beneficiaries.

In part this alliance could be explained by past associations and affinities. American generals have rarely been as nonpolitical as they have pretended, nor as political as they have sometimes hoped. MacArthur was accounted from the start a Republican general. He had been Herbert Hoover's chief of staff; he stood by Hoover during the Bonus Army affair; and Franklin Roosevelt, while retaining him in office for two extra years, later passed over the MacArthur line of descent to make George Marshall, anything but a MacArthur man, the head of the Army. In the thirties MacArthur's ringing martial rhetoric struck a responsive chord in the Hearst and McCormick press, which, despite or because of their isolationism, had always railed against pacifism and demanded military preparedness. For his part, MacArthur welcomed their support and shared at least some of their ideals.*

* He expressed his profound respect for the late Captain Joseph Patterson of the New York *Daily News* and for Colonel Robert R. McCormick, who was the happy owner of a MacArthur portrait inscribed (in 1944) "with the admiration and deep regard for his old comrade-in-arms." William Randolph Hearst, on his 87th birthday in 1950, received a prepaid wire from the General saying: "As you round out another year in the dedication of your firm voice, indomitable will, and great moral courage to the building of an invincible America . . . I send you my warm admiration and my gratitude."

Among oceans, the Pacific has always been the favorite of American isolationists: this is true partly for the simple reason that the Pacific is not the Atlantic. We are a people made up of several generations of Europe's displaced persons, and on this account, as well as for certain economic and geographical reasons, it is Europe's conflicts which have attracted our interest and stimulated our sympathies. If one wishes to have nothing to do with Europe and the Atlantic, to avert one's eyes and look the other way, one necessarily looks toward the Pacific. Not only is the Pacific across the continent from the Atlantic, but the political issues there are simpler and of less consequence in our domestic life. Isolationism is opposed to the introduction of "European ideas" in American politics; it has never had to oppose the introduction of "Asian ideas" because scarcely anyone has ever tried to introduce them. Among the more virulent isolationists, indeed, one detects almost a hatred of Europe—that continent which stands for ideas, culture, anarchy, decadence, evil, and all the troubling elements of life. If Europe were to fall, then America would be left, serene and unchallenged, the head of the world.

These emotions soon found expression in party politics. The Pacific Ocean has become in this century the Republican ocean; the Atlantic, the Democratic ocean. When the Republicans have had a foreign policy at all, it has generally been something to do with Japan and China; they are the party of the eastward orientation. The Democratic presidents in the twentieth century, on the other hand, have stood for an affirmative policy toward Europe (as they have also stood—from the Republican viewpoint—for the application of subversive European theories to the American economy).

If the isolationists have to fight anywhere, they would prefer, as they did in late 1941, a war in the Pacific to a war in the Atlantic. For some Republicans and for all isolationists, the Mac-Arthur war of 1941-45 was a godsend. It had the further advantage of being a war forced upon America by wicked Japanese (or so even the isolationists considered it at the time; later exegesis would convince them that Roosevelt had left the Japanese no alternative except a sneak attack at Pearl Harbor); and they infinitely preferred it to what they regarded as an irrelevant and gratuitous war in Europe—a war, moreover, which brought them into odious relationships with foreigners, like the British and the Russians. Above all, the grand strategy of the global war, in which priority was given to the European theater, placed MacArthur in constant opposition to Roosevelt.

The MacArthur war in the Pacific was the America First war *par excellence*. No one in it had to abate for a moment his dislike of Roosevelt, Churchill, the New Deal, the British, the Russians or Europe. It was entirely natural that such America First militants as Philip LaFollette and that brave soldier Hanford MacNider should soon show up in the MacArthur entourage; it was equally natural that when George Kenney found Colonel Charles A. Lindbergh making an unauthorized excursion into New Guinea, MacArthur, instead of bouncing him out of the theater, was (in Kenney's words) "the soul of cordiality and, after chatting for a while, asked Lindbergh if there was anything he could do for him."

It is true that Wendell Willkie first led the political fight for MacArthur in the United States.* But this alliance made no sense. MacArthur's truer friends were of another sort. They praised him on the floors of Congress; they denounced the Europe-first strategy of the administration. Some of them hoped against hope that MacArthur would be their candidate in 1944. They brought out quickie biographies of the General, bearing such titles as *MacArthur the Magnificent, MacArthur: Hero of Destiny* and *MacArthur: Fighter for Freedom*. It was in this mood that Congressman Miller of Nebraska and others wrote their letters to

---

* In February 1942 Willkie demanded that MacArthur be brought home: "Place him at the very top. Keep bureaucratic and political hands off him. Give him the responsibility and the power of co-ordinating all the armed forces of the nation. . . . Put him in supreme command. . . . Then the people of the United States will have reason to hope that skill, not bungling and confusion, directs their efforts."

MacArthur, and in the General they found, for all his other obligations, a willing and enthusiastic correspondent.

The publication of the Miller-MacArthur letters wrecked the presidential boom in 1944. But, on both sides, this was regarded as a deferment, not as a defeat. When MacArthur proclaimed on March 17, 1947, that the occupation job in Japan was substantially finished, this seemed not unrelated to the national elections in the year following. His emissaries moved back and forth between the Dai-Ichi Building and the United States, where they conferred with Colonel McCormick, Herbert Hoover and others of the General's friends; and his staff in Tokyo whiled away the dull days in speculation over who would be what when the General moved into the White House. Early in 1948 he made his candidacy public and permitted his supporters, headed by Philip LaFollette, to enter his name in the Wisconsin primaries.

But popularity becomes more difficult when free comment is permitted—a reflection that might not have occurred to Mac-Arthur in Tokyo. The Stassen machine was determined to beat him; its Wisconsin drummer, Senator Joseph McCarthy, published an open letter pointing out that the General was an old man, long out of touch with civilian problems, and that "twice before we have had Presidents who became physically weakened during their term of office and both times it had very sad results for our country." Though McCarthy was only tooling up for bigger things, his work, even at that stage, was effective. MacArthur did badly in Wisconsin, and his candidacy never recovered from the shock. In the end he received eleven out of a possible 1,094 votes at the Republican convention. Subsequently, at Wake Island, MacArthur told Truman with some bitterness that he had let the Republicans make a chump out of him in 1948 and that he had no intention of letting it happen again.

Many things changed, however, after that meeting on Wake Island. While MacArthur still seemed in 1951 unwilling to entrust his own reputation to the quicksands of party politics, there can be no question that he had restored his firm alliance with the con-

"Well, We Seem to Have Got Unification, Anyhow"

servative wing of the Republican party. Common views on domestic policy no doubt contributed to that firmness. At times,
indeed, MacArthur declared that he regarded these domestic issues as primary. "Talk of imminent threat to our national security
through the application of external force," he told the Massachusetts legislature, "is pure nonsense. It is not of any external threat
that I concern myself but rather of insidious forces working from
within which have already so drastically altered the character of
our free institutions."

Yet, while these views cemented the alliance, they were not its
essence, nor were they the cause of the fanatical enthusiasm with
which the isolationists seized upon MacArthur. The essence lay
in MacArthur's notable restatement of traditional American isolationism; the enthusiasm derived from his extraordinary success in
giving old-fashioned isolationist prejudices an embodiment which
seemed at last to make sense in a world too complex for old-fashioned isolationist doctrine. The elder prophets, like Mr. Hoover,
had continued to preach the old faith, but they were more honored than their recommendations were followed. Gibraltarism
was an appeal to obsolescence too unashamed for even Senator
Taft to observe. Indeed, the confusions of Senator Taft, the ablest
and most logical of the isolationist senators, provided a measure
of the chaos into which isolationism had fallen as a philosophy.
Within a few months in 1951, Taft managed to take several different positions on almost all the leading issues, reaching an astonishing climax when he simultaneously called for a reduction of
the Army, a reduction in the military budget and an enlargement
of the war in Asia.* But Taft could come happily to rest on the
policy of MacArthur: "I have long approved of General Mac-
Arthur's program," he said in April.

Isolationism was in a phase of perilous transition. What General MacArthur did was to supply a new crystallization. Upon the
prevailing disorder he imposed a new logic—a logic making sig-

* Unaccountably, he also wished to commit the reduced U.S. forces to the
defense of the Suez Canal.

nificant concessions, indeed, to the views of the internationalists, but still preserving the essence of old-style isolationism and thus commanding the fervent allegiance of the old-style isolationists. His triumph was to point out a way in which the United States can be in the world, yet not completely of it. If it is necessary to intervene in foreign affairs, the reasoning runs, and in this lamentable modern world it does seem to be necessary, then at least we can do it alone, unilaterally, without allies making trouble for us and wasting our resources. It is certainly essential to counter the Soviet threat with some kind of foreign policy; but it is desirable to do so quickly and on our own, not to get tangled up in messy networks of pacts, alliances and world organizations.

Unilateralism, to coin one more gobbledygook term, was the new isolationism. Go it alone; meet force with maximum counterforce; there is no substitute for victory; do not worry about consequences: these were the tenets of the new faith. It was a more vivid, more adventurous, more dangerous faith than the placid, small-town isolationism of Borah, Hiram Johnson and Herbert Hoover. It provided scope for men of global vision or of messianic bent. Moreover, it seemed to provide a clear-cut and viable alternative to the philosophy of the administration. It promised action and a victorious conclusion, against the slow death of the cold war and the swift death of the local police action. With MacArthur, American isolationism received its classical mid-century formulation.

THE FUTURE OF AMERICAN
FOREIGN POLICY

If isolationism had to await MacArthur to bring up to date its theory of foreign policy, the State and Defense Departments, bearing the awful burden of day-to-day decision, had long since worked out their theory of the nature of the threat and the best way to meet it. MacArthur could see it as "no policy at all," but that, of course, is a figure of speech; Stalin knew we had a policy, and if it was not wholly consistent, it was at least as much so as foreign policies in a confused world are likely to be. It defined the threat with precision: the enemy is the Soviet Union, a totalitarian state committed to expansion by force. It defined the techniques of expansion with almost equal precision; here the government was fortunate in having on tap the experience and intelligence of two brilliant foreign service officers, Charles E. Bohlen and George F. Kennan, who had long specialized on Soviet Russia. At an early stage Kennan set forth the government's theory of Soviet expansionism:

a fluid stream which moves constantly, wherever it is permitted to move, toward a given goal. Its main concern is to make sure that it has filled every nook and cranny available to it in the basin of world power. But if it finds unassailable barriers in its path, it accepts these philosophically and accommodates itself to them. The main thing is that there should always be pressure, unceasing constant pressure, toward the desired goal. There is no trace of any feeling in Soviet psychology that the goal must be reached at any given time.

The problem of policy, then, was to place "unassailable barriers" in the Soviet path; it was to fill the vacuums which invite Soviet expansion. Beginning in 1947, American policy systematically devoted itself to these objectives. The Truman Doctrine held out a shield in front of Greece and Turkey; the Marshall Plan began to fill the economic vacuum in Europe; the North Atlantic Pact and the rearmament programs began to fill the military vacuum. All this was part of what Kennan called the "long-term, patient but firm and vigilant containment of Russian expansive tendencies."

The first aim of the containment policy, it should be emphasized, was not to win a war: it was to contain communism without war. By creating and maintaining situations of strength in the free world, the United States proposed to show Moscow that Soviet power could not achieve its purposes. As the free world built up its strength, there would, or at least there should, come about a difference in the negotiating positions of East and West;

the realists in the Kremlin might be induced to recognize the new equilibrium of power; and the realities of power might guarantee that an agreement would last as at Yalta these realities had betrayed an agreement which did not reflect them. Or, if the Kremlin did not change, its position would become all the more insecure.

At first, the strength and unity of the free world were conceived largely in economic terms. Popular confidence in the American atomic monopoly pushed the military problem to the background; and, if the administration itself did not believe that the atomic bomb had the answer to all military contingencies and more than offset any Soviet advantages in conventional weapons, it was at any rate unwilling to tell the American people that this was not so. But in 1949 several developments severely damaged western military confidence. The Soviet Union achieved an atomic explosion; it began to develop a "peace" campaign designed to persuade our allies that the use of the atom bomb by us was the worst of all sins; and it augmented its already overpowering superiority in ground forces by adding the vast population of China to the Soviet realm.

These events compelled a reconsideration, not of the theory of American policy but of its application. If the United States were to continue its attempt both to restrain aggression and to avoid war, it must take immediate steps to restore the equilibrium of power, now tilted dangerously in Russia's direction. The National Security Council, after sober meditation, produced its famous paper, NSC No. 68. This plan called for the acceleration of American rearmament in anticipation of the build-up by the Russians of a stockpile of atom bombs.

In the balmy days of Louis Johnson, however, no one paid much attention to the NSC No. 68. On June 24, 1950, the United States had but ten and a half divisions in its Army; it had one armored division, one assembly line for B-36 bombers; its tactical air power was inadequate; its radar net was leaky. But June 25 changed all that. In the months after Korea, particularly in the months after the Chinese intervention, the build-up proceeded with speed and efficiency.

Now this policy required special qualities of patience, firmness, steadiness and understanding to make it work and keep it working. More than that, it required certain convictions: a belief in the grand coalition; a belief in the limited war as an instrument of policy; a belief in a concentration on the essential enemy and on that part of the world most needed by that enemy to perfect his war-making capacity. It is on these points above all that American policy was directly and insistently challenged in the spring of 1951. MacArthur denied that the Soviet Union is the essential enemy; he denied that Europe should have any special importance in American strategy; he denied the necessity of allies; he declared the limited war to be a species of appeasement. As the Secretary of State said, the challenge went down to bedrock.

The challenge was provoked, of course, by a difference in policy over the war in Korea. As the administration applied its theory of foreign policy to Korea, it saw in Korea one more incident in the larger struggle, greater and more costly than Berlin or Greece, but no more capable of producing a decisive result; if it might be a turning point, it still was not in itself a crucial contest. If Soviet Russia were the enemy (and, unlike MacArthur, most Americans did not have a doubt in the world what was "the source and brains" of the Communist conspiracy), then little was to be gained in investing major strength and resources in picking off satellites. "it is their third team opposing our first team," said General Wedemeyer in the hearings. If this were so, it would be a fool's game to throw away our whole first team on any engagement short of an engagement with the first team of the enemy.

While the containment policy calls for counterforce, it did not call for "maximum counterforce." It required rather what Kennan has described as "the adroit and vigilant application of counterforce at a series of constantly shifting geographical and political points, corresponding to the shifts and maneuvers of Soviet policy." It required, in other words, the use of limited force for

limited objectives, not the use of maximum force for the victory
for which there was no substitute. The objective was not to
destroy communism everywhere, a goal which would involve an
unlimited ideological crusade, or even to destroy the Soviet Union, a goal which could not be briefly attained without an atomic
holocaust; the objective was to punish aggression by lowering the
boom on individual experiments in aggression, while at the same
time refusing to generalize from the individual case to the total
war.

Korea had to remain a limited war: limited in its investment of
American forces, limited in its goals. "If anything is important,
if anything is true about the situation in Korea," Acheson said in
June 1951, "it is the overwhelming importance of not forcing a
showdown on our side in Korea and not permitting our opponents
to force a showdown." This, he went on to say, "has been the
whole heart and essence of the policy which the administration
has been following." Anything else would fatally disrupt the grand
design of American strategy. And here, of course, lay the true
danger in the MacArthur policy; for the doctrine of maximum
force and the corollary doctrine of no-substitute-for-victory
assumed that Korea was the decisive battleground, "the final crusade," that victory there was possible, that it should be won at
all cost, including the enlargement of the Asian war.

That MacArthur denied that his policy would enlarge the Asian
war seemed a fault in his own logic, not in the logic of his doctrines. He staked everything on the contention that defeating the
Chinese Communists within Korea would force Mao to sue for
peace and thus produce definite "victory." This was too easily
assumed: if China had entered the Korean War for motives of
self-protection, would not defeat in Korea increase rather than
relax Chinese determination to safeguard their homeland, their
revolution and their national survival? "Assume we embrace your
program," Senator Lyndon Johnson said to MacArthur in the
hearings, "and suppose that the Chinese were chased back across
the Yalu River, and suppose they refuse to sign a treaty and to

enter into an agreement on what their future actions will be, what course would you recommend at that stage?"

The General refused to entertain the Senator's premise. "Such a contingency," he said, "is a very hypothetical query. I can't quite see the possibility of the enemy being driven back across the Yalu and still being in a posture of offensive action. I don't believe that the hypothesis you draw is quite a reasonable and a rational one. If he ceases his depredations across the Yalu, the main purpose that we have is accomplished." Yet the Johnson hypothesis was not unreasonable; it may well have been probable; and MacArthur's last sentence suggested a curious nod toward the administration heresy that aggression, and not communism, was the enemy. The Senator returned to the attack.

JOHNSON: They go back across there, they still retain large mass formations there, what course are we going to have to take?
MACARTHUR: I don't think they could . . . I can't visualize an enemy who had been cleared of Korea staying in a state of belligerency . . . He would be subject to attack which might not only overturn the government in existence but might threaten the very security of segments of China, and that he would so recklessly defy the realisms by not accepting the defeat which would be entailed by his being forced to stop his aggressive action in Korea doesn't seem to me to be reasonable.

Yet what seemed reasonable to Douglas MacArthur might not seem reasonable to Mao Tse-tung. Maximum counterforce, far from ending the stalemate in Korea, would more probably have broadened and deepened it by involving the United States in war on the mainland against the enemy which refused to surrender when defeated on the peninsula. Similarly, if applied to crises in the past, maximum counterforce would almost invariably have expanded conflicts which both sides preferred to limit. The war in Greece from 1946 to 1949 resembled the Korean war in important respects. Communist-led guerrillas dominated the northern territory of Greece; whenever the government troops seriously threatened them, they would seek privileged sanctuary by escaping across the border into Yugoslavia or Bulgaria, where they would get hot coffee and a rubdown until they were ready to resume the war in Greece. General Van Fleet thus fought in Greece, as he would later fight in Korea, with one hand tied behind his back. The limited war, it should be noted, was a two-way affair: the enemy fought with one hand behind his back too; thus no Bulgarian or Yugoslav troops were committed, even as "volunteers," to the desperate war in Greece. (This was even true in Korea: while MacArthur protested the privileged sanctuary in Manchuria, he seemed to overlook his own privileged sanctuaries in Okinawa and in Japan.) Had MacArthur been supervising the Greek operations, he would presumably have denounced the limitations on his command; he would have advocated extending the war to Yugoslavia and Bulgaria. Maximum counterforce would similarly have altered the strategy of the Berlin airlift. From the American viewpoint, either such alteration would have been disastrous; Greece and Berlin were accounted two notable successes for the theory of limited-war.

MacArthur argued for the unlimited objective of fighting communism everywhere, without allowing that one spot may be more important than any other; this might well call for a full commitment of American strength in Korea. But the government's objective of responding to Soviet aggression demanded a more specific analysis of what Soviet requirements are for waging a modern war. Global considerations made MacArthur impatient: "Senator, I have asked you several times not to involve me in anything except my own area," he said irritably to McMahon. "My concepts on global defense are not what I am here to testify on. I don't pretend to be the authority now on those things." Yet the government could not escape so easily. For it there was a most pointed question: what, in hard fact, did Soviet Russia need before it would be in a position to confront the free world with the ultimate challenge?

This analysis bore significantly on the interpretation of the Korean war, for it issued in the firm conclusion that Asia was less important to Soviet Russia than was Europe, no matter where the fighting starts. From Asia Russia could get, no doubt, land and peasants. But Russia was already well stocked with land and peasants; and nothing in Asia repaired its glaring deficiencies. Industrial statistics told the story. Western Europe in 1951 exceeded the entire Soviet Union in the raw ingredients of power: in steel capacity, in industrial plant, in shipbuilding facilities, in electrical and chemical output, in skilled labor, in scientific and technical knowledge. The conquest of Western Europe would more than double Soviet capacities in each one of these fields. In no other way could the U.S.S.R. hope in this generation to match American industrial power. For these reasons alone, the administration was prepared to accord Europe an absolute priority over Asia in the allocation of American resources. "I believe that if we lose Western Europe," Admiral Sherman testified in the hearings, ". . . we would have an increasingly difficult time in holding our own. Whereas if we lost all of the Asiatic mainland, we could still survive and build up and possibly get it back again."

These hard facts were decisive—quite apart from what some seemed to regard as the soft fact that, for better or worse, we are in and of the civilization of the West, not the civilization of the East. Whatever doubt there might have been about official policy in this matter was resolved when Louis Johnson, who was said to have strong feelings in the MacArthur direction, was replaced as Secretary of Defense in September 1950 by a man noted for his belief that Europe was our first concern and that Russia would be the only victor in an all-out Chinese-American war. From the time of General Marshall's appointment, there could be no doubt that, while opportunity or duty may sometimes call us east, it is in Europe, if anywhere, that our dearest values will be saved. The conflict between democracy and communism would be settled on the continent which gave birth to both ideas.

The belief in the European priority was strengthened by the twin facts that the containment policy assumed the existence of a coalition, and the only reliable basis for such a coalition was to be found, not in Asia, but in Europe. Again, hard facts were decisive for those who might regard a moral or cultural concern for others as soft and sentimental. The cutting edge of the containment policy was strategic air power; and the effective application of strategic air power required the use of bases near to the Soviet Union. The B-36, it is true, could, with the aid of new refueling techniques, fly from the continental United States to Russia and return. But the B-36 was an extremely expensive plane, difficult to produce, difficult to operate; our supply of them was limited.* The main reliance of the Strategic Air Force had to be on medium range bombers, like the B-29; and these bombers could operate against the Soviet Union only from secondary bases. With the exception of the Alaska bases, all the bases upon which our strategic air superiority depended were made available to us through alliances.

Air bases constituted one hard fact; manpower, another. How could the United States, with about 6 per cent of the world's population, hope by itself to rid the world of communism? Raw materials were another hard fact: the United States was almost wholly dependent on imports from overseas for such vital materials as tin, natural rubber, chrome, manganese, industrial diamonds, hard fibers and asbestos; it also required very large imports of copper, lead, zinc, tungsten, uranium and wool. How could the United States hope to outlast the U.S.S.R. unless it established its military strength on the broadest possible foundations in terms of manpower, raw materials and strategic bastions? "The thing that the Kremlin fears most," the President had said, "is the unity of the free world."

Senator McMahon, having discovered that General MacArthur was hard put to recall the meaning of "collective security," asked

* On July 10, 1951, we had only 87 B-36's ready for action, according to testimony leaked from a closed hearing of the House Armed Services Committee. About 60 more were in process of modernization; two to three new ones a month were coming off the production lines. Clearly this was terribly inadequate for a sustained bombing offensive which must expect a high rate of attrition.

General Marshall whether he did not think that the common use with allies of certain porticns of the geography of the earth was of the utmost importance to a defense of the United States. "I would think so absolutely, sir," Marshall replied; "and that is the principle of collective security, which is the only principle that we think can carry us to peace."*

MacArthur's Korean policy thus seemed fatal to the purposes of American policy. If followed, it would have divested us of allies, destroying the grand coalition on which our national security rested; it would have involved us, in Bradley's phrase, in the wrong war in the wrong place at the wrong time against the wrong enemy; it would have wrecked our global strategy in the hope of achieving a magnificent success in a local engagement. American foreign policy, on the other hand, assuming, as Mac-Arthur did not, that time was on our side, sought in Korea to play for time—time to mobilize, time to rearm ourselves and our allies, time to bring into production new weapons and equipment and test their use, time for Europe to recover and rearm, time to build an ever-widening circle of allies and friendly neutrals, time for discontent to ferment within the sphere of Soviet power. "The basic premise of our foreign policy," Secretary Acheson said in the hearings, "is that time is on our side if we make good use of it."

Harry Truman had tried to make this point to MacArthur. In

---

* It is perhaps relevant to point out that Marshall referred here to "the principle of collective security," not to the United Nations. This did not suggest a want of faith in the United Nations, which the administration regarded as the best existing vehicle for collective security. It did perhaps suggest, however, that the United States was more interested in the substance than in the form of the grand coalition. The State Department had long believed, in an argument first put forward by Benjamin V. Cohen, the then counsellor, in 1946, that our primary commitment was to the Charter of the United Nations, not to the machinery, and that, if it became impossible to fulfill our obligations to the Charter through the machinery of the U.N., we must be prepared to act outside the machinery. Marshall did not imply, in other words, that we had forever consigned our view of our national security to a majority of the General Assembly. He did say that we could not adequately protect our national security without the co-operation and support of other nations through the world.

his telegram of January 13, 1951, he had sought patiently to explain "something of what is in our minds regarding the political factors." Through successful resistance in Korea, we could help "produce a free world coalition of incalculable value to the national security interests of the United States"; our action "should be such as to consolidate the great majority of the United Nations"; we must avoid steps, plausible in themselves, which might bring war to Japan or Western Europe; the "main threat" was the Soviet Union—all these propositions, so fundamental to the defense of American interests, were regarded with boredom, when not with exasperation, by General MacArthur. For General Bradley, Korea was "just one engagement, just one phase" of a continuing battle; for MacArthur it was the pay-off.

No one regarded this policy as infallible. "I am under no illusion," Bradley testified, "that our present strategy of using means short of total war to achieve our ends and oppose communism is a guarantee that a world war will not be thrust upon us. But a policy of patience and determination without provoking world war, while we improve our military power, is one which we believe we must continue to follow." This was fundamental: above all, American policy assumed that there is a sizable difference between an armed truce and an atomic war; it rejected the easy fatalism that general war was inevitable. "The dimness of our vision," Kennan wrote, "gives us the right neither to a total optimism nor to a total pessimism. . . . Our duty to ourselves and to the hopes of mankind lies in avoiding, like the soul of evil itself, that final bit of impatience which tells us to yield the last positions of hope before we have been pressed from them by unanswerable force."

In some quarters, of course, talk of this sort sounded like appeasement; it bordered on what *Life* magazine called the "pernicious fallacy . . . the pap of 'co-existence' with Soviet communism." Yet supporters of government policy could draw comfort from a veteran foe of appeasement. As Winston Churchill had put it in his war memoirs:

Those who are prone by temperament and character to seek sharp and clear-cut solutions of difficult and obscure problems, who are ready to fight whenever some challenge comes from a foreign power, have not always been right. On the other hand, those whose inclination is to . . . seek patiently and faithfully for peaceful compromise, are not always wrong. On the contrary, in the majority of instances they may be right, not only morally but from a practical standpoint. How many wars have been averted by patience and persisting good will! . . . How many wars have been precipitated by firebrands!"

Certainly by 1951, the results appeared more than to justify the policy. "Seen from here," the *Economist* of London reported in June 1951, "the American foreign policy of the last four years seems to have been intelligent, consistent, courageous and in a high degree successful." To say that it had been successful was not to say that it had succeeded; for the policy, in its nature, could not produce decisive results in a short period. Yet consider its achievements: the economic revival of Western Europe; the encouragement of Tito's split with Moscow; the Berlin airlift; the recovery of Western Germany; the end of civil war in Greece; the recession of the Communist threat in France and Italy; the beginnings of European rearmament; the steps toward European unification; the resistance to aggression in Korea. "Can anybody reasonably doubt," asked the *Economist*, "that, if similar courage had been shown in the years between 1933 and 1939, Hitler's war would never have happened?" The whole free world had played its part in developing this policy; "but the ideas, the money and the resolution have come from the Americans, and if the chances of avoiding war are greater today than they were in, say, 1938, it is to the American Administration that the major credit belongs."

The government, from President Truman down, seemed to know its mind well enough.* But the tragedy of the administra-

---

* In view of the fact that there was only one President while there were four Secretaries of State and three Secretaries of Defense, perhaps Mr. Truman deserves some small credit for the development and the continuity of American foreign policy.

tion was that so few other Americans understood what it was up to. Of course, the isolationists, whether old-fashioned or mid-century, could not be expected to sympathize. But even friends of the administration criticized the foreign policy as "negative" and as lacking in dynamism; or else as overestimating the material strength of America, or as overrating its psychological fortitude.

Some of this was a stale and sterile repetition of liberal clichés devised for the day when Cordell Hull was Secretary of State, and devotedly maintained in the face of later realities. The Truman Doctrine was supposed to be a blank check for reaction; yet the governments of Greece and of Turkey were far more democratic in 1951 than they had been in 1947. The Marshall Plan was supposed to freeze the status quo in Europe; yet it set Western Europe upon its most astonishing experiment in regional collaboration—an experiment which the European Payments Union and the Schuman Plan were only the first glowing manifestations. The North Atlantic Pact was supposed to cast the future of Europe in narrow military terms; yet it looked in 1951 as if it might lay the foundations for the political unification of Western Europe. Concessions to Franco and Chiang Kai-shek were not sought by the administration; they were forced upon it by the Congress. Far from being committed to a "negative" foreign policy, the United States never in its history had launched in peacetime a foreign policy so vigorous in its defense of American principles.

Other criticisms were more cogent. Walter Lippmann, for example, argued that the logic of containment must lead inexorably to a foolish dispersion of limited resources. If American power were to respond to every Soviet incitement, running one day to Iran, the next to Tibet, the next to Spitzbergen frantically plugging holes in the dike, like Charlie Chaplin trying to keep up with the accelerated assembly line, then the Soviet Union, with its interior lines of communication, could quickly enfeeble us, exhaust us, and drive us batty. Certainly, if the containment policy were to be construed in a doctrinaire way, Mr. Lippmann's argument was unanswerable. But, in practice, the problems tended to answer themselves. No one, for example, advocated the American defense of Tibet against Chinese invasion; on the other hand, the invasion of West Germany or of Yugoslavia, whether by the Soviet Union or by its satellites, would almost certainly have been resisted by the United States. The number of danger spots in between might be unlimited geographically, but they were limited practically. No one (except MacArthur) argued for global containment; selective containment, at least of the kind practiced from 1947 to 1951, seemed well within the limits of our capabilities.

Or at least within the limits of our physical capabilities. The graver question was whether it is within the limits of American emotional capabilities. Were the American people prepared for the long, burdensome years of the armed truce? Everyone agreed that they would do anything and everything in case of all-out war; but total mobilization was far simpler and easier than partial mobilization. Would not their patience at length give out at having to endure controls and constraints with no visible termination point ahead? Would they not come to feel, in a mood of exasperation and disgust, that it was better to get it over with than to live any longer in the constraint and tension of perpetual crisis?

The situation was complicated by the problem of conducting a sustained foreign policy in a democracy—a problem not peculiar to the American democracy in the late forties and early fifties, but existing there in a form of peculiar aggravation. The Truman administration had been confronted with a series of crises requiring speedy action. To stir congressmen, largely convinced that the paramount national issue was high taxes, from their complacence and lethargy, it had been necessary to shock and scare them. The Truman Doctrine message, for example, was far more melodramatic and portentous than the minor request for 300 million dollars for Greek-Turkish aid justified. Each further crisis had to be redoubled in order to seize the flickering attention of Congress: had Vishinsky and Gromyko not collaborated, Truman would long since have lost his voice with screaming and shouting.

The administration, by the careful employment of these tactics, managed to get just enough to keep its foreign policy afloat. But it was, in the idiom of Missouri, a hell of a way to run a railroad. At first people were jerked to a state of artificial exaltation from which they hurriedly relapsed to normal, like the backsliders after the revivalist has left town: thus when things were going badly in Korea, General Marshall was denounced in Congress for not getting war orders out fast enough, and, when things were going better, he was denounced for thinking that so much had to be ordered. Then, after a time, the constant clamor began to have its effect; people began to be persuaded that we were, in fact, at war and that consequently we should win it as speedily as possible, with no holds barred. Either attitude would run athwart the administration policy: many opponents of the administration, moreover, contrived to hold both.

In part, this condition was a failure in leadership, a failure in political education. President Truman had the great virtue of rising to occasions; he lacked the greater virtue of transcending them. His qualities were those of a Polk rather than a Jackson or a Roosevelt, of an Attlee rather than a Churchill. He made all the necessary decisions with great and simple courage; but he lacked the gift of illuminating them so that the people as a whole could understand their necessity. Because he did not succeed in making mid-century America comprehend its place in the great stream of history, however much he comprehended that place himself, he did not dispel the deep and agonized popular confusion. Americans could not understand why six years after the end of one great war they seemed to be on the verge of another. Since the administration did not explain this to them in terms of the deep-running moral and historical necessities, it was helpless before those who explained it in terms of bungling or of conspiracy.

Senator McCarthy's*—and later General MacArthur's—success in commanding the public ear were a measure of President Truman's failure to set forth convincingly to the American people why they were in the fix they were in. Above all, he failed to persuade them that they must learn to live with crisis.

Yet this was not a failure in policy; it was a failure in the communication of policy. One clear result of the MacArthur hearings was to improve popular understanding, not alone of the complexities of Far Eastern policy, but of the whole precise and delicate course to which the United States had committed itself. To that degree, the hearings alleviated somewhat the fear that simple impatience and simple misunderstanding might force the administration's hand and project the country and the world into atomic war. And, if atomic war were avoided, the opportunity remained that time and experience might attenuate the hostility between the democratic and communist worlds. The role of American policy, George Kennan suggested, was to seek out ways to "promote tendencies which must eventually find their outlet in either the break-up or the gradual mellowing of Soviet power." Certainly the internal contradictions of the Soviet regime were more acute than the internal contradictions of our own; nor at any of the great watersheds of history had it been possible to predict how the urgent dilemmas of the present would uncoil themselves in the future.

Because history is indeterminate, it is impossible ever to say

---

* In the long run, Senator McCarthy had a graver effect on American foreign policy than General MacArthur; and the State Department's most damaging failure may seem to be not any failure in foreign policy, but its failure to fight hard for its own against McCarthyism. The retreat before the McCarthy assault—with the public suspension of leading foreign service officers —resulted in a marked diminution of candor and outspokenness in State Department reports from the field. No one is going out on a limb when he expects that Senator McCarthy or his imitators will be freely permitted to hack the limb off, whether now or ten years from now. A premium is placed on intellectual indecision and cowardice which may cost this country dearly in the future. If McCarthyism remains unchecked, the Washington *Post* has suggested, there will be nobody left in the foreign service "except eunuchs and dimwits."

there is no alternative to war. The central object of policy has to be somehow to keep the thread of civilization alive—to avert war, if possible, but to be prepared for war, if necessary. The United States has unique obligations to the free world, as the largest and richest of free nations. It can fulfill those obligations only if it lives up to its own highest values—only if it achieves in its own inner life that vitality and clarity and serenity which are the best consequence of freedom and its surest bulwark. In the end, unless this nation repeals all its traditions and sets forth on a course of undisguised imperialism, American influence and power will stand or fall on the impression it offers to the world—not the impression projected in its propaganda broadcasts, but the impression communicated by the spirit, purpose and actuality of national life. After the confusions of the MacArthur debate of 1951 were swept away, there was reason to hope that the impression would be clearer, more faithful and more appealing.

Documentary Material

I. TEXT OF THE TRUMAN-MacARTHUR WAKE ISLAND CONFERENCE* DOCUMENT

as Released by the Senate Armed Services and Foreign Relations Committee

The following were at the table: The President; General of the Army Douglas MacArthur; Adm. Arthur W. Radford, commander in chief United States Pacific Fleet; Ambassador John Muccio; Secretary of the Army Frank Pace; Col. A. L. Hamblen; Ambassador-at-Large Philip C. Jessup; General of the Army Omar N. Bradley; Assistant Secretary of State Dean Rusk; Mr. W. Averell Harriman.

The President asked Gen. MacArthur to state the rehabilitation situation with reference to Korea.

Gen. MacArthur:

It cannot occur until the military operations have ended. I believe that formal resistance will end throughout North and South Korea by Thanksgiving. There is little resistance left in South Korea—only about 15,000 men—and those we do not destroy, the winter will. We now have about 60,000 prisoners in compounds.

In North Korea, unfortunately, they are pursuing a forlorn hope. They have about 100,000 men who were trained as replacements. They are poorly trained, led and equipped, but they are obstinate and it goes against my grain to have to destroy them. They are only fighting to save face. Orientals prefer to die rather than to lose face.

I am now driving with the 1st Cavalry Division up the line to Pyongyang, I am thinking of making up a tank and truck column and sending it up the road to take Pyongyang directly. It depends on the

* The Conference took place on October 15, 1950.

intelligence we get in the next forty-eight hours. We have already taken Wonsan, I am landing the X Corps, which will take Pyongyang in one week. The North Koreans are making the same mistake they have made before. They have not deployed in depth. When the gap is closed the same thing will happen in the North as happened in the South.

It is my hope to be able to withdraw the 8th Army to Japan by Christmas. That will leave the X Corps, which will be reconstituted, composed of the 2d and 3d Divisions and U. N. detachments. I hope the U. N. will hold elections by the first of the year. Nothing is gained by military occupation. All occupations are failures. (The President nodded agreement.) After elections are held I expect to pull out all occupying troops. Korea should have about ten divisions with our equipment, supplemented by small but competent air force and also by a small but competent navy. If we do that, I will not only secure Korea but it will be a tremendous deterrent to the Chinese Communists moving south. This is a threat that cannot be laughed off.

Again I emphasize the fact that the military should get out the minute the guns stop shooting and civilians take over.

Korea is a land of poverty. It has been knocked down for a long time and a little money goes a long way. Houses are made of mud and bamboo. When knocked down they can be put up in two weeks.

An estimate was made by E. C. A. of the cost of rehabilitation and it was estimated to be $900,000,000. Another estimate was made locally and it placed the cost at about one and one-half billion dollars. I believe these estimates are far too high. I do not believe that you can absorb and spend in Korea much more than $150,000,000 a year.

I believe three years of that will place Korea on its feet and not only make Korea self-sustaining but give a higher living standard. I believe that half a billion dollars spread over three to five years will more than make up the destruction.

Ambassador Muccio:

The general has made an important point. Korea's capacity to absorb is limited. This applies to the economic field and to other fields. We should emphasize the mental and psychological rehabilitation more than the economic.

The northern area has been under complete domination for five years. This is the first time we have moved into an area that has been dominated by Communists. We have a challenging opportunity. I want to see more emphasis on the education and information field than in the material rehabilitation.

The economy of Korea is basically a very simple one. I believe with the general that $150,000,000 a year is all she can absorb. (Turning to Gen. MacArthur) Is the cost of the armed forces included in that estimate?

Gen. MacArthur: No. Equipment and military forces are not included.

Secretary Pace: Is the directive the President sent sufficiently comprehensive?

Gen. MacArthur: Yes.

Secretary Pace: What, generally, are the critical and over-all requirements of the Army during this period? We are in a critical financial situation. Our day of reckoning is going to come in the form of a supplemental in December.

Gen. MacArthur: You give us forty days, sixty if necessary. We will have that estimate in sixty days. That will be about thirty days from now. This, you understand, is going to be some speculative guesswork, but will be accurate to within 25 per cent.

Secretary Pace: When the Army's responsibility ends, could the Army provide aid in psychological rehabilitation? Should K. M. A. G. [Korean Military Assistance Group] continue?

Gen. MacArthur: The K. M. A. G. group has been wonderful. As far as the military mission is concerned, I think it should be continued indefinitely. I want to pay high tribute to that group. I believe that 500 officers and men should be continued indefinitely. At the start of rehabilitation the Army will have to continue until the civil rehabilitation is organized. It should be organized as rapidly as possible. The U. N. should take it over. You will have a hard job getting good men to serve in Korea. It is not a nice place.

Secretary Pace: In the period of rehabilitation Gen. Walker can assess the leadership qualities of the R. O. K. men to take over civilian leadership.

Gen. MacArthur: Mr. Muccio knows more about this than I do and the Embassy has a thorough knowledge of the Koreans.

Ambassador Muccio: The Koreans are very obstinate. They have been pushed around so long they don't like it. They are convinced that we do not want Korea. The mission has done a great job training the young Koreans. They have pushed aside the old Chinese- and Japanese-trained Koreans. * * * [Asterisks here and hereafter represent censorship deletions.]

Mr. Rusk: Is it undesirable to turn K. M. A. G. into a U. N. operation? Would that spoil its effect?

Gen. MacArthur: From a political point of view it would be okay, but militarily there must be unity of doctrine. The others have different doctrines than we have.

Mr. Rusk: We might be able to work it out by using small numbers of other nationals or by getting the U. N. to ask the U. S. to take it on a contract basis. The other question I had was that we would like to see military responsibility for relief and rehabilitation end, and would also like to see the U. S. operation moved over to the U. N. On the other hand, the U. N. is trying to do something it has never done before. It is going to have some responsibility never before undertaken on the same scale. It may be necessary for an organization like E. C. A. to stand by and resume some of the responsibilities. It is fair for us to assume the basic installations of the country—railroads, water, etc.— will be in adequate use before the U. N. takes over?

Gen. MacArthur: I believe a good deal of that will be done. I believe lots will remain to be done to put them back in good condition. The Army, the minute it takes a city, gets them going, but it is only temporary. E. C. A. is continuing to do that. The president sent a letter last week to Mr. Foster and told them to go ahead with the long-term rehabilitation. E. C. A. should continue to function.

Ambassador Muccio: Heavy industries, railroads and utilities should be taken over by the Koreans and not wait for the U. N. to get in. The railroad from Pusan to Yongdungpo was put in operation within one week.

The President: What about utilities and railroads?

Gen. MacArthur: It will undoubtedly take time to put utilities back in operation. The E. C. A. is continuing to function.

Ambassador Muccio: The Army has done well operating railroads. E. C. A. has helped. The Army has had the means and has done a great job with E. C. A., putting water and trains in operation. A group of transportation men who have been with the railroad company have been most helpful. Fortunately, he had an E. C. A. man who had worked on new development for waterworks and within a short while he had water running in Seoul. A considerable number of new locomotives have been brought in.

Secretary Pace: Is there anything in terms of E. C. A. and Army co-operation that we might do to help you?

Gen. MacArthur: No commander in the history of war has ever had more complete and adequate support from all agencies in Washington than I have.

Ambassador Jessup: In regard to the figures which you suggested on the needs, does that include the cost of reconstructing industrial plants in the North?

Gen. MacArthur: Yes, except munitions making. Those plants I would not include.

Mr. Rusk: To what extent is the other side stripping plants?

Gen. MacArthur: They have to some extent. In Inchon I saw at least twenty flat cars which were loaded up with crated factory gadgets which they had not been able to get out. The North Koreans were not in the south long enough to do more than ordinary looting. I believe, however, that industry has not been seriously damaged in North Korea.

Mr. Harriman: Could we hear more about psychological rehabilitation?

Ambassador Muccio: Bring in the Koreans more. They know their own people better than we do. We should provide them with radios and text books and also scientific guidance. . . .

Mr. Harriman: What about the psychological differences between North and South Koreans?

Ambassador Muccio: Koreans are Koreans. There is no basic difference between them. Eighty per cent of them are farmers. There is no basic schism between North and South Koreans except for a few politicos and intellectuals.

Mr. Harriman: What about the 2,000,000 who came down south?

Ambassador Muccio: They were, generally, people of some means. They will be going back to North Korea and will be very helpful to us.

Gen. Bradley: What can you do with the 60,000 prisoners you now have?

Gen. MacArthur: They are the happiest Koreans in all Korea. For the first time they are well fed and clean. They have been deloused and have good jobs for which they are being paid under the Geneva Convention. I believe there is no real split, but their attitude is due only to the banner that flies over them. There is no difference in ideology and there are no North and South Korean blocs.

The President: How will Syngman Rhee take the idea of the election?

Gen. MacArthur: He won't like it.

Ambassador Muccio: The last election was an honest election, about as honest as any ever held in the Far East. How are you going to ignore that? I hope the new commission will not interpret that as requiring a nationwide election. How are you going to ignore members of the National Assembly is a major problem. The resolution was so worded that it could be interpreted in different ways. There have never been local elections or elections for provincial governors. These could be held.

Mr. Rusk: We must not undermine the present Korean government. I think it may be possible to have your local and by-elections in the South and elections in the North, and then it will be almost time for the 1952 elections throughout the country. I think it will require a good deal of patience.

Mr. Harriman: How about the interim period between elections?

Gen. MacArthur: North Korea will be under military control. The U. N. resolution calls for the maintenance of local governments wherever possible. * * * Local government will be maintained by appointing local officials recommended by R. O. K. officials.

Ambassador Muccio: There is also the problem of currency to use and what land reform laws to retain in North Korea.

Gen. MacArthur: In the interim the military will freeze land tenure, banks and currency. I will keep the North Korean currency. I will keep the North Korean currency in effect in North Korea without setting a rate to the dollar or R. O. K. won until the civilian government can take over.

The President: What are the chances for Chinese or Soviet interference?

Gen. MacArthur: Very little. Had they interfered in the first or second months it would have been decisive. We are no longer fearful of their intervention. We no longer stand hat in hand. The Chinese have 300,000 men in Manchuria. Of these probably not more than 100/125,000 are distributed along the Yalu River. Only 50/60,000 could be gotten across the Yalu River. They have no air force. Now that we have bases for our Air Force in Korea, if the Chinese tried to get down to Pyongyang there would be the greatest slaughter.

With the Russians it is a little different. They have an air force in Siberia and a fairly good one, with excellent pilots equipped with some jets and B-25 and B-29 planes. They can put 1,000 planes in the air with some 2/300 more than the 5th and 7th Soviet fleets. They are probably no match for our Air Force. The Russians have no ground troops available for North Korea. They would have difficulty in putting troops into the field. It would take six weeks to get a division across, and six weeks brings the winter. The only other combination would be Russian air support of Chinese ground troops. Russian air is deployed in a semicircle through Mukden and Harbin, but the co-ordination between the Russian air and the Chinese ground would be so flimsy that I believe Russian air would bomb the Chinese as often as they would bomb us. Ground support is a very difficult thing to do. Our Marines do it perfectly. They have been trained for it. Our own air and ground forces are not as the Marines, but they are effective. Between untrained air and ground forces an air umbrella is impossible without a lot of joint training. I believe it just wouldn't work with Chinese Communist ground and Russian air. We are the best.

Mr. Harriman: What about war criminals?

Gen. MacArthur: Don't touch the war criminals. It doesn't work. The Nurnberg trials and Tokyo trials were no deterrent. In my own right I can handle those who have committed atrocities and, if we catch them, I intend to try them immediately by military commission.

The President: Another subject—what is your idea about a Japanese peace treaty without including Russia and Communist China?

Gen. MacArthur: I would call a conference at once and invite them. If they don't come in, go ahead. After the treaty is drawn up, submit to them a draft of the treaty and if they don't sign, go ahead with the treaty. The Japanese deserve a treaty. ° ° ° The present draft of the treaty by the State Department is very good. After friction with the Joint Chiefs of Staff it has been polished until it shines like a diamond. It will call for the security of Japan to be secured by the United Nations with the United States acting as the agency of the U. N. until the U. N. is in a position to do it itself.

The President: Would we have to maintain three or four divisions in Japan until the Japanese can secure themselves?

Gen. MacArthur: I should say that they would have to be maintained there for several years. At the present time the Japanese, in accordance with the laws of war, furnish a great many things for those troops. They put up $300,000,000 a year. This includes barracks, lights, etc. When this treaty of peace is made I believe this should be changed. The troops should pay their way. We should pay rental, etc. The Japanese would not object if they didn't have to pay the bills for the support of these divisions.

Gen. Bradley: Will the Japanese who have kept the faith while our troops were gone expect to receive different treatment from the troops when they return from Korea?

Gen. MacArthur: Omar, there is complete camaraderie between the troops and the Japanese. The Japanese like our troops. I think that the presence of the troops means prosperity. They spend money and bring in so much. The 8th Army was pulled out of occupation in January. When they come back they will have nothing to do with occupation.

Gen. Bradley: The 8th Army is returning to Japan soon. We have the problem of getting additional troops to Europe. As it now stands it will be April before we can get a division into Europe. Could the 2d or the 3d Division be made available to be sent over to Europe by January?

Gen. MacArthur: Yes, I will make one available by January. I would recommend that the 2d Division be selected, as it is a veteran division, better trained, and would make a better impression.

Secretary Pace: Would Garioa end with the peace treaty?

Gen. MacArthur: Yes, Japan will be self-sufficient in 1952, treaty or no treaty.

Secretary Pace: Should S. C. A. P. continue after the treaty of peace?

Gen. MacArthur: S. C. A. P. should completely cease. I think these troops should be directly controlled by the Department of Defense, just like the troops in the United States, and their relationship with the Japanese should be the same as garrisons in America. I don't think they should have anything to do with political aspects. S. C. A. P. should discontinue entirely. I told Mr. Dulles I believed I could sell that to the Japanese. ° ° ° I think the text drawn up by the State Department is a very fine treaty.

Mr. Rusk: In connection with those troops moving back from Korea to Japan, ideally, we should have a peace treaty before military occupations in Korea wind up, but your operations in Korea are going faster than the diplomats can go in getting a treaty.

Gen. MacArthur: I hope to get the 8th Army back by Christmas. . . .

Mr. Rusk: We cannot meet that. Should you let the Japanese know we are going to have a peace treaty and make a statement to the Japanese about the treaty to facilitate the return of the troops?

Gen. MacArthur: Your thought is a good one. Last January I made some statement along those lines. . . .

Mr. Harriman: Should we begin to pay some of the expenses of occupation on return from Korea?

Gen. MacArthur: Averell, that is what we should do. If we do this we can stop the Garioa. We are taking more out than we are putting in. It is not the Japanese fault that we do not have a treaty. It is an iniquitous thing that we are taking more out than we are putting in. It is a breach among the Allies which prevents a treaty. Three years ago they did everything we asked and we have a moral obligation to them. If we pay our way in Japan for part of the cost of the troops in lieu of Garioa funds, this might be a satisfactory arrangement if it can be worked out.

Secretary Pace: I certainly think it merits consideration and no doubt it would have great psychological benefits. We have both internal problems in the Department of Defense and also with the Appropriations Committee of Congress. This isn't a final view, but my personal opinion is that it should be given consideration.

Gen. MacArthur: I am sure that you are right. Congress will not like it. All Congressional groups who came over wanted to swallow up more from the Japanese economy.

The President: You and State get together and work it out and bring it to me for approval.

Secretary Pace: Or disapproval. (Laughter.)

The President: I would like to hear your views, General, on a possible Pacific pact or some other arrangements similar to that in the Atlantic.

Gen. MacArthur: A Pacific pact would be tremendous, but due to the lack of homogeneity of the Pacific nations, it would be very difficult to put into effect. If the President would make an announcement like the Truman Doctrine, which would be a warning to the predatory nations, it would have a great effect. It is not possible to get a pact, since they are so nonhomogeneous. They have no military forces. Only the United States has the forces. All they want is the assurance of security from the United States. The President should follow up this conference with a ringing pronouncement. I believe that at this time, after the military successes and the President's trip, it would have more success than a Pacific pact.

Adm. Radford: I was in Manila last May during the conference Quirino called. I didn't attend the meetings but I spoke to a number of delegates. There was generally the same feeling that MacArthur brought out. They didn't feel they could get together but they would like to know in advance of any announcement. I am sure they would heartily agree but would like to be consulted. I believe such a pronouncement could be included in the U. N. speech and if they could be consulted, they would feel they were in on the ground floor. The peace will be upset again in six months if you do not take steps to stop it. We just have to face the facts of life. We must continue the policy followed in Korea to maintain the peace. The situation in Indo-China is the most puzzling of all as to what we can do or what we should do.

Mr. Harriman: When you speak of the Truman Doctrine, do you mean direct external aggression or do you mean the type of thing that has been going on in Indo-China and has previously occurred in Greece to which the Truman Doctrine was directed?

Gen. MacArthur: I am referring to direct aggression. * * *

The President: I have talked at some length with Gen. MacArthur about the situation in the Philippines. The General suggested that Mr. Dodge would be able to help out on this situation. I think if we could get him down there the job would be done.

Secretary Pace: Could he be spared?

Gen. MacArthur: He is doing a job now in Japan and about two or three months after he is through he could be spared.

The President: Gen. MacArthur and I have talked fully about Formosa. There is no need to cover that subject again. The General and I are in complete agreement. . . .

Gen. MacArthur: I want to take all non-Korean troops out of Korea as soon as possible. They ought to move out soon after the elections. The R. O. K. troops can handle the situation. The greatest calamity in Asia would be if the Koreans should turn against us as a result of some U. N. opposition to the Rhee government. They are quite capable of handling their own military affairs. It would be a pity if we turned them against us. I have been shaking in my boots ever since I saw the U. N. resolution which would treat them exactly on the same basis as the North Koreans. As Ambassador Muccio has said, the Koreans are a sensitive people and we might easily turn them against us. It would be bad to turn out of office a government which had stood up so well and taken such a beating, and to treat them just like the North Koreans. We have supported this government and suffered 27,000 casualties in doing so. They are a government duly elected under United Nations auspices and should not be let down.

The President: This cannot be done and should not be done. We must insist on supporting this government.

Mr. Rusk: We have been working and explaining our point of view in the United Nations but there has been an effective propaganda campaign against the Rhee government which has infected some of the U. N. delegations.

The President: We must make it plain that we are supporting the Rhee government and propaganda can "go to hell."

The President: I believe this covers the main topics. Secretary Pace, did you have anything else to take up?

Secretary Pace: Yes, sir, but I can take them up separately with Gen. MacArthur, and I imagine Gen. Bradley has some also.

The President: The communiqué should be submitted as soon as it is ready and Gen. MacArthur can return immediately. This has been a most satisfactory conference.

II. ADDRESS TO THE NATION
BY PRESIDENT TRUMAN

April 11, 1951

I want to talk plainly to you tonight about what we are doing in Korea and about our policy in the Far East.

In the simplest terms, what we are doing in Korea is this: We are trying to prevent a third world war.

I think most people in this country recognized that fact last June. And they warmly supported the decision of the Government to help the Republic of Korea against the Communist aggressors. Now, many persons, even some who applauded our decision to defend Korea, have forgotten the basic reason for our action.

It is right for us to be in Korea. It was right last June. It is right today.

I want to remind you why this is true.

The Communists in the Kremlin are engaged in a monstrous conspiracy to stamp out freedom all over the world. If they were to succeed, the United States would be numbered among their principal victims. It must be clear to everyone that the United States cannot—and will not—sit idly by and await foreign conquest. The only question is: When is the best time to meet the threat and how?

The best time to meet the threat is in the beginning. It is easier to put out a fire in the beginning when it is small than after it has become a roaring blaze.

And the best way to meet the threat of aggression is for the peace-loving nations to act together. If they don't act together, they are likely to be picked off, one by one.

If they had followed the right policies in the 1930's—if the free countries had acted together, to crush the aggression of the dictators, and if they had acted in the beginning, when the aggression was small —there probably would have been no World War II.

If history has taught us anything, it is that aggression anywhere in the world is a threat to peace everywhere in the world. When that aggression is supported by the cruel and selfish rulers of a powerful nation who are bent on conquest, it becomes a clear and present danger to the security and independence of every free nation.

This is a lesson that most people in this country have learned thoroughly. This is the basic reason why we joined in creating the United Nations. And since the end of World War II we have been putting that lesson into practice—we have been working with other free nations to check the aggressive designs of the Soviet Union before they can result in a third world war.

That is what we did in Greece, when that nation was threatened by the aggression of international communism.

The attack against Greece could have led to general war. But this country came to the aid of Greece. The United Nations supported Greek resistance. With our help, the determination and efforts of the Greek people defeated the attack on the spot.

Another big Communist threat to peace was the Berlin blockade. That too could have led to war. But again it was settled because free men would not back down in an emergency.

The aggression against Korea is the boldest and most dangerous move the Communists have yet made.

The attack on Korea was part of a greater plan for conquering all of Asia.

I would like to read to you from a secret intelligence report which came to us after the attack. It is a report of a speech a Communist army officer in North Korea gave to a group of spies and saboteurs last May, one month before South Korea was invaded. The report shows in great detail how this invasion was part of a carefully prepared plot. Here is part of what the Communist officer, who had been trained in Moscow, told his men: "Our forces," he said, "are scheduled to attack South Korean forces about the middle of June. . . . The coming attack on South Korea marks the first step toward the liberation of Asia."

Notice that he used the word "liberation." That is Communist doubletalk meaning "conquest."

I have another secret intelligence report here. This one tells what another Communist officer in the Far East told his men several months before the invasion of Korea. Here is what he said: "In order to successfully undertake the long awaited world revolution, we must first unify Asia. . . . Java, Indochina, Malaya, India, Tibet, Thailand, Philippines, and Japan are our ultimate targets. . . . The United States is the only obstacle on our road for the liberation of all countries in southeast Asia. In other words, we must unify the people of Asia and crush the United States."

That is what the Communist leaders are telling their people, and that is what they have been trying to do.

They want to control all Asia from the Kremlin.

This plan of conquest is in flat contradiction to what we believe. We believe that Korea belongs to the Koreans, that India belongs to the Indians—that all the nations of Asia should be free to work out their affairs in their own way. This is the basis of peace in the Far East and everywhere else.

The whole Communist imperialism is back of the attack on peace in the Far East. It was the Soviet Union that trained and equipped the North Koreans for aggression. The Chinese Communists massed 44 well-trained and well-equipped divisions on the Korean frontier. These were the troops they threw into battle when the North Korean Communists were beaten.

The question we have had to face is whether the Communist plan of conquest can be stopped without general war. Our Government and other countries associated with us in the United Nations believe that the best chance of stopping it without general war is to meet the attack in Korea and defeat it there.

That is what we have been doing. It is a difficult and bitter task.

But so far it has been successful.

So far, we have prevented World War III.

So far, by fighting a limited war in Korea, we have prevented aggression from succeeding and bringing on a general war. And the ability of the whole free world to resist Communist aggression has been greatly improved.

We have taught the enemy a lesson. He has found out that aggression is not cheap or easy. Moreover, men all over the world who want to remain free have been given new courage and new hope. They know now that the champions of freedom can stand up and fight and that they will stand up and fight.

Our resolute stand in Korea is helping the forces of freedom now fighting in Indochina and other countries in that part of the world. It has already slowed down the timetable of conquest.

In Korea itself, there are signs that the enemy is building up his ground forces for a new mass offensive. We also know that there have been large increases in the enemy's available air forces.

If a new attack comes, I feel confident it will be turned back. The United Nations fighting forces are tough and able and well equipped. They are fighting for a just cause. They are proving to all the world that the principle of collective security will work. We are proud of all these forces for the magnificent job they have done against heavy odds. We pray that their efforts may succeed, for upon their success may hinge the peace of the world.

The Communist side must now choose its course of action. The Communist rulers may press the attack against us. They may take further action which will spread the conflict. They have that choice, and with it the awful responsibility for what may follow. The Communists also have the choice of a peaceful settlement which could lead to a general relaxation of tensions in the Far East. The decision is theirs, because the forces of the United Nations will strive to limit the conflict if possible.

We do not want to see the conflict in Korea extended. We are trying to prevent a world war—not to start one. The best way to do that is to make it plain that we and the other free countries will continue to resist the attack.

But you may ask: Why can't we take other steps to punish the aggressor? Why don't we bomb Manchuria and China itself? Why don't we assist Chinese Nationalist troops to land on the mainland of China?

If we were to do these things we would be running a very grave risk of starting a general war. If that were to happen, we would have brought about the exact situation we are trying to prevent.

If we were to do these things, we would become entangled in a vast conflict on the continent of Asia and our task would become immeasurably more difficult all over the world.

What would suit the ambitions of the Kremlin better than for our military forces to be committed to a full-scale war with Red China?

It may well be that, in spite of our best efforts, the Communists may spread the war. But it would be wrong—tragically wrong—for us to take the initiative in extending the war.

The dangers are great. Make no mistake about it. Behind the North Koreans and Chinese Communists in the front lines stand additional millions of Chinese soldiers. And behind the Chinese stand the tanks, the planes, the submarines, the soldiers, and the scheming rulers of the Soviet Union.

Our aim is to avoid the spread of the conflict.

The course we have been following is the one best calculated to avoid an all-out war. It is the course consistent with our obligation to do all we can to maintain international peace and security. Our experience in Greece and Berlin shows that it is the most effective course of action we can follow.

First of all, it is clear that our efforts in Korea can blunt the will of the Chinese Communists to continue the struggle. The United Nations forces have put up a tremendous fight in Korea and have inflicted very heavy casualties on the enemy. Our forces are stronger now than they have been before. These are plain facts which may discourage the Chinese Communists from continuing their attack.

Second, the free world as a whole is growing in military strength every day. In the United States, in Western Europe, and throughout the world, free men are alert to the Soviet threat and are building their defenses. This may discourage the Communist rulers from continuing the war in Korea—and from undertaking new acts of aggression elsewhere.

If the Communist authorities realize that they cannot defeat us in Korea, if they realize it would be foolhardy to widen the hostilities beyond Korea, then they may recognize the folly of continuing their aggression. A peaceful settlement may then be possible. The door is always open.

Then we may achieve a settlement in Korea which will not compromise the principles and purposes of the United Nations.

I have thought long and hard about this question of extending the war in Asia. I have discussed it many times with the ablest military advisers in the country. I believe with all my heart that the course we are following is the best course.

I believe that we must try to limit the war to Korea for these vital reasons: to make sure that the precious lives of our fighting men are not wasted; to see that the security of our country and the free world is not needlessly jeopardized; and to prevent a third world war.

A number of events have made it evident that General MacArthur did not agree with that policy. I have therefore considered it essential to relieve General MacArthur so that there would be no doubt or confusion as to the real purpose and aim of our policy.

It was with the deepest personal regret that I found myself compelled to take this action. General MacArthur is one of our greatest military commanders. But the cause of world peace is more important than any individual.

The change in commands in the Far East means no change whatever in the policy of the United States. We will carry on the fight in Korea with vigor and determination in an effort to bring the war to a speedy and successful conclusion.

The new commander, Lieutenant General Matthew Ridgway, has already demonstrated that he has the great qualities of military leadership needed for this task.

We are ready, at any time, to negotiate for a restoration of peace in the area. But we will not engage in appeasement. We are only interested in real peace.

Real peace can be achieved through a settlement based on the following factors:

> One: the fighting must stop.
> Two: concrete steps must be taken to insure that the fighting will not break out again.
> Three: there must be an end to the aggression.

A settlement founded upon these elements would open the way for the unification of Korea and the withdrawal of all foreign forces.

In the meantime, I want to be clear about our military objective. We are fighting to resist an outrageous aggression in Korea. We are trying to keep the Korean conflict from spreading to other areas. But at the same time we must conduct our military activities so as to insure the security of our forces. This is essential if they are to continue the fight until the enemy abandons its ruthless attempt to destroy the Republic of Korea.

That is our military objective—to repel attack and to restore peace.

In the hard fighting in Korea, we are proving that collective action among nations is not only a high principle but a workable means of resisting aggression. Defeat of aggression in Korea may be the turning point in the world's search for a practical way of achieving peace and security.

The struggle of the United Nations in Korea is a struggle for peace.

The free nations have united their strength in an effort to prevent a third world war.

That war can come if the Communist rulers want it to come. But this Nation and its allies will not be responsible for its coming.

We do not want to widen the conflict. We will use every effort to prevent that disaster. And in so doing we know that we are following the great principles of peace, freedom, and justice.

III. ADDRESS BY GENERAL MacARTHUR

to a Joint Meeting of Congress, April 19, 1951

Mr. President, Mr. Speaker and distinguished members of the Congress:

I stand on this rostrum with a sense of deep humility and great pride —humility in the wake of those great American architects of our history who have stood here before me, pride in the reflection that this forum of legislative debate represents human liberty in the purest form yet devised.

Here are centered the hopes and aspirations and faith of the entire human race. I do not stand here as advocate for any partisan cause, for the issues are fundamental and reach quite beyond the realm of partisan consideration. They must be resolved on the highest plane of national interest if our course is to prove sound and our future protected.

I trust, therefore, that you will do me the justice of receiving that which I have to say as solely expressing the considered viewpoint of a fellow American.

I address you with neither rancor nor bitterness in the fading twilight of life with but one purpose in mind: to serve my country.

The issues are global and so interlocked that to consider the problems of one sector, oblivious to those of another, is but to court disaster for the whole.

While Asia is commonly referred to as the gateway to Europe, it is no less true that Europe is the gateway to Asia, and the broad influence of the one cannot fail to have its impact upon the other. There are those who claim our strength is inadequate to protect on both

270

fronts, that we can not divide our effort. I can think of no greater expression of defeatism.

If a potential enemy can divide his strength on two fronts, it is for us to counter his effort. The Communist threat is a global one. Its successful advance in one sector threatens the destruction of every other sector. You cannot appease or otherwise surrender to Communism in Asia without simultaneously undermining our efforts to halt its advance in Europe.

Beyond pointing out these general truisms, I shall confine my discussion to the general areas of Asia. Before one may objectively assess the situation now existing there, he must comprehend something of Asia's past and the revolutionary changes which have marked her course up to the present.

Long exploited by the so-called colonial powers, with little opportunity to achieve any degree of social justice, individual dignity, or a higher standard of life such as guided our own noble administration of the Philippines, the peoples of Asia found their opportunity in the war just past to throw off the shackles of colonialism, and now see the dawn of new opportunity, a heretofore unfelt dignity, and the self-respect of political freedom.

Mustering half of the earth's population and 60 per cent of its natural resources, these peoples are rapidly consolidating a new force, both moral and material, with which to raise the living standard and erect adaptations of the design of modern progress to their own distinct cultural environments.

Whether one adheres to the concept of colonization or not, this is the direction of Asian progress and it may not be stopped. It is a corollary to the shift of the world economic frontiers, as the whole epicenter of world affairs rotates back toward the area whence it started.

In this situation it becomes vital that our own country orient its policies in consonance with this basic evolutionary condition rather than pursue a course blind to the reality that the colonial era is now passed and the Asian peoples covet the right to shape their own free destiny. What they seek now is friendly guidance, understanding and support, not imperious direction; the dignity of equality and not the shame of subjugation. Their prewar standard of life, pitifully low, is infinitely lower now in the devastation left in war's wake.

World ideologies play little part in Asia thinking and are little understood. What the people strive for is the opportunity for a little more food in their stomachs, a little better clothing on their backs, and a little firmer roof over their heads, and the realization of the normal nationalist urge for political freedom.

These political-social conditions have but an indirect bearing upon our own national security but do form a backdrop to contemporary planning which must be thoughtfully considered if we are to avoid the pitfalls of unrealism.

Of more direct and immediate bearing upon our national security are the changes wrought in the strategic potential of the Pacific Ocean in the course of the past war. Prior thereto, the western strategic frontier of the United States lay on the littoral line of the Americas with an exposed island salient extending out through Hawaii, Midway and Guam to the Philippines.

That salient proved not an outpost of strength but an avenue of weakness along which the enemy could and did attack. The Pacific was a potential area of advance for any predatory force intent upon striking at the bordering land areas.

All this was changed by our Pacific victory. Our strategic frontier then shifted to embrace the entire Pacific Ocean, which became a vast moat to protect us as long as we held it.

Indeed, it acts as a protective shield for all of the Americas and all free lands of the Pacific Ocean area. We control it to the shores of Asia by a chain of islands extending in an arc from the Aleutians to the Marianas held by us and our free allies.

From this island chain we can dominate with sea and air power every Asiatic port from Vladivostok to Singapore—with sea and air power, as I said, every port from Vladivostok to Singapore—and prevent any hostile movement into the Pacific. Any predatory attack from Asia must be an amphibious effort. No amphibious force can be successful without control of the sea lanes and the air over those lanes in its avenue of advance.

With naval and air supremacy and modest ground elements to defend bases, any major attack from continental Asia toward us or our friends in the Pacific would be doomed to failure. Under such conditions the Pacific no longer represents menacing avenues of approach for a prospective invader. It assumes instead the friendly aspect of a peaceful lake.

Our line of defense is a natural one and can be maintained with a minimum of military effort and expense. It envisions no attack against anyone, nor does it provide the bastions essential for offensive operations, but properly maintained would be an invincible defense against aggression.

The holding of this littoral defense in line in the Western Pacific is entirely dependent upon holding all segments thereof. For any major breach of this line by an unfriendly power would render vulnerable to determined attack every other major segment.

This is a military estimate as to which I have yet to find a military leader who will take exception.

For that reason I have strongly recommended in the past as a matter of military urgency that under no circumstances must Formosa fall under Communist control.

Such an eventuality would at once threaten the freedom of the Philippines and the loss of Japan, and might well force our western frontier back to the coast of California, Oregon and Washington.

To understand the changes which now appear upon the Chinese mainland, one must understand the changes in Chinese character and culture over the past 50 years. China, up to 50 years ago, was completely nonhomogeneous, being compartmented into groups divided against each other. The warmaking tendency was almost nonexistent, as they still follow the tenets of the Confucian ideal of pacifist culture. At the turn of the century, under the regime of Chang Tso-lin, efforts toward greater homogeneity produced the start of a nationalist urge. This was further and more successfully developed under the leadership of Chiang Kai-shek but has been brought to its greatest fruition under the present regime to the point that it has now taken on the character of a united nationalism, of increasingly dominant aggressive tendencies.

Through these past 50 years the Chinese people have thus become militarized in their concepts and in their ideals. They now constitute excellent soldiers with competent staffs and commanders. This has produced a new and dominant power in Asia which, for its own purposes, is allied with Soviet Russia, but which in its own concepts and methods has become aggressively imperialistic, with a lust for expansion and increased power normal to this type of imperialism. There is little of the ideological concept either one way or another in the Chinese make-up. The standard of living is so low and the capital accumulation has been so thoroughly dissipated by war that the masses are desperate, unable to follow any leadership which seemed to promise an alleviation of local stringencies.

I have from the beginning believed that the Chinese Communist support of the North Koreans was the dominant one. Their interests are at present parallel to those of the Soviet, but I believe that the aggressiveness recently displayed not only in Korea but also in Indo-China and Tibet and pointing potentially toward the south reflects predominantly the same lust for the expansion of power which has animated every would-be conqueror since the beginning of time.

The Japanese people, since the war, have undergone the greatest reformation recorded in modern history. With a commendable will, eagerness to learn, and marked capacity to understand, they have, from the ashes left in war's wake erected in Japan an edifice dedicated to the primacy of individual liberty and personal dignity, and in the ensuing process there has been created a truly representative Government committed to the advance of political morality, freedom of economic enterprise, and social justice.

Politically, economically and socially, Japan is now abreast of many free nations of the earth and will not again fail the universal trust. That it may be counted upon to wield a profoundly beneficial influence over the course of events in Asia is attested by the magnificent manner in which the Japanese people have met the recent challenge of war, unrest and confusion surrounding them from the outside, and checked Communism within their own frontiers without the slightest slackening in their forward progress.

I sent all four of our occupation divisions to the Korean battlefront without the slightest qualms as to the effect of the resulting power vacuum upon Japan. The results fully justified my faith. I know of no nation more serene, orderly and industrious nor in which higher hopes can be entertained for future constructive service in the advance of the human race.

Of our former ward, the Philippines, we can look forward in confidence that the existing unrest will be corrected and a strong and healthy nation will grow in the longer aftermath of war's terrible destructiveness. We must be patient and understanding and never fail them as in our hour of need they did not fail us.

A Christian nation, the Philippines stands as a mighty bulwark of Christianity in the Far East, and its capacity for high moral leadership in Asia is unlimited.

On Formosa, the Government of the Republic of China has had the opportunity to refute by action much of the malicious gossip which so undermined the strength of its leadership on the Chinese mainland.

The Formosan people are receiving a just and enlightened administration with majority representation on the organs of government; and politically, economically and socially appear to be advancing along sound and constructive lines.

With this brief insight into the surrounding areas, I now turn to the Korean conflict.

While I was not consulted prior to the President's decision to intervene in support of the Republic of Korea, that decision, from a military standpoint, proved a sound one. As I say, it proved a sound one, as we hurled back the invader and decimated his forces. Our victory was complete and our objectives within reach when Red China intervened with numerically superior ground forces.

This created a new war and an entirely new situation, a situation not contemplated when our forces were committed against the North Korean invaders, a situation which called for new decisions in the diplomatic sphere to permit the realistic adjustment of military strategy.

Such decisions have not been forthcoming.

While no man in his right mind would advocate sending our ground forces into continental China, and such was never given a thought, the new situation did urgently demand a drastic revision of strategic planning if our political aim was to defeat this new enemy as we had defeated the old.

Apart from the military need, as I saw it, to neutralize the sanctuary protection given the enemy north of Yalu, I felt that military necessity in the conduct of the war made necessary, first, the intensification of our economic blockade against China; second, the imposition of a naval blockade against the China coast; third, removal of restrictions on air reconnaissance of China's coastal areas and of Manchuria; fourth, removal of restrictions on the forces of the Republic of China on Formosa with logistical support to contribute to their effective operations against the Chinese mainland.

For entertaining these views, all professionally designed to support our forces committed to Korea and bring hostilities to an end with the least possible delay at a saving of countless American and Allied lives, I have been severely criticized in lay circles, principally abroad, despite my understanding that from a military standpoint the above views have been fully shared in the past by practically every military leader concerned with the Korean campaign, including our own Joint Chiefs of Staff.

I called for reinforcements, but was informed that reinforcements were not available. I made clear that, if not permitted to destroy the enemy-built-up bases north of the Yalu, if not permitted to utilize the friendly Chinese force of some 600,000 men on Formosa, if not permitted to blockade the China coast to prevent the Chinese Reds from getting succor from without, and if there were to be no hope of major reinforcements, the position of the command from the military standpoint forbade victory.

We could hold in Korea by constant maneuver, and at an approximate area where our supply-line advantages were in balance with the supply-line disadvantages of the enemy. But we could hope at best for only an indecisive campaign with its terrible and constant attrition upon our forces if the enemy utilized his full military potential.

I have constantly called for the new political decisions essential to a solution. Efforts have been made to distort my position. It has been said in effect that I was a warmonger. Nothing could be further from the truth.

I know war as few other men now fighting know it, and nothing, to me, is more revolting. I have long advocated its compete abolition, as its very destructiveness on both friend and foe has rendered its useless as a means of settling international disputes. Indeed, on the second day of September, 1945, just following the surrender of the Japanese nation on the battleship *Missouri,* I formally cautioned as follows:

"Men, since the beginning of time, have sought peace. Various methods, through the ages, have been attempted to devise an international process to prevent or settle disputes between nations. From the very start, workable methods were found insofar as individual citizens were concerned, but the mechanics of an instrumentality of larger international scope have never been successful. Military alliances, balances of power, leagues of nations, all in turn failed, leaving the only path to be by way of the crucible of war."

The utter destructivenes of war now blots out this alternative. We have had our last chance. If we will not devise some greater and more equitable system, Armageddon will be at our door.

The problem basically is still logical and involves a spiritual recrudescence and improvement of human character that will synchronize with our almost matchless advances in science, art, literature, and all material and cultural developments of the past 2,000 years. It must be of the spirit if we are to save the flesh.

But once war is forced upon us, there is no other alternative than to apply every available means to bring it to a swift end. War's very object is victory, not prolonged indecision.

In war there is no substitute for victory. There are some who, for varying reasons, would appease Red China. They are blind to history's clear lesson, for history teaches, with unmistakable emphasis, that appeasement but begets new and bloodier war. It points to no single instance where this end has justified that means, where appeasement has led to more than a sham peace. Like blackmail, it lays the basis for new and successively greater demands until, as in blackmail, violence becomes the only other alternative. Why, my soldiers asked of me, surrender military advantages to an enemy in the field? I could not answer.

Some may say to avoid spread of the conflict into an all-out war with China. Others, to avoid Soviet intervention. Neither explanation seems valid, for China is already engaging with the maximum power it can commit, and the Soviet will not necessarily mesh its actions with our moves. Like a cobra, any new enemy will more likely strike whenever it feels that the relativity in military or other potential is in its favor on a world-wide basis.

The tragedy of Korea is further heightened by the fact that its military action is confined to its territorial limits. It condemns that nation, which it is our purpose to save, to suffer the devastating impact of full naval and air bombardment while the enemy's sanctuaries are fully protected from such attack and devastation.

Of the nations of the world, Korea alone, up to now, is the sole one which has risked its all against communism. The magnificence of the courage and fortitude of the Korean people defies description. They have chosen to risk death rather than slavery. Their last words to me were: "Don't scuttle the Pacific."

I am closing my fifty-two years of military service. When I joined the Army, even before the turn of the century, it was the fulfillment of all my boyish hopes and dreams.

The world has turned over many times since I took the oath on the plain at West Point, and the hopes and dreams have long since vanished, but I still remember the refrain of one of the most popular barracks ballads of that day which proclaimed most proudly that old soldiers never die; they just fade away.

And like the old soldier of that ballad, I now close my military career and just fade away, an old soldier who tried to do his duty as God gave him the light to see that duty. Good bye.

IV. ADDRESS BY PRESIDENT TRUMAN
TO CIVIL DEFENSE CONFERENCE

May 7, 1951

This conference is being held to consider one of the most important tasks facing our country. The lives of many millions of our fellow citizens may depend on the development of a strong civil defense. The threat of atomic warfare is one which we must face, no matter how much we dislike it. We can never afford to forget that the terrible destruction of cities, and of civilization as we know it, is a real possibility.

There are two things our country must do in the face of this awesome and terrible possibility. One of them is to look to our civil defense. So long as there is any chance at all that atomic bombs may fall on our cities, we cannot gamble on being caught unprepared. And let's not fool ourselves—there is such a chance. We must prepare for it.

The other thing we must do is to try to prevent atomic war from coming. That is what I have been working for ever since I became President. That is what our foreign policy is all about. The foreign policy of the United States is based on an effort to attain world peace. Every action we have taken has had this aim.

We are right in the midst of a big debate on foreign policy. A lot of people are looking at this debate as if it were just a political fight. But the stakes are a lot more important than the outcome of an election. The thing that is at stake in this debate may be atomic war. Our foreign policy is not a political issue. It is a matter of life and death. It is a matter of the future of mankind.

These two things—civil defense and foreign policy—are what I will talk about tonight. As you see, they are closely tied together. And they

278

are both concerned with a form of warfare which is more destructive than anything the world has ever known before.

Our civil-defense problem starts with a few basic facts. Because there was an atomic explosion in the Soviet Union in 1949, we must act on the assumption that they do have atomic bombs. They have planes that could drop atomic bombs upon our cities. No matter how good our air defense may be, or how big an air force we build, a determined air attack by the Soviet Union could drop bombs upon this country. Our air force experts say planes would get through, however good our defenses may be. . . .

The best defense against atomic bombing is to prevent the outbreak of another world war and achieve a real peace. We must bend all our energy to the job of keeping our free way of life, and to doing it without another war. We can have peace only if we have justice and fair dealing among nations. The United Nations is the best means we have for deciding what is right and what is wrong between nations. It is a great attempt to make the moral judgment of mankind effective in international affairs. Nothing is more important if mankind is to overcome the barbarian doctrine that might makes right.

Our best chance of keeping the peace and staying free is for nations that believe in freedom to stick together and to build their strength together. This is what we call collective security. We have been trying since the last war was over and even before to build a system of collective security among all those countries that really believe in the principles of the United Nations. I think we have made a lot of progress. I know that some people have become impatient with our efforts to establish collective security, because we have not yet succeeded in attaining world peace. But we are on the right road.

There are cynics who scorn the United Nations, who are indifferent to the need for co-operation among the free peoples. They do not understand that our best hope for peace is to bind together the nations that are striving for peace and to increase their strength to stop aggression. The United Nations is being severely tested today because of the Korean conflict. The fighting there is requiring great sacrifices. In a time of crisis, there is a tendency to look for some easy way out regardless of the consequences. But we must not be misled. We must not lose sight of the world picture and the critical importance of the United Nations if we are to reach a permanent solution.

Communist aggression in Korea is part of the world-wide strategy of the Kremlin to destroy freedom. It has shown men all over the world that Communist imperialism may strike anywhere, anytime. The defense of Korea is part of the world-wide effort of all the free nations to maintain freedom. It has shown free men that if they stand together, and pool their strength, Communist aggression cannot succeed. The firm stand of the United Nations in Korea has checked the advance of Communist imperialism throughout Asia. It is using up the military resources of these Chinese Communists to such an extent that they are not able to carry out the designs of Communist imperialism against the independence of other Asian countries. And the people of those countries who have been resisting Communist aggression have now been given new hope and new courage.

The Communist assault in Indochina has been checked by the free people of Indochina with the help of the French. In Malaya, the British are holding firm against Communist guerrilla attacks. In the Philippines, in Burma, and in other places in Asia, Communist-led guerrillas are being blocked.

The fight against aggression in Korea has also dealt a heavy blow to the Kremlin conspiracy outside of Asia. It has brought new hope and courage to free men in Europe, and in the Middle East, who face the Soviet menace across their frontiers. The fight against Communist aggression in the Far East is the fight against Communist aggression in the West as well.

The struggle in Korea is a long and hard one. But it can be won—and our policy is designed to win it.

The Chinese rulers are losing large numbers of their soldiers. As these losses increase it will become clearer and clearer to them that aggression does not pay. They can have peace when they give up their aggression and stop the fighting.

Meanwhile, the strength of all the free nations is growing. The Soviet plan of world conquest is becoming more and more impossible to achieve. If we stick to our guns, and continue to punish the aggressors, we can end the aggression in Korea and restore peace.

We have been urged to take measures which would spread the fighting in the Far East. We have been told that this would bring the Korean conflict to a speedy conclusion; that it would save the lives of our troops. In my judgment, this is not true. I believe we have a better chance of stopping the aggression in Korea, at a smaller cost in the lives of our troops and those of our allies, by following our present course. Let me tell you that I have studied this question for a long time. It is not a question that can be decided in the light of Korea alone. It does not affect the Far East alone. It is not a local question. It affects Korea and Japan, and the security of our troops in those places. But it also

reaches Europe, and the future of the North Atlantic Treaty, and the security of free people there and everywhere else in the world. It is a decision that affects the future of the United Nations and the future of the whole world.

I have refused to extend the area of the conflict in the Far East, under the circumstances which now prevail, and I am going to tell you exactly why. I have refused first on military grounds. The best military advice I have been able to obtain—the best collective military advice in this country—is that this course of action would not lead to a quick and easy solution of the Korean conflict.

On the contrary, it could very well lead to a much bigger and much longer war. Such a war would not reduce our casualties in the Far East. It would increase them enormously. Such a war would expose our troops to devastating air and submarine attacks. It would seriously endanger Japan and the Philippines. It would unite the Chinese people behind their Communist rulers.

Furthermore, a deep involvement on our part in a war in China, whatever the outcome there, would have critical military consequences in Europe. There is nothing that would give the Kremlin greater satisfaction than to see our resources committed to an all-out struggle in Asia, leaving Europe exposed to the Soviet armies.

These are some of the military dangers.

Moreover, there are other dangers. The Kremlin is trying, and has been trying for a long time, to drive a wedge between us and the other free nations. It wants to see us isolated. It wants to see us distrusted. It wants to see us feared and hated by our allies. Our allies agree with us in the course we are following. They do not believe that we should take the initiative to widen the conflict in the Far East. If the United States were to widen the conflict, we might well have to go it alone.

If we go it alone in Asia, we may destroy the unity of the free nations against aggression. Our European allies are nearer to Russia than we are. They are in far greater danger. If we act without regard to the danger that faces them, they may act without regard to the dangers that we face. Going it alone brought the world to the disaster of World War II. We cannot go it alone is Asia and go it in company in Europe. The whole idea of going it alone is the opposite of everything we have stood for and worked for since World War II. In this way, going it alone in Asia might wreck the United Nations, The North Atlantic Treaty, and the whole system of collective security we are helping to set up.

That would be a tremendous Soviet victory. We do not intend to fall into that trap. I do not propose to strip this country of its allies in the face of the Soviet danger. The path of collective security is our only sure defense against the dangers that threaten us. Moreover, it is the path to peace in Korea, to peace in the world.

We are determined to do our utmost to limit the war in Korea. We will not take any action which might place upon us the responsibility for initiating a general war. But if the aggressor takes further action which threatens the security of the United Nations forces in Korea, we will counter that action.

I repeat: I am convinced that the course we are now following in Korea is achieving the most for peace—and at the least cost in American lives. All of us wish that no Americans had to fight and die. But by fighting on a limited scale now, we may be able to prevent a third world war later on.

Remember this. If we do have another world war, it will be an atomic war. We could expect many atomic bombs to be dropped on American cities. And a single one of them could cause many times more casualties than we have suffered in all the fighting in Korea. I do not want to be responsible for bringing that about.

Some people do not understand how the free world can ever win this long struggle, without fighting a third world war. These people overlook the inner weaknesses of the Soviet dictatorship. They forget that the free world is stronger—stronger in its determination, stronger in its staying power, stronger in its human resources—than any system of slavery.

The Kremlin's system of terror, which appears to be its main strength, is one of its greatest weaknesses. Dictatorships are based on fear. They cannot give their people happiness and peace. They have nothing to offer except aggression and slavery.

As the aggressive tactics of the Kremlin are checked by the collective defenses of the free world, the futility of the whole Communist program is becoming more and more apparent to the people under Soviet control. We can already see this process at work. In China, the failure of the Korean adventure is weakening the hold of the Communist government. Wholesale arrests and executions are taking place. In the same way, the pressure of the police state is increasing in the other satellite countries. Yugoslavia has thrown off the Kremlin yoke. Every day refugees flee across the border from the Iron Curtain countries into the free countries of Europe.

There are growing signs of internal tension and unrest behind the Iron Curtain.

We must remember that the peoples under the Soviet rule of terror are not only our friends, but our silent allies. They are the victims of a terrible tyranny. We do not hate them. We have had friendly relations with them in the past; we can have such friendship again.

As the free nations build their strength and unity, this fact will compel a change in the Soviet drive for power and conquest. The Soviet rulers are faced with the growing strength of the free world, the increasing cost of aggression, and the increasing difficulty of driving their people to greater and greater hardships. They will be forced by these pressures from within and without to give up aggression. It will then be possible to make progress with a program for international control and reduction of armaments and for the peaceful settlement of disputes.

Our programs of economic aid and technical assistance, and our campaign of truth, not only strengthen the free peoples; they weaken the dictatorships. They remind the victims of tyranny that a better world lies outside their prison. They build up the hope of freedom everywhere.

Everything we do to strengthen the free world; every dollar we spend for assistance to other free nations; every effort we make to resist aggression in Korea, and around the world, brings closer the day of genuine peace.

We are not engaged in a struggle without end. We are engaged in a struggle which has the definite goal of peace. Peace under law is the victory we seek. To achieve this goal we must work together, steadfastly and patiently. We must not be led astray. The real issue is whether we stand alone, or whether we stand and work with the other free peoples of the world.

I am confident that the American people will not yield either to impatience or defeatism. I am sure that our courage and wisdom are equal to the great test we are now undergoing. And I believe that with all of our resources, our human energies, and our common sense, we shall be successful in the great objective of defending freedom and bringing peace to the world.

V. GENERAL BRADLEY'S OPENING STATEMENT BEFORE THE SENATE ARMED SERVICES AND FOREIGN RELATIONS COMMITTEES

May 15, 1951

. . . At the very outset, I want to make it clear that I would not say anything to discredit the long and illustrious career of General Douglas MacArthur. We may have different views on certain aspects of our government's military policy, but that is not unusual.

Certainly there have been no personal considerations in our differences of opinion. In matters of such great scope and of such importance many people have different ideas and might consequently recommend different courses of action.

As Chairman of the Joints Chiefs of Staff, I am one of the military advisers to the President, the Secretary of Defense, and the National Security Council. I pass on to them the collective advice and recommendations of the Joint Chiefs.

When the Joint Chiefs of Staff express their opinion on a subject, it is from the military point of view, and is given with a full realization that considerations other than military may be overriding in making the final decision. The relative importance of the military aspect varies. In some cases it is greatly overshadowed by other considerations. In other cases, the military aspects may be the decisive ones.

When all of these aspects are considered the Government's policy is determined. As military men we then abide by the decision.

Before your interrogation on the details of our Government's policies in Korea and the Far East, I would like to ask myself this question: What is the great issue at stake in this hearing?

Principally I would say that you are trying to determine the course we should follow as the best road to peace. There are military factors

284

which must be evaluated before a sound decision can be made. At present the issue is obscured in the public mind by many details which do not relate to the task of keeping the peace and making America secure.

The fundamental military issue that has arisen is whether to increase the risk of a global war by taking additional measures that are open to the United States and its allies. We now have a localized conflict in Korea. Some of the military measures under discussion might well place the United States in the position of responsibility for broadening the war and at the same time losing most if not all of our allies.

General MacArthur has stated that there are certain additional measures which can and should be taken, and that by so doing no unacceptable increased risk of global war will result.

The Joint Chiefs of Staff believe that these same measures do increase the risk of global war and that such a risk should not be taken unnecessarily. At the same time we recognize the military advantages that might accrue to the United Nations' position in Korea and to the United States position in the Far East by these measures. While a field commander very properly estimates his needs from the viewpoint of operations in his own theatre or sphere of action, those responsible for higher direction must necessarily base their actions on broader aspects, and on the needs, actual or prospective, of several theatres.

The Joint Chiefs of Staff, in view of their global responsibilities and their perspective with respect to the world-wide strategic situation, are in a better position than is any single theatre commander to assess the risk of general war. Moreover, the Joint Chiefs of Staff are best able to judge our own military resources with which to meet that risk.

In order that all may understand the strategy which the Joint Chiefs of Staff believe the United States must pursue, I would like to discuss in broad terms this perspective in which we view our security problems.

As a background to our consideration of global strategy, we must realize that human beings have invented a great variety of techniques designed to influence other nations. Right now, nations are being subjected to persuasion by propaganda, and coercion by force of arms. It is my conviction that broad and comprehensive knowledge of the strength, aims, and the policies of nations is basic to understanding the problem of security in a world of tension.

We must understand—as we conduct our foreign affairs and our military affairs—that while power and nationalism prevail, it is up to us to gain strength through co-operative efforts with other nations which have common ideals and objectives with our own. At the same time, we must create and maintain the power essential to persuasion, and to our own security in such a world. We must understand the role and nature, including the limitations, of this power if we are to exercise it wisely.

One of the great power potentials of this world is the United States of America and her allies. The other great power in this world is Soviet Russia and her satellites. As much as we desire peace, we must realize that we have two centers of power supporting opposing ideologies.

From a global viewpoint—and with the security of our nation of prime importance—our military mission is to support a policy of preventing communism from gaining the manpower, the resources, the raw material and the industrial capacity essential to world domination. If Soviet Russia ever controls the entire Eurasian land mass, then the Soviet-satellite imperialism may have the broad base upon which to build the military power to rule the world.

Three times in the past five years the Kremlin-inspired imperialism has been thwarted by direct action.

In Berlin, Greece and Korea the free nations have opposed Communist aggression with a different type of action. But each time the power of the United States had been called upon and we have become involved. Each incident has cost us money, resources and some lives.

But in each instance we have prevented the domination of one more area and the absorption of another source of manpower, raw materials and resources.

Korea, in spite of the importance of the engagement, must be looked upon with proper perspective. It is just one engagement, just one phase of this battle that we are having with the other power center in the world which opposes us and all we stand for. For five years this "guerrilla diplomacy" have been going on. In each of the actions in which we have participated to oppose this gangster conduct we have risked World War III. But each time we have used methods short of total war. As costly as Berlin and Greece and Korea may be, they are less expensive than the vast destruction which would be inflicted upon all sides if a total war were to be precipitated.

I am under no illusion that our present strategy of using means short of total war to achieve our ends and oppose communism is a guarantee that a world war will not be thrust upon us. But a policy of patience and determination without provoking world war, while we improve our military power, is one which we believe we must continue to follow.

As long as we keep the conflict within its present scope, we are holding to a minimum the forces we must commit and tie down.

The strategic alternative, enlargement of the war in Korea to include Red China, would probably delight the Kremlin more than anything else we could do. It would necessarily tie down additional forces, especially our sea power and our air power, while the Soviet Union would not be obliged to put a single man into the conflict.

Under the present circumstances, we have recommended against enlarging the war. The course of action often described as a "limited war" with Red China would increase the risk we are taking by engaging too much of our power in an area that is not the critical strategic prize.

Red China is not the powerful nation seeking to dominate the world. Frankly, in the opinion of the Joint Chiefs of Staff, this strategy would involve us in the wrong war, at the wrong place, at the wrong time and with the wrong enemy.

There are some other considerations which have tended to obscure this main issue. Some critics have not hesitated to state that the policy our Government is following, and its included strategy, is not that which has been recommended by the Joint Chiefs of Staff.

Statements have been made that the President as Commander in Chief, and the Secretary of State and the Secretary of Defense, have a policy all their own, and that the Joint Chiefs of Staff have been overridden.

This is just not so. The Joint Chiefs of Staff have continually given their considered opinion—always from a military viewpoint—concerning our global capabilities and responsibilities and have recommended our present strategy in and for Korea. This has been the course of action which the Secretary of Defense and the Commander in Chief have adopted as far as practicable.

I pointed out earlier that many times the international policy considerations, including the views of our allies, are also considered and in some instances modify the course of action.

In other instances, even after the international considerations and the views of our allies have been considered, the proposed military strategy has not been altered.

Our over-all policy has been one of steadfast patience and determination in opposing Communist aggression without provoking unnecessarily a total war.

There are many critics who have been impatient with this strategy and who would like to call for a "showdown." From a purely military viewpoint, this is not desirable. We are not in the best military position to seek a showdown, even if it were the nation's desire to forfeit the chances for peace by precipitating a total war.

Undoubtedly, this statement will be misconstrued by some critics who will say, "Why are the Joint Chiefs of Staff advertising the fact that we are not militarily in a position to have a showdown?"

I can assure those critics that with the methods we must pursue in a democracy in order to support a military establishment—including this present investigation of our strategy in the Far East—our capabilities are not unknown to the Communists.

They are apt students of military power, and fully realize that although we are not prepared to deliver any ultimatum, we could hurt them badly if they attacked us or our friends.

They also know that with our potential, and the strength of our allies, in the long run they could not win a war with a United States that is alert, and continuously prepared.

I would not be a proponent of any policy which would ignore the military facts and rush us headlong into a showdown before we are ready. It is true that this policy of armed resistance to aggression, which we pursue while we are getting stronger, often risks a world war. But so far we have taken these risks without disastrous results.

I think our global strategy is paying off and I see no reason to let impatience alter it in the Far East. Certainly the course of action we are pursuing has avoided a total war which could only bring death and destruction to millions of Americans, both in the United States and on the battlefield. Our present course of action has at the same time won us respect and admiration everywhere in the world, both inside and outside the Iron Curtain.

There are also those who deplore the present military situation in Korea and urge us to engage Red China in a larger war to solve this problem. Taking on Red China is not a decisive move, does not guarantee the end of the war in Korea, and may not bring China to her knees.

We have only to look back to the five long years when the Japanese, one of the greatest military powers of that time, moved into China and had almost full control of a large part of China, and yet were never able to conclude that war successfully. I would say that from past history one would only jump from a smaller conflict to a larger deadlock at greater expense. My own feeling is to avoid such an engagement if possible because victory in Korea would not be assured and victory over Red China would be many years away. We believe that every effort should be made to settle the present conflict without extending it outside Korea. If this proves to be impossible, then other measures may have to be taken.

In my consideration of this viewpoint, I am going back to the basic objective of the American people—as much peace as we can gain without appeasement.

Some critics of our strategy say if we do not immediately bomb troop concentration points and airfields in Manchuria, it is "appeasement." If we do not immediately set up a blockade of Chinese ports—which to be successful would have to include British and Russian ports in Asia—it is "appeasement." These same critics would say that if we do not provide the logistical support and air and naval assistance to launch Chinese Nationalist troops into China, it is "appeasement."

These critics ignore the vital questions:

Will these actions, if taken, actually assure victory in Korea?

Do these actions mean prolongation of the war by bringing Russia into the fight?

Will these actions strip us of our allies in Korea and in other parts of the world

From a military viewpoint, appeasement occurs when you give up something, which is rightfully free to an aggressor without putting up a struggle, or making him pay a price. Forsaking Korea—withdrawing from the fight unless we are forced out—would be an appeasement to aggression. Refusing to enlarge the quarrel to the point where our global capabilities are diminished, is certainly not appeasement but is a militarily sound course of action under the present circumstances.

It is my sincere hope that these hearings will encourage us as a nation to follow a steadfast and determined course of action in this world, which would deny any free nation to Soviet imperialism, and at the same time preserve the peace for which so many men died in World War I, World War II, and in Greece, Indochina, Malaya and Korea.

VI. SECRETARY ACHESON'S REVIEW OF CHINA POLICY BEFORE THE SENATE ARMED SERVICES AND FOREIGN RELATIONS COMMITTEES

June 4, 1951

. . . I should like to state at the outset what I am going to try to do, and that is, I want to present to the committee the problem which confronted the United States of China in 1945, and in doing that I shall have to give some of its roots in history.

I should like to point out what the times of decision were. There were moments in this period from 1945 on, moments of decision, and I should like to point out those moments. I should like to point out the considerations which were taken under advisement when decisions were made, and I should like to say what the decisions were and how they were made.

One further preliminary observation I think is important, and that is that American aid cannot in itself insure the survival of a recipient Government or the survival of a people that this Government is trying to help against aggression.

What our aid must do and can do is to supplement the efforts of that recipient Government and of that people itself. It cannot be a substitute for those efforts. It can only be an aid and a supplement to them.

The United States Government, in aiding another government, does not have power of decision within that country or within that Government. That power of decision remains with the Government, the people in it. Those are thoughts I think we should have in mind.

With those preliminary statements, we come to the problem which faced the Chinese and American Governments in 1945.

The Japanese had been defeated. The Chinese Government was in the extreme southwestern part of China. The task which had to be solved by the Chinese Government was, in effect, how to create a nation, and how to have the authority of the Chinese Government exercised throughout that nation.

Now, I do not say re-create a nation; I say, advisedly, *create a nation;* because for almost an indefinite period in the past there had not been in our sense a nation in the territory which we call China, and I will come to and explain to you why that is so, a nation in the sense of a Government in control throughout that area.

Therefore, the question which had to be faced was how to create that nation and how to create the authority of the nation in that area. . . .

The Chinese Government that we are talking about—the Nationalist Government—had not had authority—indeed, no Chinese Government had had authority, by which I mean substantial authority—throughout China since the period of the Manchus.

Here is the picture which confronted everybody at the time I am talking about. The great northern area of China, Manchuria, was occupied by the Soviet Union, with its own armed forces. In the second place, the north central and southeast parts of China were in the control of the Communists and the Japanese.

I say both the Communists and the Japanese because the Japanese held the cities and the major lines of communication; whereas, the surrounding areas were occupied by the Communists.

That part of China included what we call North China, swinging down through Central China into the southeast and coming quite far south and southeast in China.

The south central and southern part of China was occupied by the Japanese, who had troops along the coast and for considerable areas inland and the Government itself was, as I said before, in the extreme southwestern part of China.

Another important fact, which must never be lost sight of in our consideration, is that in addition to these facts of who actually occupied and exercised authority in certain parts of China, all of China was in the grip of a very profound social revolution. . . .

It grew out of a similiar experience in almost all wars, that as the Governments concerned have to make tremendous efforts, as, in some areas, the controls of Government become weakened, and promises are made, people move forward in social economic ways, at least they move forward in acquiring new social and economic rights; and this was going on in China, in the age-long battle between the peasants and the landlords.

The peasants had made advances and there was a new idea of profound importance.

If I may speak briefly, on the general area of Communist control:

The Communists controlled an area containing 116,000,000 people, which was one-fourth of the population of China. The geographical area was 15 per cent of the country we call China, exclusive of Manchuria.

This area included in it some of the most heavily populated areas of China, the area which had most of the railway communications, important industrial developments and important cities.

Now, let us take a look at Manchuria.

Manchuria, except in a wholly nominal way, and then only for a period of two or three years, part of '28, '29, '30 and part of '31, had never been in any way under the control of the present Nationalist Government of China; and, until his death in 1927 or '28, the old Marshal had been the war lord of Manchuria, and controlled it absolutely.

Upon his death, the young Marshal took over his authority, and in 1928 after Chiang Kai-shek had taken Peking and defeated the Communists and the northern war lords, the young Marshal announced his adherence to the National Government. That was a pretty nominal adherence.

It meant that he recognized the Government of Chiang Kai-shek as the National Government of China, but the Administration in Manchuria did not change, and he continued to exercise the authority.

However, that authority continued for a very short period of time, and in 1931 the Japanese invaded Manchuria and set up their puppet state, and all Chinese authority disappeared from Manchuria, a very important thing for us to remember.

When we come to North China, we find that in 1927 the struggle between the Left Wing of the Kuomintang party, which was established at Hangkow, and the Right Wing of the party under Chiang Kai-shek came to a head. The Chiang Kai-shek forces won, the Russians, [including] Borodin, who was then advising the Government, had to flee from China, and in 1928 Chiang Kai-shek moved into Peking and there announced the official unification of China. That was in 1928.

The battle with the Communists which began in 1927 in open warfare continued until '36, and in the period of '34 and '35 the Communists were forced to make their long march from the southeastern portion of China to the northwestern portion of China. There they established themselves in the period '34-'35.

In the meantime, however, the Japanese who were in Manchuria were moving into North China, and in 1935 the Japanese undertook to set up another puppet state in North China which would comprise the five northern provinces of China; and at that time they had sufficient physical control of the area to do that.

I point all of this out to make clear to you again that in North China the authority of Chiang Kai-shek's Government, which was established in 1928, had been in very large part eliminated by 1935, and instead of his Government having power in North China, that was in part controlled through Japanese puppets, Japanese, and in part was controlled by the Communists in the northwest.

With this review then, let us just mention once more the principal problems which confronted the Chinese Government and confronted the American Government in its efforts to help the Chinese Government.

These were: the Soviets in Manchuria, the Japanese and the Communists struggling against one another to control a vast area in Northwest, North Central and Southeast China—the Communists I have already mentioned—and at the same time this great problem of the revolution in thought and in social relationships which was going on throughout all China.

So the first period of decision, the first time after the war when important decisions were made and had to be made, was the period 1945 and 1946. Now I do not mean for a moment that important decisions were not made before and after, but that was the first great moment of decision.

The situation was stated in a nutshell by General Wedemeyer in November, 1945, very shortly after V-J Day, and I should like to read, not very much, but I should like to read the report.

He says:

"Chinese Communist guerrillas and saboteurs can, and probably will, if present activities are a reliable indication, restrict and harass the movements of National Government forces to such an extent that the result will be a costly and extended campaign. Logistical support for the National Government forces, and measures for their security in the heart of Manchuria have not been fully appreciated by the Generalissimo or his Chinese staff. These facts, plus the lack of appropriate forces and transport, have caused me to advise the Generalissimo that he should concentrate his efforts on the recovery of North China and the consolidation of his military and political position there, prior to any attempt to occupy Manchuria. I received the impression that he agreed with this concept."

Now, General Wedemeyer has given conclusions to this report of 1945:

1. The Generalissimo will be able to stabilize the situation in South China, provided he accepts the assistance of foreign administrators and technicians, and engages in political, economic and social reforms through honest, competent civilian officials.

2. He will be unable to stabilize the situation in North China for months, and perhaps, even years, unless a satisfactory settlement with the Chinese Communists is achieved, and followed up realistically by the kind of action suggested in Paragraph One—that is the paragraph which has just been talked about, the political, economic and social reforms.

3. He will be unable to occupy Manchuria for many years unless satisfactory agreements are reached with Russia and the Chinese Communists.

4. Russia is in effect creating favorable conditions for the realization of Chinese Communist and possibly their own plans in North China and Manchuria. These activities are violations of the recent Sino-Soviet treaty and related agreements.

5. It appears remote that a satisfactory understanding will be reached between Chinese Communists and the National Government.

Now, in short, what General Wedemeyer reported and advised was, first of all, that the Generalissimo must consolidate his own position in South China and to do that he must take into consideration this revolution that I have been talking about. And General Wedemeyer stressed then—and you will see over and over again he stresses—the same point, that there must be political, economic and social reforms in order that the Chinese Government might put itself at the head of this great demand for improvement, which was existing in China, and not allow the Communists or anybody else to take that advantage away from them.

In the second place, he points out that to establish himself in North China he must come to agreement with the Communists.

In the third place, he points out the only way to establish himself in Manchuria is through agreement with the Russians.

He ends up by saying that the outlook on all of these fronts is dark, and he points out that force is not available to accomplish these efforts, partly because force can not accomplish some of them, and secondly, because there is not enough force available to take on the problems which I have already mentioned.

Now, in that situation the United States Government had three choices open to it.

One choice was to pull out of China and say, "we have defeated the Japanese. The Chinese from now on must paddle their own canoe, and we have to wash our hands of it."

That was an impossible choice to take because with the presence of 1,235,000 armed Japanese troops in China, exclusive of Manchuria, and of another 1,700,000 Japanese civilians—government officials, economic people, clerks and businessmen, one thing or another—there was a Japanese force and a Japanese influence so great in China that by throwing its weight to either side in this civil war it could have taken over the administration of the country, and Japan in defeat would have found itself in actual control of China, a result which we could not, of course, help to bring about.

The second choice was that the United States Government might have put into China unlimited resources and all the necessary military power to try and defeat the Communists, remove the Japanese, and remove the Russians from Manchuria.

That was a task so great and so repugnant to the American people that the Government could not undertake it, and it was one which was not in accord with American interests.

The third choice, and the one which was chosen, was to give important assistance of all sorts to the Chinese Government and to assist in every way in the preservation of peace in China and the working out of the agreements which were so necessary to enable the Chinese Government to re-establish itself in those parts of China where it had been before and to get, for the first time, into areas of China where it never had been.

Now, I should like briefly to talk about the Chinese Communist situation and the background of that as it existed in 1945 and then I will take up each of the other elements of this problem.

The relations between the Nationalist Government and the Communists have had a long history in China. I shall not take time to go through it all.

Prior to 1927, there was a period of collaboration. From 1927 to 1937 there was a period of war. From 1937 onward there was again a period in which the official attitude of both the Government and the Communists was that the differences between them were political in nature, had to be settled by political means; and beginning in 1937 they worked out arrangements for collaboration in fighting the Japanese, which never were very effective, but were agreements between them.

Later on, as you will see, they began working very vigorously at arrangements to bring about a settlement by negotiation in China. This official view was stated by the Generalissimo on Sept. 13, 1943, where he said—and this is one of many times when he said this from 1937 on:

"I am of the opinion that first of all we should clearly recognize that the Chinese Communist problem is a purely political problem and should be solved by political means."

As I said, there was an agreement reached between them in 1937 for their joint efforts against the Japanese. That agreement did not work, and reports were made over and over again that a very large part of the Communist armed forces and a very large part of the Nationalist armed forces were immobilized so far as the war against Japan was concerned because they stood facing one another and maneuvering against one another.

It was the effort of our Government throughout the war period to try and reach some kind of an arrangement so that these two forces instead of watching one another would both fight the Japanese. If they did that, there was a very important contribution to the war.

I will not go into all the efforts that were made by General Stilwell and others in the early period.

In the spring of 1944 Vice President Wallace went on a mission for President Roosevelt. Among other places, he went to China, and there he had talks with the Generalissimo, and they talked about two of the great important problems that I have been discussing. One was Manchuria and the other was the Communists.

The Generalissimo was most anxious to get help of the United States in improving relations, as he stated it, between the United States and the Soviet Union because without that improvement the prospects for China were very difficult indeed. They discussed what could be done along that line.

They also discussed the Communist problem, and the Generalissimo pointed out vigorously that the Communists were, as he stated it, not people of good faith, claimed that they were not Chinese, that they had their interests with an alien power. But, nevertheless, he said, "This is a political problem and we have got to settle it by political means."

He stated that he would not regard any help from the United States, in attempting that, to be meddling into the internal affairs of China, and he would be grateful for help.

And finally, before Vice President Wallace left China, he reversed the position which he had taken earlier in which he had opposed any American military people having any relations with the Communists, and withdrew his objection to that.

Now in the fall of 1944 and after these discussions, the President sent another personal representative to China, and that was General Hurley. General Hurley was not then Ambassador. He became Ambassador in the early part of '45, but he went out as the personal representative of the President in order to try and unify this military effort, and there, with the consent and approval of the Generalissimo and of his cabinet, he undertook to act as mediator between the Yenen Communist authorities and the Chungking Nationalist authorities, and they had meetings, some in Yenan at which General Hurley was present, some in Chungking in which they worked out a series of agreements.

Some of these agreements had to do with the conduct of the war, and then some of them went beyond that, and a very important and basic agreement was worked out.

The beginning of it was under the mediation of General Hurley. It was announced on Oct. 11, 1945, and that was the agreement on the general principles of a peaceful settlement of the differences between the Chinese Communists and the Chinese Nationalists.

It was announced after General Hurley's departure from China and was made public, as I said, on Oct. 11. This called for the convening of the National Assembly and for a political consultative conference of all party and nonparty leaders.

It called for the inauguration of a Constitution Government for all of China; for the formation of a committee of Government and Communist representatives to discuss the reorganization of the armies and the reduction of all the armed forces in China.

Now, these agreements were of the greatest possible importance, and they established the basis for the efforts which General Marshall later took on.

May I just pause again for a moment to point out that the problem between the Chinese Government and the Chinese Communists differed in one important respect from the relations between—from the problems of Governments, say, to Europe after the war with Communists in their country, because in China the Communists were not scattered through the population as an element of the population.

They were people who had a defined area, with a large population subject to their control, 116,000,000.

They had a government of their own; they had an army of their own; and, in effect, they had a separate country within China, and the task was to put these two things together so that there would be one country and one Government. Now, that was what they were working on. . . .

Now, I have dealt with the background of this Communist business, and I am coming back to that, when we get to the mission of General Marshall.

I now want to go back and deal with a problem that has to do with another important aspect of this thing, and that is, Manchuria.

I want to talk about Yalta.

The Yalta agreements were made in the very early part of 1945. Later on, in August of '45, treaties were signed between the Chinese Nationalist Government, and the Soviet Union, which grew out of and were based upon these Yalta agreements.

Now, first of all, the Yalta agreements, from the point of view of the wartime effort, and the interest of the United States and its major fighting allies—I think this has been referred to many times, and I shall make it brief—at the time these agreements were entered into at Yalta, we did not know whether we had an atomic bomb or not. That was not proved until some months later, that we had one, and it was not used until considerably later.

It was the then military opinion, concurred in by everyone, that the reduction of Japan would have to be brought about by a large scale landing on the islands of Japan, and the forecast of that fighting, which came from the fighting on the other islands in the Pacific, indicated that it would be a very bloody and terrible battle.

It was of the utmost importance that the Russians should come into the war in the Far East, in time.

Now, there was very little doubt that they would come in, but the grave danger was that they would really wait until the war was over, and until we had expended our effort and blood to win the war, and they would come in and do what they wished.

It was very important, in the view of the military people, and the others too present that they should come in in time so that none of the 700,000 Japanese troops in Manchuria, and none, if possible of the 1,235,000 Japanese troops in China, would come back to strengthen the troops on the main islands of Japan; but that they would be occupied with the Russian effort on the mainland.

That was the purpose and in making the agreements the price which was paid for the agreements was that three months after the end of the European war, the Russians would enter the Far East war; that they should have the southern half of Sakhalin, the Kuriles; that their former rights in Port Arthur and Dairen should be returned to them; and their former interest in the two railways in Manchuria.

The Russians took the same attitude toward these rights that the Chinese took toward their rights in Formosa.

The Russians had lost theirs to the Japanese by war in 1904; the Chinese had lost theirs to the Japanese by war in 1895.

Russia made its claim for those rights, and the claims were granted at this meeting at Yalta. . . .

One of the other things that I should like to point out about Yalta was that unquestionably the Russians had it in their power not only to take what was conceded to them, but much more, besides.

There was very little likelihood that anybody would have the will, and few people could have the power, to throw them out of any area on the mainland which they might occupy, and where they might wish to remain, so that this agreement gave them the basis for a legal claim to something considerably less than they might have taken without a legal claim.

I should also like to point out that at the time the Chinese entered into this treaty with the Russians, a few months after Yalta, that is, in August 1945, they regarded the arrangements which they had made with the Russians on the basis of Yalta as very satisfactory.

Such statements were expressed by the Generalissimo, Chiang Kai-shek, and by the Chinese Foreign Minister, in fact, in 1947 the Chinese Foreign Minister expressed grave apprehension that the Soviet Union might cancel the treaty with China of 1945, in which China had conferred these rights to the bases in Port Arthur, the interests in Dairen, and the interest in the railway.

They regarded that as a very valuable treaty because it also carried with it the obligation of the Russians to evacuate Manchuria, to recognize the Chinese Nationalist Government, and to aid in the reestablishment of Chinese Sovereignty in Manchuria.

Now these agreements, as I shall point out later on, did have a very important effect and bearing when it came to the question of the reoccupation of Manchuria by the Chinese, because it was on the basis of these agreements that both the Chinese Communists and the Russians agreed to occupation by the National Government's forces. . . .

I have pointed out to you the very great importance of the presence of the Japanese in China, the 1,235,000 troops, 1,700,000 civilians. It was divided very early in the game, between the Chinese Government, the Nationalist Government and ourselves, that one of our major efforts must be to get these people out of China and back into Japan.

That wouldn't have been too hard a job to do if they were all just marching on to ships. The great difficulty about it was that these armed soldiers controlled most of the important cities in Central China, in Southeast China and East China, and also the main lines of communication.

If they had been told to drop their guns on the ground and march to the coast at once, those areas would have been occupied by the Communists and the Nationalist Government forces would have never gotten in there without fighting.

Therefore the task was to have the Japanese evacuate the areas which they held at the time when the Government forces could be moved and were moved by us into those areas. That was the task to perform.

In order to do that we landed 50,000 Marines in China. The function of these Marines was to occupy the principal seaports, to guard the principal rail lines close to those seaports, and later to take over the areas along the eastern coast where coal was produced and guard the lines along which the coal came to the principal consuming centers. That was to allow the industrial life of China to continue, and those coal areas and the coal railroads were being constantly raided by the Communists.

So the Marines had to go in there, hold coal, which was the heart of the industrial life of China, hold the seaports so that they would not be captured by Communists, and then receive the Japanese as they were marched to the railheads and down their railroads, and put them on ships and take them back to Japan.

At the same time our armed forces *airlifted* Chinese armies, whole armies from South China into the areas to be evacuated and which were being evacuated by the Japanese. Now, that was a tremendous undertaking most skillfully carried out, and it was that undertaking which permitted the Chinese Government to really get back into areas of China which it would have had the utmost difficulty in even getting into without that colossal effort.

By the end of '46 we had removed 3,000,000 Japanese, just a few thousand under 3,000,000, from China to Japan—one of the great mass movements of people.

After the agreements between the Chinese Nationalists and the

Chinese Communists that I have spoken of in 1945, Oct. 11, 1945, armed clashes broke out again between the two parties; and both the Government authorities, and the American Government authorities, were gravely disturbed that civil war would break out.

If that happened, then the whole chance of dealing with any of the problems which you and I have been discussing this morning would disappear.

If there was civil war going on in China, fighting between the Government forces and the Communist forces, all possibility of removing the Japanese either disappeared or was gravely diminished.

The possibility of occupying North China became much dimmer; the possibility of moving into Manchuria became non-existent; and the possibility of really getting any reforms in South China or any other part of China would be greatly diminished. So, the peace became a major objective of both the Chinese Government and the United States Government in its efforts to help the Chinese Government.

It was in that situation that General Marshall was asked by the President to go to China at the end of 1945. . . .

At the outset I will go into a matter of detail which really is quite out of place in the broad picture which I am trying to paint for you here; but since it has been talked about a great deal, I think it is important to clear it up, and that is the preparation of the instructions which were issued to General Marshall.

I think he was questioned about that, and there have been various charges and countercharges having to do with the preparation of those instructions. The story is very simple.

At the end of November, 1945, Secretary Byrnes and General Marshall met. This was after General Marshall had been asked to go.

Secretary Byrnes read him a memorandum suggesting the outline of instructions for him. General Marshall did not approve of it.

General Marshall said that he would wish to try his own hand, assisted by some of his associates, in drafting the instructions.

This he did; and a draft was prepared by him, in conjunction with four Generals who were working very closely with General Marshall. This was submitted to Secretary Byrnes.

On the 8th of December Secretary Byrnes made his suggestions to General Marshall—that is, suggestions of changes or alterations or additions to the draft prepared by General Marshall.

General Marshall's draft, with Secretary Byrnes' suggestions, was discussed at a meeting in Secretary Byrnes' office on Sunday morning Dec. 9, 1945, by Secretary Byrnes, General Marshall, Mr. John Carter

Vincent, General Hull, and myself. I was then Under Secretary of State.

Those of us went over the instructions. General Marshall approved the suggestions made by Secretary Byrnes, and we then had a completely agreed draft.

In the course of that meeting the outline of a letter from the President to General Marshall was discussed and directions were given for its preparation.

There was also approved at the meeting a memorandum from Secretary Byrnes to the Secretary of War, requesting certain help in connection with the removal of the Japanese and the movement of Chinese armies into the north and laying down certain restrictions of those movements.

There was also agreed upon the form of a press release, I believe —it was agreed that day or a few days later—but the important papers were agreed at that meeting.

They were taken up by Secretary Byrnes with the President, who went over them; and they were put in final shape, unchanged from the agreements of Dec. 9.

The President then had a meeting with General Marshall, at which I was present—there were three of us at that meeting, the President, General Marshall, and myself—and at that point the signed letter and the inclosures were handed to General Marshall.

It was ascertained by the President at that meeting that these papers were unanimously approved and agreeable to all concerned, and to himself.

Now, that is the account of the preparation of these instructions.

All the papers concerned are printed in the White Book. With one exception, the press release, which I mentioned a moment ago, which was given out on the 15th of December—everything in the press release was in General Marshall's instructions. In other words, the press release was a verbatim statement of what was in the instructions to General Marshall, except that certain paragraphs in the instructions were omitted from the press release.

One of those omissions had to do with what is printed in the White Paper and in the memorandum from Secretary Byrnes to the Secretary of War. That was the discretion and authority given to General Marshall in not moving Nationalist Government troops into areas in which there was fighting until he thought that that was a wise thing to do.

That was not to be stated and released because obviously it wouldn't work if it were.

Another omission, two other omissions had to do with things which we would do if the Chinese Government asked us to do it. Obviously you do not print in the newspapers that you will do something if somebody else asks you to. You leave it to the other person to ask you to do that if they wish. That is the story of the instructions.

General Marshall arrived in China at the very end of December, 1945. By February 1946 three major agreements had been reached between the Chinese Government and the Communists. These agreements grew out of the earlier agreements of Oct. 11, 1945, which discussed the general principles for working out peacefully the difference between the Communists and the Government.

The agreements of January and February, 1946, carried into considerable detail how this should be done. In regard to these three agreements which I shall describe, General Marshall had a part only in one, and that was in the first one.

The first agreement was for the cessation of hostilities, it provided that all fighting should cease, and it provided for the setting up of an executive headquarters in which there would be an American chairmanship and Nationalist and Communist representation, the purpose of this Executive Headquarters being to bring the fighting to an end, and these tripartite teams were set up which went to every area where there was any clashing between the troops, and together they brought that fighting to an end and tried to have that truce develop into a more substantial truce.

General Marshall played a very considerable part in working this out. The Executive Headquarters was the really great instrumentality which set up and worked very well until the two parties fell apart—then nothing worked.

The second agreement was an agreement for governmental reorganization and for a constitutional government, and the third agreement was for a military reorganization and the integration of the Communist forces into the National Government.

As I said, General Marshall participated in the negotiations for the cessation of hostilities, but he did not participate in working out the second or the third agreement.

The second agreement for working out a constitutional government recognized the preponderant strength of the Kuomintang position in the Nationalist Government. It provided that there was to be an Interim State Council, sort of a provisional government, which would govern until the new constitution was established and elections were held throughout China and a constitutional government was set up in which all the people of China would have their representatives, and which would function on a two-party or multi-party system.

The Interim State Council was to function in this interim period as the supreme organ of the state. The Kuomintang party was given twenty of the forty seats in this National Council. The other twenty seats were distributed among the Communists and the other parties and to some nonparty people.

It was provided that the Generalissimo, Generalissimo Chiang Kai-shek, as the President of China, should select all the members of the Council, that is, he would select those from his own party and those from all the other parties. However, he would have to appoint a certain number from these other minority parties. That would leave him with twenty people whom he had selected from the other parties, including the Communists, and it would also leave him with a veto over any action of this Council which could only be overriden by a three-fifths vote, which could not be done if his own party stayed with him.

Now, that, I say, was the temporary government. That was to continue until the constitution was to be agreed upon on May 4 through the National Assembly, May 4, 1946, and it was hoped that at an early date, sometime in '46 or '47, I believe it was, there could be an election, and they would then set up a regular constitutional government with legislative, judicial and executive branches, in which all parts of China would be represented, so that this country would have a government extending over all of the area.

The third agreement had to do with the amalgamation of the forces, and that was the most important one. It provided that there should be a great reduction in forces on both sides, because China could not support the tremendous military establishment which existed on the Nationalist side and on the Communist side together.

The Army was to consist of sixty divisions. Of these sixty divisions fifty were to be National Government divisions and ten were to be Communist divisions. These divisions were to be grouped together in armies, armies which would contain three divisions, or whatever the Chinese military order of battle is. There would be several divisions in each army.

The divisions were to be stationed in certain numerical strengths in various parts of China.

The important thing here about the agreement, as we look back on it, was that so far as Manchuria was concerned, the agreement provided that in Manchuria there should be fifteen divisions of the new government's troops. Of those fifteen divisions, fourteen should be National Government divisions and one should be a Communist division. That was of the greatest possible importance. If that could have been carried out, the whole situation might have been very different.

In 1946 the situation of comparative peace, which had been brought about as a result of the agreements in the early part of the year, began to deteriorate. Fighting broke out in various places.

General Marshall, in trying to stop this fighting, through the Executive Headquarters, got drawn into greater detail in some of the political negotiations between the two parties, because this fighting rapidly took on political aspects.

One side or the other would believe that it could gain an advantage by capturing this or that city or area, and believed it could strengthen itself in the negotiations; and then would start an attack. Either the Communists would attack the Nationalists or the Nationalists would attack the Communists, and in that way this situation became worse and worse; and General Marshall's efforts were unable to deal with it.

Therefore, the whole discussions between the Communists and the Nationalists in the attempt to work out the interim government, and the long-term constitutional government, got into more and more and more confusion and trouble.

The Prime Minister of China, Doctor Sun Fo, has an interesting comment on this period. In a New Year's message which he delivered on Jan. 1, 1949, speaking of the period which I have been discussing, he said:

"The Government had decided to call this conference because it was generally realized that the country and the people needed recuperation and peace so that rehabilitation work could be started. Had these measures been carried out at that time all of us would have seen more prosperity and happiness in our midst. Unfortunately all the parties concerned could not completely abandon their own selfish ends and the people in general did not exert sufficient influence in promoting this peace movement."

The result of the breakdown was that the situation developed into one of very considerable fighting by the end of 1946 and when General Marshall left China in 1947, January 1947, to return to Washington, the American effort to mediate in this struggle between the Government and the Communists ended.

General Marshall issued a long statement, which I shall not bother to read to you now, but it sums up very clearly his understanding of the difficulties which brought failure to his mission, and his understanding of the difficulties in the Chinese Government, which could not really permit it to function unless they were removed.

These difficulties, in some respects, had their roots in the fact that the liberal elements in the Kuomintang party were the ones which were dealt with much more severely by the war and the inflation. Inflation and war tend to eliminate the middle class, and that is where the liberal elements came into the Kuomintang, and as the inflation and the war went forward, the power in the party shifted more to the extreme right wing; and General Marshall, in his farewell message, spoke of the importance of more liberal leadership in the Kuomintang party itself.

But as I say, the effort to mediate came to an end with his departure. From then on, we go into the military period of the struggle between the two governments. The Nationalist Government reached a peak of its military holdings toward the end of 1946. In the middle of '46, it had approximately 3,000,000 men under arms. These were opposed by something over 1,000,000 Communist troops, of whom about 400,000 were not regulars but were guerrilla troops.

Until the end of '46 and the early part of '47, the gains, the military gains made by the Nationalist Government, appeared to be impressive, but in fact they were not, and General Marshall repeatedly pointed out to the Government that what it was doing was over-extending itself militarily and politically, since it neither had sufficient troops to garrison this whole area nor did it have sufficient administrators to administer the areas that it was taking over.

Therefore, what it was doing by this military advance was weakening itself both militarily and through administrative ineptitude, because it didn't have the necessary administrators; it was not giving the people of the occupied areas what they had been led to expect when the National Government came in, so politically it was doing itself harm, and militarily it was doing itself harm.

General Barr points out it was during this period that what he calls the war psychology took possession of the Chinese Nationalist army. He had pointed out over and over again that in modern warfare the most disastrous of all things to do is to retreat into a city behind walls and take a defensive position. Modern warfare must be a war of maneuver.

Therefore, time and time and time again these Nationalist lines get pushed away forward; finally the troops at the end take up defensive positions behind some kind of walls, a long line of communication has to be guarded, which eventually is cut, and over and over again the troops at the end of the line either go over to the side of the enemy without firing a shot, or sufficient of them do so that those who want to fight can't fight.

That was the story of the war from 1946 on. At first, it looked very successful—lots of areas occupied, important cities taken—but the armies all go to garrison, they become immobilized, and maneuver and initiative is left with the Communists.

At the end of '46 the Government had 2,600,000 men under arms and the Communists had about 1,100,000 of regulars.

However, in firepower, in rifle firepower, the Government still enjoyed a superiority of three or four to one over the Communists.

In '46, when this fighting started, General Marshall was acting as mediator. He called on both sides to stop the fighting. Both professed to want to do it, but did not do it.

Therefore, General Marshall asked for and obtained from this Government an embargo in the shipment of combat matériel into China. That embargo lasted from the time it was imposed in '46, . . . until May, 1947. During that time the Nationalists were winning the battles, they won the fights they had, they occupied the cities, but they immobilized themselves.

We have talked from time to time here about the great necessity for reform in China. General Marshall, during his mission to China, stressed that over and over again with the Generalissimo, pointing out that the whole possibility of any kind of armed action against the Communists must at last rest upon a belief in the country and their own belief that they had something which was worth fighting for, and was progressive and good, and that if we did not have reform in China, we were never going to get this spirit which was necessary to fight and defeat the Communists.

After General Marshall returned in the summer of 1947, the President, on the recommendation of General Marshall, sent General Wedemeyer to China on a fact-finding mission. General Wedemeyer, before he left, stressed again, as he had in 1945, the great importance and the necessity for reform.

He said before he left the United States:

"To regain and maintain the confidence of the people, the Central Government will have to effect immediately drastic and far-reaching political and economic reforms. Promises will no longer suffice. Performance is absolutely necessary. It should be accepted that military force in itself will not eliminate communism."

General Wedemeyer went to China and returned. He made recommendations which are printed in the White Paper, in which he recommended assistance of economic and military equipment for a five-year period, which would require Congressional authorization. Although his actual recommendations do not call for a grant of military aid, it is possible to read that in. He does talk about the desirability of that.

However, General Wedemeyer recognized the desirability and importance of avoiding direct United States involvement in the civil war in China by stating:

"Although advice indicated above"—that is, technical military advice —"does provide advice indirectly to tactical force, it should be carried on outside operational areas to prevent the criticism that American personnel are actively engaged in fratricidal warfare."

And he took the position, strongly, that the United States Government had to be extremely careful that it did not commit itself to a policy involving the absorption of its resources to an unpredictable extent by assuming a direct responsibility for the civil war in China, and for the Chinese economy.

He also pointed out that we must be prepared to face the possibility that the Chinese Government might not be able to maintain itself against the Chinese Communist forces.

That was stated quite clearly by General Marshall. In fact, he said:

"An attempt to underwrite the Chinese economy and the Chinese Government's military efforts will result in a burden on the United States economy and a military responsibility which I cannot recommend as a course of action for this Government."

Now, the program of aid which General Marshall presented was a program of $570 million in economic assistance over a fifteen-month period. He pointed out that the experience gained in the program would throw light on the possibilities of future programs.

There are other recommendations in the Wedemeyer Report which I shall not dwell upon at the present time. We are now directing our attention to the aid part of it.

The Secretary of State, General Marshall, then had prepared, and with the approval of the President sent to Congress, a recommendation for aid to China. He made before the Foreign Relations Committee a very frank statement of the problems facing the United States Government in considering aid to China.

He made it clear that there were steps which had to be taken and could only be taken by the Chinese Government which were essential to meet the Communist threat.

The program was sufficient in size, it was thought, to free the major portion of the Chinese Government's own foreign exchange assets for the purchase of such military supplies, from foreign sources, as it might need.

It was not recommended that we should have military advisers in combat areas.

It was not recommended that we should take measures of military aid which would lead to United States military intervention in China, or direct involvement in the civil war.

Now, this question was very carefully considered in the Executive Branch, at a meeting in June, 1948, attended by Secretary Marshall, Secretary of the Army Royall, General Bradley and General Wedemeyer, and the decision which I have just spoken of was taken.

There was already a United States military advisory group in China that had been established in 1946, and in 1947 the commanding officer of this group had been authorized to give advice on a confidential basis to the Generalissimo, advice of a strategic nature, but the United States was not willing to assume responsibility for the strategic direction of the war.

General Marshall in a message to General Barr pointed out one reason why. He said:

"I think you will agree that implications of our accepting that responsibility would be very far-reaching and grave, and that such responsibility is in logic inseparable from the authority to make it effective. Whatever the Generalissimo may feel moved to say with respect to his willingness to delegate necessary powers to Americans, I know from my own experience that advice is always listened to very politely but not infrequently ignored when deemed unpalatable."

Therefore we did not take responsibility for the strategic direction of the war, nor did we recommend that American officers should be with troops in combat areas.

This recommendation was considered by the Eightieth Congress. The Eightieth Congress—and I shall not go through a whole long story—the Senate bill reduced the period of time from fifteen months to twelve months. It reduced, split the appropriations and recommended $338,000,000 for economic aid and $125,000,000 as a special grant to be used at the discretion of the Chinese Government.

The debate indicates that the Chinese Government would probably use this 125 for military aid. In the course of the legislative history, the House put in a provision authorizing military advice on the so-called Greek model, that is, having officers with troops in combat areas and strategic advice. That was stricken out by the Senate, and in speaking about it Senator Vandenberg said:

"As in the case of Greece and Turkey, your committee recognizes that military aid is necessary in order to make economic aid effective. It proposes to make military supplies available at China's option. Your committee believes that as a matter of elementary prudence that this process must be completely clear of any implication that we are underwriting the military campaign of the Nationalist Government."

And, as I say, the House provision was stricken out.

That was agreed to in conference, and the bill was passed chiefly as written by the Senate.

I said that the bill authorized $338,000,000 for economic aid. However, when it came to the appropriation process, Congress only appropriated $275,000,000 for economic aid and $125,000,000 for military aid. So a total was actually made available by the Congress of $400,000,000 as against $570,000,000 requested.

I shall not go in detail through the campaigns of 1947 more than I have already done. The real collapse of the Government in a military way began in the latter part of 1948. The first large-scale defection and collapse occurred in September, 1948, with the fall of Tsinan, where Government forces without any effort at all went over to the other side and surrendered with all their matériel.

The U. S. Army Intelligence review of military developments in 1948, in January, 1949, sums it up this way:

"The Nationalists entered 1948 with an estimated strength of 2,723,000 troops. Recruitment and replacement of combat losses kept this figure constant through mid-September. By Feb. 1, 1949, however, heavy losses had reduced Nationalist strength to 1,500,000, of which approximately 500,000 were service troops. This represents a reduction of 45 per cent of the Nationalist Government's total strength in a four and one-half month period.

"Communist strength, estimated at 1,150,000 a year ago, has mounted to 1,622,000, virtually all combat effectives. Whereas the Nationalists began 1948 with almost a three-to-one numerical superiority, the Communist forces now outnumber the total Nationalist strength and have achieved better than a one and a half to one superiority in combat effectives.

"The events of the last year, and more specifically those of the last four and a half months, have resulted in such overwhelming losses to the Nationalist Government that, acting alone, its military position has declined beyond possible recoupment.

"On the other hand, these same events have so enhanced the position and capabilities of the Communists that they are now capable of achieving a complete military victory over the Nationalist forces."

In mid-November, 1948, General Barr, who was the head of the military mission to China, reported to the Department of the Army:

"I am convinced that the military situation has deteriorated to the point where only the active participation of United States troops could effect a remedy. No battle has been lost since my arrival due to lack of ammunition or equipment. Their military debacles, in my opinion, can all be attributed to the world's worst leadership and many other morale-destroying factors that led to a complete loss of the will to fight."

In another report early in 1949, he explained some of the causes for National Government defeats. He says:

"The Government committed its first politico-military blunder by concentrating on the purely military reoccupation of former Japanese-held areas. It gave very little realization to the regional areas or the creation of efficient loyal administrations. Its strategy was burdened by an unsound strategy conceived by a politically influenced and militarily inept high command.

"Throughout the structure and machinery of the National Government there are interlocking ties of interests, family, financial and political. No Chinese, no matter how efficient, can hope for a position of authority because he is the best qualified man. He must have other backing. In too many cases, such backing was the support and loyalty of the Generalissimo and his army comrades, which kept them in posts of responsibility regardless of their qualifications. The direct result has been the unsound strategy and faulty tactics of the Nationalists in their fight against the Communists.". . .

By the end of 1948 the struggle in North China had virtually ended with the complete collapse of the Nationalist armies. Eighty per cent of all the matériel which we had furnished, both during the war and after, to the National Government, was lost; and seventy-five per cent of that is estimated to have been captured by the Communists.

One reason for this large capture General Barr points out when he says "that the Chinese Nationalist Government never destroyed any— the troops never destroyed any of the matériel when they were about to surrender or run."

He says, "The Chinese seemed inherently unable to destroy anything of value."

Now, at the very end of my remarks here, I briefly sum up some of the things, material and otherwise, which the United States did in aid of its policy in China.

Speaking, first, of things on which it is impossible to put a dollar value, first is the aid rendered by the United States forces in China in planning and in carrying out the movement of the Chinese Government forces into the areas occupied by the Japanese.

Second is the evacuation of the Japanese troops from those areas.

Third is the aid rendered by the United States Marines in North China in occupying key areas and maintaining control for the Government of essential railway lines until the Government was able to take over.

Fourth, the aid provided by the United States military advisory group.

Apart from this, the United States Government, in the period from V-J Day until early 1949, authorized grants and credits to China totaling approximately $2,000,000,000, of which approximately $1,600,-000,000, were grants and $400,000,000 were on credit terms.

This total is divided almost equally between military and economic aid. The amounts do not include United States surplus property, except where the sales were on credit terms.

Surplus property, with a total estimated procurement cost of over $1,000,000,000, has been sold to China for the agreed realization to the United States of $230,000,000, of which $95,000,000 were on credit terms.

By the spring of 1949 the military position of the Chinese Government collapsed to the point where the Chinese Communists controlled the major centers of population and railways from Manchuria south to the Yangtze.

The military collapse of the Chinese Government had, for the most part, been the consequence of inept political and military leadership, and lack of the will to fight on the part of its armies, rather than inadequate military supplies.

It was at that time the considered judgment of responsible United States Government observers in China that only the extension of unlimited American economic and military aid involving the use of our own troops and operations which might require the extensive control of Chinese Government operations would enable the Nationalist Government to maintain a foothold in South China.

It was believed that United States involvement in Chinese civil war under the existing conditions would be clearly contrary to American interests.

As the last note of this tragic story, I should like to read you the message of the Acting President of China, Gen. Li Tsung-jen.

In a letter [of May 5, 1945] which he addressed to President Truman. He says: "This policy"—he had described our help to China during the war, and then he had discussed our aid to China after the war, as I have described it to you. He says:

"This policy of friendly assistance was continued when, some years ago, General Marshall, under instructions from your good self, took up the difficult task of mediation in our conflict with the Chinese Communists, to which he devoted painstaking effort. All this work was unfortunately rendered fruitless by the lack of sincerity, on the part of both the then Government and the Chinese Communists.

"In spite of this, your country continued to extend its aid to our Government. It is regrettable that owing to the failure of our then Government to make judicious use of this aid and to bring about appropriate political, economic, and military reforms, your assistance has not produced the desired effect. To this failure is attributable the present predicament in which our country finds itself."

VII. ADDRESS BY GENERAL MacARTHUR BEFORE THE MASSACHUSETTS LEGISLATURE IN BOSTON

July 25, 1951

In this historic forum I recall vividly and reverently the memory of those great architects and defenders of liberty who immortalized the Commonwealth of Massachusetts. To this section of the country men point as the cradle of our freedom.

For here was established more than three centuries ago a declaration of rights from which ultimately came the constitutional mandate guaranteeing our civil liberties. Here men arose militantly in protest against the tyranny of oppressive rule of burdensome taxation. Here men engaged in formal combat to sever the distasteful bonds of colonial rule.

Here men etched the patriot's pattern which all races who harbored in their hearts a love for freedom have since sought to emulate. Here men, by their courage, vision and faith, forged a new concept of modern civilization.

Before the descendants of these early American patriots I am honored, indeed, to address this legislative assembly in response to its thoughtful and kind invitation. I do so with neither partisan affiliation nor political purpose.

But I have been warned by many that an outspoken course, even if it be solely of truth, will bring down upon my head ruthless retaliation —that efforts will be made to destroy public faith in the integrity of my views—not by force of just argument but by the application of the false methods of propaganda. I am told in effect I must follow blindly the leader—keep silent—or take the bitter consequences.

I had thought Abraham Lincoln had pinned down for all time this·

ugly code when he declared: "To sin by silence when they should protest makes cowards of men."

I shall raise my voice as loud and as often as I believe it to be in the interest of the American people. I shall dedicate all of my energies to restoring to American life those immutable principles and ideals which your forebears and mine handed down to us in sacred trust. I shall assist in the regaining of that moral base for both public and private life which will restore the people's faith in the integrity of public institutions and the private faith of every man in the integrity of his neighbor.

I shall set my course to the end that no man need fear to speak the truth. I could not do less, for the opportunities for service my country has given me and the honors it has conferred upon me have imposed an obligation which is not discharged by the termination of public service.

Much that I have seen since my return to my native land after an absence of many years has filled me with immeasurable satisfaction and pride. Our material progress has been little short of phenomenal.

It has established an eminence in material strength so far in advance of any other nation or combination of nations that talk of imminent threat to our national security through the application of external force is pure nonsense.

It is not of any external threat that I concern myself but rather of insidious forces working from within which have already so drastically altered the character of our free institutions—those institutions which formerly we hailed as something beyond question or challenge—those institutions we proudly called the American way of life.

Foremost of these forces is that directly, or even more frequently indirectly, allied with the scourge of imperialistic communism. It has infiltrated into positions of public trust and responsibility—into journalism, the press, the radio and the schools.

It seeks through covert manipulation of the civil power and the media of public information and education to pervert the truth, impair respect for moral values, suppress human freedom and representative government and, in the end, destroy our faith in our religious teachings.

This evil force, with neither spiritual base nor moral standard, rallies the abnormal and subnormal elements among our citizenry and applies internal pressure against all things we hold decent and all things that we hold right—the type of pressure which has caused many Christian nations abroad to fall and their own cherished freedoms to languish in the shackles of complete suppression.

As it has happened there it can happen here. Our need for patriotic fervor and religious devotion was never more impelling. There can be no compromise with atheistic communism—no half-way in the preservation of freedom and religion. It must be all or nothing.

We must unite in the high purpose that the liberties etched upon the design of our life by our forefathers be unimpaired and that we maintain the moral courage and spiritual leadership to preserve inviolate that mighty bulwark of all freedom, our Christian faith.

It was the adventurous spirit of Americans which despite risks and hazards carved a great nation from an almost impenetrable wilderness; which established the pattern for modern industrialization and scientific development; which built our own almost unbelievable material progress and favorably influenced that of all others; which through the scientific advance of means of communication closed the international geographic gap to permit rapid and effective trade and commerce among the peoples of the world; which raised the living standard of the American people beyond that ever before known; and which elevated the laborer, the farmer and the tradesman to their rightful station of dignity and relative prosperity.

This adventurous spirit is now threatened as it was in the days of the Boston Tea Party by an unconscionable burden of taxation. This is sapping the initiative and energies of the people and leaves little incentive for the assumption of those risks which are inherent and unescapable in the forging of progress under the system of free enterprise.

Worst of all, it is throwing its tentacles around the low income bracket sector of our society, from whom is now exacted the major share of the cost of government. This renders its paper income largely illusory.

The so-called "forgotten man" of the early Thirties now is indeed no longer forgotten as the Government levies upon his income as the main remaining source to defray reckless spendthrift policies.

More and more we work not for ourselves but for the state. In time, if permitted to continue, this trend cannot fail to be destructive. For no nation may survive in freedom once its people become the servants of the state, a condition to which we are now pointed with dreadful certainty. Labor, as always, will be the first to feel its frightful consequences.

It is quite true that some levy upon the people's earnings to pay the cost of government is unavoidable. But the costs of government, even discounting extraordinary military requirements, have risen at an accelerated, alarming and reckless rate.

Nothing is heard from those in supreme executive authority concerning the possibility of a reduction or even limitation upon these mounting costs. No suggestion deals with the restoration of some semblance of a healthy balance. No plan is advanced for easing the crushing burden already resting upon the people.

To the contrary, all that we hear are the plans by which such costs progressively may be increased. New means are constantly being devised for greater call upon the taxable potential as though the resources available were inexhaustible. We compound irresponsibility by seeking to share what liquid wealth we have with others.

In so doing we recklessly speak of the billions we would set aside for the purpose, as though they were inconsequential. There can be no quarrel with altruism. Such has never been a predominant quality making up the nobility of the American character. We should do all in our power to alleviate the suffering and hardship of other peoples, and to support their own maximum effort to preserve their freedom from the assaults of Communist imperialism.

But when this effort is carried beyond the ability to pay, or to the point that the attendant burden upon our own people becomes insufferable, or places our own way of life and freedom in jeopardy, then it ceases to be altruism and becomes reckless imprudence. I have yet to see evidence that such vast outlays were preceded by the slightest concern for the ultimate effect it will have upon our own liberties and standards of life.

This nation's material wealth is built upon the vision and courage, the sweat and toil, hope and faith of our people. There has been no magic involved upon which we might again call to replenish our denuded coffers.

We can either advance upon the security of sound principles or we can plunge on to the precipice of disaster toward which we are now headed in the dangerous illusion that our wealth is inexhaustible—and can therefore be limitlessly shared with others.

It is argued that we must give boundlessly if we are to be insured allies in an emergency.

I reject this reasoning as an unwarranted calumny against well-tested friends of long standing. The survival of the free world is infinitely more dependent upon the maintenance of a strong, vigorous, healthy and independent America as a leavening influence than upon any financial aid which we might provide under our own existing stringencies.

The free world's one great hope for survival now rests upon the maintaining and preserving of our own strength. Continue to dissipate it and that one hope is dead. If the American people would pass on the standard of life and the heritage of opportunity they themselves have enjoyed to their children and their children's children they should ask their representatives in government:

"What is the plan for the easing of the tax burden upon us? What is the plan for bringing to a halt this inflationary movement which is progressively and inexorably decreasing the purchasing power of our currency, nullifying the protection of our insurance provisions, and reducing those of fixed income to hardship and even despair?"

I fear these questions, if asked, would be met by stony silence. For just as in Korea there has been no plan. We have long drifted aimlessly with the sole safeguard against the ineptitude of our leaders resting upon American enterprise, American skill and American courage. But once the incentive for the maximizing of these great attributes is lost the bulwark to support our failures is gone and the American way of life as we have known it will be gravely threatened.

Indivisible from this trend and probably contributory to it is a growing tendency to overlook certain forms of laxity in high quarters. Petty corruption in the public administration is a disease unfortunately common to all nations but I refer to an even more alarming situation.

Men of significant statute in national affairs appear to cower before the threat of reprisal if the truth be expressed in criticism of those in higher public authority.

For example, I find in existence a new and heretofore unknown and dangerous concept that the members of our armed forces owe primary allegiance and loyalty to those who temporarily exercise the authority of the executive branch of government, rather than to the country and its Constitution which they are sworn to defend.

No proposition could be more dangerous. None could cast greater doubt upon the integrity of the armed services.

For its application would at once convert them from their traditional and constitutional role as the instrument for the defense of the Republic into something partaking of the nature of a pretorian guard, owing sole allegiance to the political master of the hour.

While for the purpose of administration and command the armed services are within the executive branch of the Government, they are accountable as well to the Congress, charged with the policy making responsibility, and to the people, ultimate repository of all national power.

Yet so inordinate has been the application of the executive power that members of the armed services have been subjected to the most arbitrary and ruthless treatment for daring to speak the truth in accordance with conviction and conscience.

I hesitate to refer to my own relief from the Far Eastern Commands as I have never questioned the legal authority underlying such action. But the three sole reasons publicly stated by the highest authority clearly demonstrate the arbitrary nature of the decision.

The first reason given was that, contrary to existing policy, I warned of the strategic relationship of Formosa to American security and the dangers inherent in this area's falling under Communist control. Yet this viewpoint has since been declared by the Secretary of State, under oath before Congressional committees, to have been and to be the invincible and long standing policy of the United States.

The second reason given was that I communicated my readiness to meet the enemy commander at any time to discuss acceptable terms of a cease-fire arrangement. Yet, for this proposal, I was relieved of my command by the same authorities who since have received so enthusiastically the identical proposal when made by the Soviet Government.

The third and final reason advanced was my replying to a Congressman's request for information on a public subject then under open consideration by the Congress. Yet both Houses of Congress promptly passed a law confirming my action, which indeed had been entirely in accordance with a long existing and well recognized though unwritten policy.

This law states that no member of the Armed Forces shall be restricted or prevented from communicating directly or indirectly with any member or members of Congress concerning any subject unless such communication is in violation of law or the security and safety of the United States. And this formal enactment of basic public policy was approved without the slightest dissent by the President.

Is there wonder that men who seek an objective understanding of American policy thinking become completely frustrated and bewildered? Is there wonder that Soviet propaganda so completely dominates American foreign policy? And, indeed, what is our foreign policy?

We hear impassioned appeals that it be bipartisan—violent charges that sinister efforts are being made to obstruct and defeat it—but I defy you or any other man to tell me what it is. It has become a mass of confused misunderstandings and vacillations. It has meant one thing today—another tomorrow. It has almost blown with every wind, changed with every tide.

The sorry truth is we have no policy. Expediences as variable and shifting as the exigencies of the moment seem to be the only guide. Yesterday, we disarmed, today we arm and what of tomorrow? We have been told of the war in Korea that it is the wrong war, with the wrong enemy, at the wrong time and in the wrong place. Does this mean that they intend and indeed plan what they would call a right war, with a right enemy, at a right time and in a right place?

If successful in mounting the North Atlantic pact in 1953 or 1954 or at one of the ever-changing dates fixed for its consummation, what comes then? Do we mean to throw down a gauge of battle? Do we mean to continue the fantastic fiscal burden indefinitely to our inevitable exhaustion?

Is our only plan to spend and spend and spend? Do we intend to resist by force Red aggression in South East Asia if it develops? Do we intend to take over commitments in the explosive Middle East? Do we intend to enter into a series of military alliances abroad? Do we intend to actually implement by force of arms the so-called Truman Plan? These are questions that disturb us because there is no answer forthcoming. We do want and need unity and bipartisanship in our foreign policy—but when there is no policy we can but dangerously drift.

In Korea, despite the magnificent performance of our fighting forces, the result has been indecisive. The high moral purpose which so animated and inspired the world a year ago yielded to the timidity and fear of our leaders as after defeating our original enemy a new one entered the field which they dared not fight to a decision. Appeasement thereafter became the policy of war on the battlefield.

In the actual fighting with this new enemy we did not lose but neither did we win. Yet, it can be accepted as a basic principle proven and reproven since the beginning of time that a great nation which enters upon war and fails to see it through to victory must accept the full moral consequences of defeat.

Now that the fighting has temporarily abated the outstanding impression which emerges from the scene is the utter uselessness of the enormous sacrifice in life and limb which has resulted. A million soldiers on both sides and unquestionably at least a like number of civilians are maimed or dead. A nation has been gutted and we stand today just where we stood before it all started.

The threat of aggression upon the weak by those callously inclined among the strong has not diminished. Indeed, nothing has been settled. No issue has been decided.

This experience again emphasizes the utter futility of modern war —its complete failure as an arbiter of international dissensions. Its threat must be abolished if the world is to go on—and if it does not go on it will go under.

We must finally come to realize that war is outmoded as an instrument of political policy, that it provides no solution for international suicide. We must understand that in final analysis the mounting cost of preparation for war is in many ways as materially destructive as war itself. We must find the means to avoid this great sapping of human energy and resource.

This requires leadership of the highest order—a spiritual and moral leadership—a leadership which our country alone is capable of providing. While we must be prepared to meet the trial of war if war comes, we should gear our foreign and domestic policies toward the ultimate goal—the abolition of war from the face of the earth.

This is what practically all mankind—all the great masses which populate the world—long and pray for. Therein lies the road, the only road, to universal peace and prosperity. We must lead the world down that road however long and tortuous and illusory it may now appear.

Such is the role as I see it for which this great nation of ours is now cast. In this we follow the Cross. If we meet the challenge we cannot fail. But no end may be achieved without first making a start —no success without a trial.

On this problem of greatest universal concern, unless we address ourselves to the fundamentals we shall get no farther than the preceding generations which have tried and failed. Convention after convention has been entered into, designed to humanize war and bring it under the control of rules dictated by the highest human ideals. Yet each war becomes increasingly savage as the means for mass killing are further developed.

You cannot control war; you can only abolish it. Those who shrug this off as idealistic are the real enemies of peace—the real warmongers. Those who lack the enterprise, vision and courage to try a new approach when none others have succeeded fail completely the most simple test of leadership.

As I have traveled through the country since my return, I find a great transformation in American thought to be taking place. Our apathy is disappearing. American public opinion is beginning to exert its immense power. The American people are expressing themselves with dynamic force on foreign policy. This is exerting a profound influence upon the Soviet course of action.

Few events in the life of our Republic have been of more significant importance nor more heartening than this rallying of the collective will of the American people. They are putting pressure upon their own leaders and upon the leaders of those with whom we are directly or indirectly engaged. And just as it has cast its influence upon policy and events abroad it can be brought to bear with no less telling effect upon policy and events at home.

Therein lies our best hope in the battle to save America—the full weight of an aroused, informed and militant public opinion. I stated in Texas:

"If it be that my relief was the spark which ignited this great power of American public expression; which caused our people to rise above the level of narrow partisanship to unite in a common crusade to effect a spiritual rebirth in American life; which restored to the American people the full glory and dignity of self-rule under those same high principles and ideals which animated our fathers; which restored a lost faith in ourselves and our free institutions; which provided the symbol for rallying the mighty forces for good throughout the land—then I would be thankful, indeed, to a farseeing and merciful Providence and could not ask for more."

We stand today at a critical moment of history—at a vital crossroad. In one direction is the path of courageous patriots seeking in humility but the opportunity to serve their country; the other that of those selfishly seeking to entrench autocratic power.

The one group stands for implacable resistance against communism; the other for compromising with communism. The one stands for our traditional system of government and freedom; the other for a socialist state and slavery.

The one boldly speaks the truth; the other spreads propaganda, fear and deception. The one denounces excessive taxation, bureaucratic government and corruption; the other seeks more taxes, more bureaucratic power, and shields corruption.

The people, as the ultimate rulers, must choose the course our nation shall follow. On their decision rests the future of our free civilization and the survival of our Christian faith. Not for a moment do I doubt that decision or that it will guide the nation to a new and fuller greatness. Good night.

VIII. STATEMENT OF W. AVERELL HARRIMAN ON THE YALTA AGREEMENT

July 13, 1951*

To the Committees on Armed Services and Foreign Relations
of the Senate:

A myth has grown up that what President Roosevelt and Prime Minister Churchill did at Yalta has led to our postwar difficulties with the Soviet Union. This myth is without foundation in fact.

The discussion at Yalta and the understandings reached there were an integral part of our negotiations with the Soviet Union throughout the war to bring the desperate struggle to a victorious and early conclusion and to find a way in which the United States, Great Britain and the U.S.S.R. could live together in peace. The postwar problems have resulted not from the understandings reached at Yalta but from the fact that Stalin failed to carry out those understandings and from aggressive actions by the Kremlin. . . .

The primary objective of the American and British governments in our relations with the Soviet Union during the war was to keep the Soviet Army as an effective fighting force against Hitler. We sought to do this through the shipment of essential supplies and through the coordination of our military strategy. . . . There are those who now contend that we should not have supported the Soviet armies. They contend that we should have let Germany and the Soviet Union kill each other off. These people forget the real danger was that Hitler would knock Russia out of the war. The Germans were only a few miles from Moscow when I was there in October 1941. That year the

* Made public August 17, 1951.

winter saved the city. I was in Moscow again in August 1942 when the Russians were again facing disaster. The supplies from the British and ourselves may have been decisive in helping the Russians to hold Leningrad, to prevent the encirclement of Moscow, and to stop the onslaught on Stalingrad and the oil fields of the Caucasus. With the increased flow of our supplies, by the spring of 1944 the Russians had been able to throw the Germans back on all fronts.

These people forget that on June 6, 1944, when the Allies landed on the Normandy beaches, there were about 60 German divisions in France and the Low Countries, whereas there were 199 German divisions and 50 satellite divisions engaged on the eastern front. In accordance with Stalin's agreement at Teheran, the Russian armies launched a major offensive on June 22 and tied down and broke through this formidable Nazi force.

If we had failed to come to the support of the Soviet Union, the Germans would have rendered the Russian armies ineffective and would have been able to throw their full power against an allied invasion of the continent. In this case it is doubtful whether such an invasion could have been attempted, and no one can now tell how long the war with Hitler might have lasted.

These tremendous and courageous operations by the Soviet Army and the fact that Stalin had honored such a vital military commitment influenced the attitude of British and American representatives in subsequent negotiations with the Soviet Union—and built up favorable opinion for the Soviet Union among the people of the United States and the other Western Allies.

In addition to maintaining the Soviet Union as an effective fighting ally against Hitler, it was our objective to encourage the Soviet Union to join in the war against Japan at the earliest possible date. Because of their ambitions in the East, there was never any doubt in my mind that the Soviets would attack the Japanese in Manchuria in their own due time. The question was whether they could come in early enough to be of any help to us and to save American lives. I raised the subject with Stalin as early as August 1942. He told me then that it was his intention to come into the Pacific war when he was in a position to do so. Stalin was gravely concerned by the possibility of a premature attack by the Japanese. He had weakened his Siberian forces for the defense of Stalingrad. Furthermore, the Japanese Navy alone could have cut off the vital line of our supplies coming through Vladivostok.

The question of Soviet participation in the Pacific war was discussed in some detail at Teheran. Roosevelt proposed to Stalin the basing of American heavy bombers in the Maritime Provinces north of Vladivostok. This was deemed a necessary requirement by our Air Force in order to cover the Japanese Islands. In addition, Roosevelt suggested the possible use of Soviet ports for our naval forces and requested the immediate exchange of military intelligence concerning Japan. Stalin agreed that these matters should be studied. Shortly thereafter we established exchange of combat intelligence. The other matters continued to be the subject of discussion on my part with Stalin in Moscow during the ensuing year.

Concurrently with our negotiations for the conduct of the war, President Roosevelt sought to come to an understanding regarding postwar problems with the Soviet Union. It was clear that unless these problems were settled we would have difficulties once the war was ended. President Roosevelt attempted to use our relationship as allies to develop a basis on which world peace could be maintained, and to settle in advance differences which we were likely to have over the treatment of territories occupied by the Red Army. . . .

Although Stalin had on several occasions mentioned Soviet political objectives in the East, it was not until December 1944 that he outlined these objectives to me in detail. He said that Russia's position in the East should be generally re-established as it existed before the Russo-Japanese War of 1905. The lower half of Sakhalin should be returned to the Russians, as well as the Kurile Islands, in order to protect Soviet outlets to the Pacific. The Russians wished again to lease the ports of Dairen and Port Arthur and to obtain a lease on those railroads in Manchuria built by the Russians under contract with the Chinese, specifically, the Chinese Eastern Railway, which was the direct line from the Trans-Siberian Railroad through to Vladivostok, and the South Manchurian Railroad making a connection to Dairen. He stated that the Soviet Union would not interfere with the sovereignty of China over Manchuria. In addition Stalin asked for the recognition of the status quo in Outer Mongolia. I pointed out to Stalin that the talks at Teheran had envisaged internationalization of the Port of Dairen, rather than a lease. Stalin replied that this could be discussed. I immediately reported Stalin's proposals to President Roosevelt, and they became the basis of the discussions at Yalta.

It was against this background, which I have briefly sketched, that President Roosevelt and Prime Minister Churchill met with Stalin at Yalta in early February 1945. . . . Unquestionably, he was not in good health and the long conferences tired him. Nevertheless, for many months he had given much thought to the matters to be discussed and, in consultation with many officials of the Government, he had blocked out definite objectives which he had clearly in mind. He came to Yalta determined to do his utmost to achieve these objectives and he carried on the negotiations to this end with his usual skill and perception.

The discussions at Yalta covered a wide range of topics, including final plans for the defeat of Hitler, the occupation and control of Germany, reparations, the United Nations Conference to meet at San Francisco on April 25th, the restoration of sovereign rights and self-government to the liberated peoples of Europe, and the establishment of a free, independent and democratic Poland through the holding of free and unfettered elections. By the Declaration on Liberated Europe, Roosevelt and Churchill obtained the pledge of Stalin for joint action to secure the fundamental freedoms for the people in territories overrun by the Red Army.* . . .

Had Stalin honored these commitments taken at Yalta, Eastern Europe would be free today and the United Nations would be a truly effective organization for world security.

The last understanding to be reached was that relating to the Far East. The crucial issue was not whether the Soviet Union would enter the Pacific War, but whether it would do so in time to be of help in the carrying out of the plans of the Joint Chiefs of Staff for an invasion of the Japanese home islands. The great danger existed that the Soviet Union would stand by until we had brought Japan to her knees at great cost in American lives, and then the Red Army could march into Manchuria and large areas of Northern China. It would then have been a simple matter for the Soviets to give expression to "popular demand" by establishing People's Republics of Manchuria and Inner Mongolia. President Roosevelt sought to reduce the general assurances which Stalin had previously given to specific undertakings for the early entry of Russia in the Pacific War, to limit Soviet ex-

---

* "To foster the conditions in which the liberated peoples may exericse these rights [of sovereignty and self-government], the three Governments will jointly assist the people in any European liberated state or former Axis satellite state in Europe where in their judgment conditions require (a) to establish conditions of internal peace; (b) to carry out emergency measures for the relief of distressed peoples; (c) to form interim governmental authorities broadly representative of all democratic elements in the population and pledged to the earliest possible establishment through free elections of governments responsive to the will of the people; and (d) to facilitate where necessary the holding of such elections."

pansion in the East and to gain Soviet support for the Nationalist Government of China.

It should be recalled that it was only on the second day of the Yalta Conference that General MacArthur entered Manila. The bloody battles of Iwo Jima and Okinawa still lay ahead. It was not until more than five months later that the first and only experimental explosion of the atomic bomb was successfully concluded at Alamogordo. The military authorities estimated that it would take 18 months after the surrender of Germany to defeat Japan, and that Soviet participation would greatly reduce the heavy American casualties which could otherwise be expected. The Joint Chiefs of Staff were planning an invasion of the Japanese home islands, and were anxious for the early entry of Russia in the war to defeat the Japanese Kwantung Army in Manchuria and in order that our bombers could operate from bases in Eastern Siberia.

These plans were outlined in two memoranda which were before the President at Yalta.

In a memorandum for the President, dated 23 January 1945, the Joint Chiefs of Staff stated:

> The Joint Chiefs of Staff have been guided by the following basic principles in working toward U.S.S.R. entry into the war against Japan:
>
> Russia's entry at as early a date as possible consistent with her ability to engage in offensive operations is necessary to provide maximum asistance to our Pacific operations. The U.S. will provide maximum support possible without interfering with our main effort against Japan.
>
> The objective of Russia's military effort against Japan in the Far East should be the defeat of the Japanese forces in Manchuria, air operations against Japan proper in collaboration with U.S. air forces based in eastern Siberia, and maximum interference with Japanese sea traffic between Japan and the mainland of Asia.

In a memorandum dated 22 January 1945, the Joint Chiefs of Staff stated:

> 1. The agreed over-all objective in the war against Japan has been expressed as follows:
> To force the unconditional surrender of Japan by
> (1) Lowering Japanese ability and will to resist by establishing sea and air blockades, conducting intensive air bombardment, and destroying Japanese air and naval strength.
> (2) Invading and seizing objectives in the industrial heart of Japan.

2. The United States Chiefs of Staff have adopted the following as a basis for planning in the war against Japan:
The concept of operations for the main effort in the Pacific
a. Following the Okinawa operation to seize additional positions to intensify the blockade and air bombardment of Japan in order to create a situation favorable to:
b. An assault on Kyushu for the purpose of further reducing Japanese capabilities by containing and destroying major enemy forces and further intensifying the blockade and air bombardment in order to establish a tactical condition favorable to:
c. The decisive invasion of the industrial heart of Japan through the Tokyo Plain.
3. The following sequence and timing of operations have been directed by the United States Chiefs of Staff and plans prepared by theater commanders:—

Objectives	*Target Date*
Continuation of operations in the Philippines (Luzon, Mindoro, Leyte)	_____
Iwo Jima	19 February 1945
Okinawa and extension therefrom in the Ryukyus	1 April-August 1945

4. Until a firm date can be established when redeployment from Europe can begin, planning will be continued for an operation to seize a position in the Chusan-Ningpo area and for invasion of Kyushu-Honshu in the winter of 1945–1946.
5. Examination is being conducted of the necessity for and cost of operations to maintain and defend a sea route to the Sea of Okhotsk when the entry of Russia into the war against Japan becomes imminent. Examination so far has shown that the possibility of seizing a position in the Kuriles for that purpose during the favorable weather period of 1945 is remote due to lack of sufficient resources. The possibility of maintaining and defending such a sea route from bases in Kamchatka alone is being further examined.
6. The United States Chiefs of Staff have also directed examination and preparation of a plan of campaign against Japan in the event that prolongation of the European war requires postponement of the invasion of Japan until well into 1946.

These military considerations had been the subject of careful study by Roosevelt for a long time and they were uppermost in his mind at Yalta. President Roosevelt personally carried on with Stalin the negotiations leading up to the understanding on the Far East. I was present at the meetings when these matters were discussed and, under President Roosevelt's direction, I took up certain details with Stalin and with Molotov. Neither Secretary of State Stettinius nor any of his advisers, except for Charles E. Bohlen who acted as the President's interpreter, had anything to do with these negotiations. Any suggestion to the contrary is utterly without foundation in fact.*

The first conversations took place on February 8th, at which Stalin brought up with Roosevelt the proposals which he had presented to me the previous December in Moscow. Stalin contended that these proposals should be accepted. Roosvelt said that he believed there would be no difficulty in regard to the Kurile Islands and the return to Russia of the southern half of Sakhalin. He said that, although he could not speak for Chiang Kai-shek, he believed that Dairen might be made a free port under an international commission, and that the Manchurian railroads might be operated jointly. The President and Stalin also discussed internal conditions in China. Stalin reiterated his recognition of the need for a united China under Chiang Kai-shek's leadership.

Stalin suggested that the proposals be put in writing and be agreed to before the conference ended. . . . [On] February 10, Roosevelt and Stalin met again. Stalin agreed to the modifications as proposed by Roosevelt, except that he maintained that a lease on Port Arthur would be required, as it was to be used for a naval base. Stalin accepted the requirement for Chiang Kai-shek's concurrence and said that he wanted his concurrence also to the status quo in Outer Mongolia. President Roosevelt and Stalin concluded that the matter should be discussed with Chiang when Stalin was prepared to have this done, having in mind the need for secrecy and lack of security in Chungking.† . . .

* [Mr. Harriman is here laying the ghost of Alger Hiss.]
† The full text of the controversial Far Eastern accord, signed February 11, 1945, by Stalin, Roosevelt and Churchill, is as follows:

"The leaders of the three Great Powers—the Soviet Union, the United States of America and Great Britain—have agreed that in two or three months after Germany has surrendered and the war in Europe has terminated the Soviet Union shall enter into the war against Japan on the side of the Allies on condition that:

1. The status quo in Outer-Mongolia (The Mongolian People's Republic) shall be preserved;

2. The former rights of Russia violated by the treacherous attack of Japan in 1904 shall be restored, viz.:

(a) the southern part of Sakhalin as well as all the islands adjacent to it shall be returned to the Soviet Union,

Stalin also agreed to joint planning for military operations in the Pacific and to the use by the United States Army Air Force of bases in the Maritime Provinces at Komsomolsk and Nikolaevsk.

President Roosevelt felt that he had achieved his principal objectives. He had obtained the agreement of the Soviet Union to enter the war against Japan within three months after the defeat of Germany. This was the period required to move Soviet troops from the European front to Siberia. It was considered to be in good time, and conformed to the plans of the Joint Chiefs of Staff which involved the redeployment of our forces from Europe to the Pacific. Roosevelt had also obtained Stalin's pledge of support for Chiang Kai-shek and recognition of the sovereignty of the Chinese National Government over Manchuria.

In recent years several objections have been leveled at the terms of the Yalta understanding on the Far East and the circumstances under which it was concluded.

It has been asserted that the understanding was a mistake because, as it turned out, Russian participation had no influence on the defeat of Japan. To President Roosevelt at Yalta, the lives of American fighting men were at stake. He had been advised by the Joint Chiefs of Staff that the defeat of Japan would take many months after V.E. day and that if the Soviet Union came in soon enough countless American lives would be saved. Furthermore, up to that time, Stalin had carried out vital military undertakings. Roosevelt, therefore, considered that

---

(b) the commercial port of Dairen shall be internationalized, the preeminent interests of the Soviet Union in this port being safeguarded and the lease of Port Arthur as a naval base of the U.S.S.R. restored,

(c) the Chinese-Eastern Railroad and the South-Manchurian Railroad which provides an outlet to Dairen shall be jointly operated by the establishment of a joint Soviet-Chinese Company it being understood that the preeminent interests of the Soviet Union shall be safeguarded and that China shall retain full sovereignty in Manchuria;

3. The Kurile Islands shall be handed over to the Soviet Union.

It is understood, that the agreement concerning Outer-Mongolia and the ports and railroads referred to above will require concurrence of Generalissimo Chiang Kai-shek. The President will take measures in order to obtain this concurrence on advice from Marshal Stalin.

The Heads of the three Great Powers have agreed that these claims of the Soviet Union shall be unquestionably fulfilled after Japan has been defeated.

For its part the Soviet Union expresses its readiness to conclude with the National Government of China a pact of friendship and alliance between the U.S.S.R. and China in order to render assistance to China with its armed forces for the purposes of liberating China from the Japanese yoke."

a definite commitment from Stalin was of supreme importance and would be of great value.

Another criticism is that Chiang Kai-shek was not consulted before the understanding was signed and that the understanding was kept secret. The question of consulting Chiang was a difficult one. Secrecy was a military necessity. Experience had shown that whatever was known in Chungking got to the Japanese. Stalin was unwilling to risk Japanese knowledge of his plans until he had been able to strengthen his forces in Siberia. At Roosevelt's insistence, however, the understanding specified that Chiang's concurrence was required where China's direct interests were affected and that Chiang should be notified at the appropriate time.

I am sure that Roosevelt would have much preferred to have consulted Chiang in advance, if he had thought it was feasible for him to do so. On the other hand, he had had certain general talks with Chiang on some of the points involved, and knew of Chiang's desire to come to a permanent understanding with the Soviet Union. For these reasons, and also because of the strong support that he had given Chiang in the past, Roosevelt felt that he could work things out with Chiang when the time came.

Because of the prior conversations with Stalin, Roosevelt was convinced that the requirement for Chiang's concurrence qualified the provision that the claims of the Soviet Union "shall be unquestionably fulfilled," and that Stalin so understood. Events proved that Roosevelt was correct. The Yalta understanding provided a framework for negotiaions between the Soviet Union and the Chinese National Government in the summer of 1945, looking toward a settlement of the long standing difficulties between the two countries. . . .

Subsequent to the Yalta Conference certain events took place during the late winter and spring of 1945.

At the end of February, Ambassador Hurley, who was then United States Ambassador to China, returned to Washington for consultation. He has testified that he saw President Roosevelt on two occasions in March and that Roosevelt instructed him to go to London and attempt to ameliorate the Yalta understanding. (Printed Record, Part 4, p. 2885.) It does not appear that Ambassador Hurley correctly recalls the facts.

I am convinced that President Roosevelt's concern after Yalta was to see to it that friendly relations were developed between the Soviet Union and the National Government of China.

Ambassador Hurley came through Moscow on his way to Chungking in April. He stayed with me during his visit. At no time did he indicate to me that President Roosevelt was disturbed about the understanding reached at Yalta or that he desired that this understanding be ameliorated. On the contrary, the purpose of Ambassador Hurley's visit to Moscow, as he stated it to me and to Stalin, was to find out from Stalin when Chiang could be told about the Yalta understanding and to help further cement the relations between the Soviet Union and the Chinese National Government. . . .

In a cable to President Truman from Chungking on May 10, 1945, Ambassador Hurley outlined in some detail his conception of the mission which he had been given by President Roosevelt in March. There is nothing in this cable which indicates that Roosevelt had instructed Ambassador Hurley to attempt to ameliorate the Yalta understanding. The paraphrased text of the cable is as follows:

> . . . In my last conference with President Roosevelt he entrusted me with two specific missions in addition to my duties as Ambassador to China. The first mission was to bring Churchill and Stalin to an agreement on the policy that the United States has been pursuing in China. Namely (1) to take all necessary action to bring about unification under the National Government of all anti-Japanese armed forces in China. (2) To endorse the aspirations of the Chinese people for the establishment of a free united Democratic Chinese Government. (3) To continue to insist that China furnish her own leadership, make her own decisions and be responsible for her own policies and thus work out her own destiny in her own way. As you have not doubt been advised by the Secretary of State I obtained concurrence of Churchill and Stalin on the plan outlined. . . .

The second mission, entrusted to me by President Roosevelt in my last conference with him pertains to a decision affecting China reached at the Yalta Conference. . . . All of the problems decided, except No. one in the prelude, have been raised by the Generalissimo and discussed fully with me. I am convinced that he will agree to every one of the requirements but will take exceptions to the use of two words "preeminent" and "lease." . . . Both Roosevelt and Stalin advised me that it was agreed between them that I would not open the subject of the Yalta decision with Chiang Kai-shek until the signal was given me by Stalin. Stalin said he would give me carte blanche and let me use my own judgment as to when and how to present the subject. However, both Harriman and I were of the opinion that it would be best to delay the presentation because of the possibility of leakage which in turn might bring undesirable results.

With regard to Ambassador Hurley's comments on the words "pre-eminent" and "lease" in the Yalta understanding, I can personally state that neither Roosevelt nor Stalin intended that the phrase "preeminent interests" should go beyond Soviet interests in the free transit of exports to and imports from the Soviet Union. President Roosevelt had told me at Yalta that this was his interpretation and, when I took this position with Stalin in August 1945, he agreed. As to the lease on Port Arthur, Roosevelt looked upon this as an arrangement similar to privileges which the United States had negotiated with other countries for the mutual security of two friendly nations. . . .

At Potsdam, more than five months after Yalta, the Joint Chiefs of Staff were still planning an invasion of the Japanese home islands and still considered Soviet participation in the Pacific war essential. On July 24, 1945, the Combined Chiefs of Staff reported to the President and the Prime Minister that . . . our policy should be to: "Encourage Russian entry into the war against Japan. Provide such aid to her war-making capacity as may be necessary and practicable in connection therewith."

On the basis of this overall plan, extensive discussions were carried on with the Soviet Chiefs of Staff for the attack on Manchuria by the Soviet forces about two months prior to landings by U.S. forces on the Japanese home islands.

In the meantime the Chinese Government had been informed of the Yalta understanding. . . .

By this time it had been agreed that negotiations would start promptly in Moscow between China and the Soviet Union regarding the matter dealt with in the Yalta understanding. . . . Stalin, at the outset, made demands that went substantially beyond the Yalta understanding. While [T. V.] Soong was not prepared to accede to all of these demands, he made it clear to me that his Government was anxious to reach an agreement with the Soviet Union, and to this end he was prepared to make concessions which we considered went beyond the Yalta understanding.

At no time did Soong give me any indication that he felt the Yalta understanding was a handicap in his negotiations. I repeatedly urged him not to give in to Stalin's demands. At the same time, during this period, I had several talks with Stalin and Molotov in which I insisted that the Soviet position was not justified. This action I took on instructions from Washington. Also, on instructions, I informed Soong that the United States would consider that any concessions which went beyond our interpretation of the Yalta understanding, would be made because Soong believed they would be of value in obtaining Soviet support in other directions. Soong told me that he thoroughly understood and accepted the correctness of this position. The fact is that, in spite of the position I took, Soong gave in on several points in order to achieve his objectives.*

Soong told me in Moscow he was gratified at the results obtained and expressed his gratitude for the active support the United States had given him in his negotiations. Ambassador Hurley informed the Secretary of State on August 16 from Chungking that Chiang Kai-shek was "generally satisfied with the treaty." Ambassador Hurley went on to state that at his suggestion, Chiang had invited Mao Tse-tung, Chairman of the Chinese Communist party to a conference in Chungking. His cable concluded by stating that "Chiang Kai-shek will now have an opportunity to show realistic and generous leadership." On September 6, Ambassador Hurley cabled the Department of State that: "The publication of these documents has demonstrated conclusively that the Soviet Government supports the National Government of China and also that the two governments are in agreement regarding Manchuria." . . .

Nothing that was done at Yalta contributed to the loss of control over China by Chiang Kai-shek. The Yalta understanding was implemented by the Sino-Soviet agreements, which had they been carried out by Stalin, might have saved the Chinese National Government. The inability of the Chinese National Government to maintain control over China was due to the fact that the Sino-Soviet agreements were not honored by Stalin, and to other factors which have been dealt with before these Committees in great detail. . . .

Some people claim that we "sold out" to the Soviet Union at Yalta. If this were true, it is difficult to understand why the Soviet Union has gone to such lengths to violate the Yalta understandings. The fact is that these violations have been the basis of our protests against Soviet actions since the end of the war. There would have been a sellout if Roosevelt and Churchill had failed to bend every effort to come to an understanding with the Soviet Union and had permitted the Red

---

* An exchange of notes between Molotov and Wang Shi-chieh, the Chinese Foreign Minister, accompanying the treaty, specified: "In accordance with the spirit of the aforementioned Treaty, and in order to put into effect its aims and purposes, the Government of the U.S.S.R. agrees to render to China moral support and aid in military supplies and other material resources, such support and aid to be *entirely given to the National Government as the central government of China.*" (Italics supplied.)

Army to occupy vast areas, without attempting to protect the interests of people in those areas.

Only by keeping our military forces in being after Germany and Japan surrendered could we have attempted to compel the Soviet Union to withdraw from the territory which it controlled and to live up to its commitments. The people of the United States and the war-weary people of Europe were in no mood to support such an undertaking. This country certainly erred in its rapid demobilization in 1945, but this is an error for which the entire American people must share the responsibility. I cannot believe that anyone seriously thinks that the move to bring the boys home could have been stopped. I still recall my grave concern when I was in Moscow at the cold reception the Congress gave to President Truman's recommendation for Universal Military Training in the fall of 1945.

The most difficult question to answer is why Stalin took so many commitments which he subsequently failed to honor. There can be no clear answer to this question. I believe that the Kremlin had two approaches to their post-war policies, and in my many talks with Stalin I felt that he himself was of two minds. One approach emphasized reconstruction and development of Russia, and the other external expansion.

On the one hand, they were discussing possible understandings with us which would lead to peaceful relations and result in increased trade and loans from the West for the reconstruction of the terrible devastation left in the wake of the war. If they had carried out this program, they would have had to soft-pedal for the time at least the Communist designs for world domination—much along the lines of the policies they had pursued between the two wars.

On the other hand, we had constant difficulties with them throughout the war and they treated us with great suspicion. Moreover, there were indications that they would take advantage of the Red Army occupation of neighboring countries to maintain control, and they were supporting Communist Parties in other countries to be in a position to seize control in the post-war turmoil.

The Kremlin chose the second course. It is my belief that Stalin was influenced by the hostile attitude of the peoples of Eastern Europe toward the Red Army, and that he recognized that governments established by free elections would not be "friendly" to the Soviet Union. In addition, I believe, he became increasingly aware of the great opportunities for Soviet expansion in the post-war economic chaos. After our rapid demobilization, I do not think that he conceived that the

United States would take the firm stand against Soviet aggression that we have taken the past five years.

The one great thing accomplished by our constant efforts during and since the war to reach a settlement with the Soviet Union is that we have firmly established our moral position before the world. Had these efforts not been made, many people of the free world would still be wondering whether we and not the Kremlin were to blame for the tensions that have developed. The fact that the Soviet Union did not live up to its undertakings made clear the duplicity and the aggressive designs of the Kremlin. This fact has provided the rallying point for the free world in their collective effort to build their defenses and to unite against aggression.

Acknowledgment

Most of the books, periodicals, and documents we have drawn on are identified in the text. There are certain works, however, of which we have made wider use than the identifications show— among them David Bernstein's *The Philippine Story;* James K. Eyre, Jr.'s, *The Roosevelt-MacArthur Conflict;* John Gunther's *The Riddle of MacArthur;* George M. McCune's *Korea Today; Newsweek's History of Our Times: Events of 1950;* Edwin O. Reischauer's *The United States and Japan;* Richard P. Stebbins' *The United States in World Affairs:* 1950; the State Department's *United States Relations with China;* and the memoirs by Lewis H. Brereton, James F. Byrnes, Robert L. Eichelberger, Dwight D. Eisenhower, William F. Halsey, Allison Ind, George C. Kenney, Clark Lee, E. B. Miller, Robert E. Sherwood, Holland M. Smith, Edward R. Stettinius, Jr., Jonathan M. Wainwright, and others. We have also made extensive use of the New York *Times,* the New York *Herald Tribune,* the Washington *Post, United States News & World Report,* the *Economist,* the *Reporter,* and *Time.* Here and there, we have adapted certain parts of articles we have written for *Harper's,* the New York *Post,* and *The New Yorker.*

We are especially pleased that Herbert Block has joined with us and that a selection of his remarkable cartoons illuminates our text. A number of friends and colleagues have supplied us with excellent advice and information, among them Will Chasan,

337

Thomas Govan, Trumbull Higgins, Julie Armstrong Jeppson, Eric Larrabee, Charles Lichenstein, Milton MacKaye, Leonard Miall, Joseph L. Rauh, Jr., Edwin O. Reischauer, Arthur M. Schlesinger, William Shawn, and Charles H. Taylor. Throughout the preparation of this volume we have been very patient and understanding with our wives, Eleanor Burgess Rovere and Marian Cannon Schlesinger.

August 15, 1951

Index

Index